ABBOTT:
AS DELIVERED

THE DEFINING SPEECHES

Edited by David Furse-Roberts and Paul Ritchie

Connor Court Publishing

CONTENTS

FOREWORD

Rt Hon Stephen Harper

As a head of government, you connect with some global leaders and not with others. That should not be too surprising. It can reflect different personalities, different politics, or different perspectives. Sometimes though, you find another leader with whom you just click. Tony Abbott and I clicked.

I did not share his well-known enthusiasm for surfing, but we had other commonalities that caused us to see the world similarly and to work well together on behalf of our two countries. We both saw former Australian Prime Minister John Howard as a political mentor whose career exemplified a model of effective conservative leadership. We both understood that governing requires real-world trade-offs rather than a slavish adherence to intellectual abstractions. And we were both conservatives who sought to apply conservative insights and principles to the opportunities and challenges facing regular citizens.

These shared perspectives were reflected in similar policy priorities during our respective terms in office. We both consistently lowered taxes on families and low- and middle-income earners. We both reformed regulations and cut red tape to unleash resource development and promote entrepreneurialism. We both signed free trade agreements to expand market access for businesses and workers in our countries. And we both opposed carbon taxes as economically damaging, environmentally ineffective, and harmful to the interests of regular working citizens.

It is no surprise, then, that we got along so well. It was an honour to serve with Tony. And this compilation of speeches underscores the reasons I feel that way.

Readers are able to see Tony's depth of knowledge, commitment to principle, senses of humour and decency, and, of course, his concern for Australia and its people. These admirable traits and more have been present throughout his impressive record of public service chronicled here. And I do not just say that because he praises my own record in 'Together as comrades'!

There is a good distillation of Tony's ambitious record, including his 'We've laid a solid foundation' speech of February 2015. There is an expression of his emphasis on long-term growth and dynamism, including major infrastructure investments, reflected in his 'We're now readier to take the long view' in November 2014. And, of course, there is his sense of history and its foundational role for our societies, from 'We wonder at their selflessness' back in April 2015.

But what strikes me most is how rooted his political vision is in the interests of regular Australians, and his unfailing optimism in them and their future. Even in his solemn remarks about the end of Holden manufacturing in 2013, one can still discern this sense of confidence.

I believe his perspective comes from a recognition of the extraordinary contributions made by ordinary Australians over the years. His speech, 'Ordinary men did extraordinary things', to mark the centenary of the Gallipoli landing, was therefore more than just an eloquent commemoration. It points to the heart of Tony's politics. As he concluded: "They were as good as they could be in their time; now, let us be as good as we can be in ours."

Such an outlook ought to animate policymakers and regular citizens alike. Yes, we face real challenges – the threat of terrorism, bouts of economic disruption, and so on – but we have, as he rightly observed, "won the lottery of life." We live in free, dynamic, and wealthy countries, during the best era ever to be alive. Our people are hard-working, ingenious, and good. We have the means to tackle the challenges we will invariably confront. Our future can be bright.

The enclosed speeches can serve as a roadmap for navigating that future, that is, by drawing on the lessons of the past and applying them forward. It is no accident that the 2015 speech at Gallipoli channeled Edmund Burke's insight that healthy societies are compacts between the "dead, the living and the yet-to-be-born." Ronald Reagan's famous observation: "I do not want to go back to the past; I want to go back to the past way of facing the future," reflects the same fundamentally conservative perspective that Tony shares.

The one constant along this spectrum of past, present, and future is Tony's faith and trust in democratic citizenry. He summed it up in his speech to the World Economic Forum in 2014. He reminded the attendees that government is ultimately about people – whom he called "our masters." It was a prescient warning of the growing elite disconnection that has since precipitated the populist uprising across the western world.

It is this loyalty to the interests, aspirations, and challenges of everyday citizens that distinguished Tony's prime ministership and ought to guide future policymakers. It is a reminder that public officials can neither serve their own interests nor the interests of ideology. Good governance is ultimately about serving the people. Tony understands this very well, as this brilliant compilation powerfully displays. I was grateful to serve with him and am even more grateful to call him a friend.

Stephen J. Harper was the 22nd prime minister of Canada, from 2006 to 2015. His new book, *Right Here, Right Now: Politics and Leadership in the Age of Disruption*, was published on 9 October 2018.

PREFACE

Nick Cater

Robert Menzies set a high bar. His weekly radio broadcasts delivered during the hardest days of World War II, including the defining 'Forgotten People' speech of May 1942, became a precise manifesto for the Liberal Party established two years later.

The Menzies Research Centre republished transcripts of those broadcasts in 2017. This year we are posting nine of them as podcasts thanks to technology that Menzies could scarcely have imagined. We also published *Menzies: The Forgotten Speeches*, an anthology spanning more than 40 years in public life of speeches rescued from obscurity in the archives.

For a politician who aspires to lead, a public speech is no mere ornament. It is an opportunity to shape and share a vision and provide a solid foundation for governance. They are also a vehicle for persuasion, a skill mastered by John Howard and captured in *Howard: The Art of Persuasion* published last year.

This year we turn our attention to Tony Abbott's brief but productive period as Prime Minister. The influences of Menzies and Howard are clear, but so too is Abbott's literary skill, honed as a journalist. Like Menzies and Howard, Abbott achieved the remarkable task of leading his party out of opposition. These speeches reveal he also had a strong plan for government, accomplishing the tasks he had laid before the electorate while developing further plans for reform of the federation, taxation, welfare, indigenous affairs, health funding and more.

This volume, like the others in the series, is, if you like, a self-portrait. *Abbott: As Delivered* is an intimate picture of politician who thought deeply about the purpose of government and its role in creating a more prosperous and just society not with its own energy but by releasing the potential of its people. We present it as a template for others who aspire to serve.

Nick Cater

Executive Director, Menzies Research Centre

INTRODUCTION

Paul Ritchie

Tony Abbott had been in the Parliament for almost twenty years before he had a speechwriter. I was his first.

Abbott, the Rhodes Scholar, author and journalist is a man of the written word. He lived out the admonition of his high school teacher "to read with a voracious appetite" and writes with similar passion. He reminded me on many occasions of Churchill's sentiment that words are the only things that last forever. In the world of the internet, that's truer than ever.

Like his prime ministerial predecessors, Alfred Deakin and John Curtin, he was trained as a journalist and shared Sir Robert Menzies' obstinate objection to having others put words into his mouth. The grey speeches written by bureaucrats were invariably too long, focused on the processes of government and were inclined to regard the amount of money spent by government as proof of an underlying value. Abbott, by his own admission, is 'word proud' believing that 'good writing is good thinking'.

He knew, however, that you can rarely 'wing it' as prime minister, because a wrong name, an incorrect fact or a misquoted source quickly becomes the story of the day. Still, there are moments when a prime minister himself must own the text. When Holden announced in late 2014 that it was closing its Australian operations, Tony Abbott was in the VIP jet returning from the funeral of former South African President Nelson Mandela. As the he alighted from his car in Canberra I attempted to hand him some notes. "I know what I want to say" and he headed directly to the Chamber. On the Friday that news came through that Flight MH17 had been brought down, the House was sitting to deal with procedural business. Again, the words of that morning were all his own work.

Speeches matter. They shape the arguments, values and thinking that underpins a government. They give meaning, set direction and allow us to weigh the intellectual strength and character of the speaker.

Abbott was never banal or empty. His speeches were polished, cohesive, checked and mostly hit the mark, even if his audiences did not always know it at the time. In his address to the 25th Anniversary of the Sydney Institute, Abbott chose not to give a philosophical speech or one to tickle the audience's ears but to set out the direction and scope of the forthcoming 2014 Budget. We knew the Budget would be significant, we didn't realise it would be the pivot point of the Abbott Government. The audience was, by most reports, disappointed on the night. With hindsight, however, it was a place mark in history, clearly signalling the government's determination to tackle the economic and fiscal challenges that are holding back Australia from fulfilling its potential.

Edmund Burke's famous speech about political judgement might well have been intended for parliamentarians like Abbott who believe that the business of the nation should be conducted in the Chamber, not holding court at the local pub or handing out fliers at local railway stations. While Abbott thrived in such settings, and could scull a beer almost as quick as Bob Hawke, he sees the essence of his job as to shape the debate and thereby shape the direction of the country. That is why he is still in politics today.

INTRODUCTION

David Furse-Roberts

Honing his writing skills as a Rhodes Scholar, seminarian, journalist, political staffer, campaign director, parliamentarian and cabinet minister, Tony Abbott brought a facility with words to the prime ministership. Like Winston Churchill, John F Kennedy and Robert Menzies, Abbott appreciated the power of the pen and its importance to good statecraft. As both a seasoned writer and a parliamentarian, he instinctively knows speech can inspire, persuade and encourage in equal measure.

As a journalist-turned-politician, Abbott observed that writing speeches on key topics, many of which were published in the press, was his way of combining writing with politics. For Abbott as both a journalist and a politician, what mattered "was the impact of ideas on events and the critical importance of a written argument in shaping people's ideas". From this collection of speeches, it is evident that Abbott brought this same approach to the prime ministership.

Abbott: As Delivered showcases the speeches of Australia's twenty-eighth Prime Minister. In his twenty-four months as Prime Minister, Abbott abolished the carbon and mining taxes, stopped the people-smuggling trade, launched a humanitarian program to resettle 12,000 refugees from Syria, restored fiscal restraint to the budget, repealed gratuitous regulations to maximise the freedom of individuals and businesses, initiated a royal commission into trade union corruption, brokered free-trade agreements with China, Japan and South Korea, and instigated a UN-led investigation into the MH17 tragedy.

As well as chronicling Abbott's policy achievements as Prime Minister, this volume provides an insight into the conservative-liberal principles that inspired Abbott to enter public life. Acknowledged by supporters and opponents alike as a "conviction politician", Abbott believed that politics was not only a noble vocation through which to serve the common good but a theatre for the battle of ideas. Inspired by the Catholic faith of his upbringing, together with mentors such as Emmet Costello and B.A. Santamaria, Abbott's political philosophy was forged on an impregnable spiritual foundation that affirmed the divine image of every human being, the equality of all people before God, the importance of the family, the "golden rule" of treating others as you would have them treat you, and the "subsidiarity principle" of Catholic social thought which favours localised government over centralised administration.

Added to this was indeed his liberal-conservative philosophy imbibed from his chief political lodestars, John Hewson and John Howard. With its natural home in the Liberal Party, this tradition favours free market capitalism over socialism, individual initiative over state coercion, personal freedom over government regulation, limited government over bloated bureaucracy and free trade over tariff protection. Drawing inspiration from Edmund Burke, it typically combines these liberal principles with the conservative defence of such institutions as the Crown, the Constitution and the flag. As Abbott once remarked, "Simple self-respect demands some appreciation of and sympathy for the history and cultures that have made modern Australia".

Like Menzies and also Alfred Deakin, Abbott never subscribed to an atomistic individualism that regarded individuals as simply ends in themselves. Drawing from the Australian Liberal tradition of Deakin and Menzies, and to some degree the continental European tradition of Christian Democracy embodied by the likes of Santamaria, Abbott's own credo stresses the importance of the individual but also appreciates that they are part of a social fabric that has to be respected and preserved. Accordingly, for individuals to be fulfilled, they normally need families and communities, whose members' interests also need to be considered.

From the very beginnings of his parliamentary career in 1994, Abbott has been a consistent exponent of Liberal Party values. In a well-received preselection speech for the seat of Warringah that enabled him to "come through the middle" of a crowded field of budding candidates, Abbott articulated his Liberal philosophy:

> I'm a Liberal because I believe that government's role is to give people a hand up, not a handout. I believe in limited government and unlimited opportunity, because for getting things done free enterprise beats red tape every time…I'm a Liberal because our party has always stood for the decent, the humane and usually for the practical too.

As to putting his liberal creed into practice, Abbott's guiding approach to policy was always "What are the Liberal Party's best values and how can they be translated into policy". This volume of speeches reveals Abbott doing precisely that as his prime ministerial pronouncements across a wide range of policy fronts evidently stemmed from his party's core principles.

Prior to becoming Prime Minister, Abbott frequently pondered what the essence and orientation of Australia's next centre-right government would be. In his 2009 book, *Battlelines*, he contemplated whether it would be one focused on "single-mindedly cutting public expenditure and striving to deliver smaller government" or one that would "morph into compassionate conservatism, stressing solidarity with those who are doing it tough". As this collection of speeches reveals, it appears that the centre-right government he eventually led from 2013 to 2015 exhibited both traits. On the one hand, the Abbott government had a clear agenda to rein in the budget and scale back regulation, whilst on the other it expressed its resolve to help the lot of the disadvantaged, not least Indigenous Australians and the unemployed.

For all his fidelity to his core principles and values, nonetheless, Abbott appreciated that their application needed to adapt to the times. As much as he admired his Liberal forebears such as Menzies and Howard, he never regarded it as wise to merely ape their policies since they had governed in different times. To take the example of Indigenous affairs, Abbott adopted an appreciably different approach to that of the previous Liberal government under Howard. As Abbott once remarked in *Battlelines*, "The challenge is to express enduring ideals and aspirations in new policies that apply those age-old values to contemporary problems". In short, Abbott believed that the job of government was to respond intelligently and practically to the problems of the day and, in so doing, to help our country to reflect better its best values. This mindset of Abbott is certainly apparent in the collection of speeches that follow.

The speeches in this collection are categorised thematically to allow readers to appreciate the considerable policy breadth that Abbott brought to the prime ministership. Beginning with his maiden speech of 1994 where he articulated the values and ideals that inspired his career in politics, the volume features the speeches where Abbott articulated the philosophy and approach of the modern Liberal Party. Like his predecessors Howard and Menzies, Abbott was a great believer in expounding the Liberal creed and bringing it to bear on the great policy questions of the day from social welfare to education and employment.

While Abbott was frequently criticised for his perceived lack of economic policy nous, his speeches on economic matters revealed his sustained vision for a stronger Australian economy. Abbott's policy agenda for strengthening the economy entailed budgetary repair and fiscal restraint, lower taxes, less regulation and the necessary support for businesses to grow and flourish.

Turning to foreign affairs, the speeches in this section reveal that Abbott more or less continued Howard's approach of not having to choose between Australia's geography and history. Accordingly, Abbott combined an active engagement in the Asia Pacific region with an emphasis on nourishing Australia's traditional Trans-Tasman and North Atlantic alliances. In addition, Abbott focused on strengthening important yet underdeveloped friendships with nations such as Canada and India.

Returning to the domestic sphere, the speeches on Indigenous affairs shed light on the priority for Abbott of both tackling Indigenous disadvantage and enshrining the First Australians in our founding document and national story. To a greater extent than his Liberal predecessor, John Howard, Abbott managed to combine the practical with the symbolic in his government's approach to empowering Aboriginal and Torres Strait Islander Australians.

As a journalist and literary enthusiast, Abbott appreciated firsthand the importance of quality journalism and literature to enriching the nation's cultural capital. As the leader of a party that has occasionally been chided for its perceived indifference to the arts and culture, the speeches in this section reveal Abbott's abiding love for the written word and the power of literature to transmit the culture of our civilisation from one generation to the next.

Central to modern Australia's cultural identity, of course, is the legend of Anzac. Abbott's speeches on the Anzacs and their legacy speak powerfully to the national soul. Again, he appreciates not only the gallant deeds of the original Anzacs, but the legacy of writers such as Charles E.W. Bean that have kept the spirit of Anzac alive.

For Abbott, the historic legend of Anzac informed his contemporary outlook on veterans affairs and defence. His speeches to returned service personnel demonstrated his esteem for Australia's successive generations of veterans as worthy heirs to the Anzacs of Gallipoli. At the same time, his approach to Australia's defence was dictated by the geostrategic imperatives of the day but inspired by the ethos of Anzac.

With his prime ministership coinciding with the rise of Daesh in the Middle East and the ever-present spectre of radical Islamic terrorism, the security of Australia and its people emerged as one of the chief policy priorities of Abbott during his term in office. His speeches on national security, counter-terrorism and air safety in the wake of the MH17 and MH370 tragedies convey both his resolve to keep Australians safe and his refusal to yield to the demands of terrorists.

As a lifelong Catholic educated in the Jesuit tradition, Abbott instinctively recognised the importance of religious faith to the moral fibre, meaning and purpose of even a relatively secular country such as Australia. Abbott's speeches on faith reveal his personal indebtedness to the Catholic faith tradition of his upbringing as well as his respect for other faith traditions in Australia such as Buddhism.

Serving as a former health minister under Howard, medical research surfaced as an important priority for Abbott as did health care providers such as the community pharmacy. The speeches in this section express his commitment to these priorities, and impressively for a humanities-educated prime minister, his pledge to support the "STEM" disciplines of science, technology, engineering and mathematics in Australian schools and research institutes.

As an avowed conservative, his philosophical instincts extended to the conservation of the natural environment, but at the same time, he acknowledged that this needed to be delicately balanced with the interests of industries that generated the jobs, growth and infrastructure necessary for Australia's livelihood. As such, his speeches on the environment, energy and infrastructure reveal the mind of a prime minister who sees no conflict between the necessity to conserve Australia's natural environment but also the imperative to utilise the country's natural resources appropriately for development and growth.

Whilst not of a rural background himself, Abbott recognised the importance of Australia's primary industries for not only regional development and employment but also for overseas trade. In this section are speeches where Abbott affirms his government's commitment to supporting Australian agriculture, fostering regional development and promoting freer trade, especially with Australia's trading partners.

During his prime ministership, there were fewer instances where Abbott's Liberal philosophy of smaller government was more evident than in his agenda to reduce red-tape and burdensome regulations. In these speeches on deregulation, Abbott explains that his rationale for cutting red-tape and rolling back regulations is to maximise personal freedom and to create a climate where businesses can thrive and flourish.

On the place of women in society, Abbott acknowledged that his views had evolved from the more traditionalist attitudes of his early adulthood. His speeches on women reveal a Prime Minister who is serious about empowering all Australians to be active contributors to the social, cultural, economic and public life of the nation.

With almost two decades in parliament prior to becoming Prime Minister after careers in journalism and political staffing, Abbott had been a lifelong and studious observer of political leadership. In these speeches on leadership, governance and direction, he appraised the successes and failures of recent Australian governments, reflected on the relationship between politics and the media, assessed his own government's performance and flagged future reforms to Australia's federation.

The eulogies and tributes capture both Abbott's reflection of the national mood during a period of mourning and his conception of politics as a parade of public leaders who help define the course of history. In his tribute to the victims of the Martin Place siege, Abbott articulated the sentiments of a nation in shock and grief, whilst his condolences to Gough Whitlam and Malcolm Fraser paid homage to the legacy of his departed predecessors.

The collection concludes with Tony Abbott's final speech as prime minister, delivered on the morning after he was defeated by his challenger Malcolm Turnbull in a Liberal party room ballot. In this address, Abbott came full circle back to his maiden speech where he quoted again the text of Psalm 116 to declare that he had "rendered all" in his service as Prime Minister.

This volume of Tony Abbott's speeches seeks to cut through all the media commentary to provide readers with a firsthand insight into the principles, ideals and aspirations that drove Australia's twenty-eighth Prime Minister. From perusing these pages, readers will gain a more authentic and comprehensive portrait of a statesman who combined a commanding intellect with practical know-how to deliver tangible benefits to the lives of ordinary Australians.

Although his prime ministership of twenty-four months was relatively brief, this volume of speeches reveals an Australian leader who accomplished so much on both the domestic and foreign policy fronts. Whatever the circumstances attending the abrupt end to his prime ministership in September 2015, this formidable record of delivery ensures that his legacy can never be easily erased or forgotten. His exposition and, most importantly, his execution of liberal-conservative principles into practical policy initiatives, as evidenced by these speeches, assures his place in history as one of Australia's great conviction Prime Ministers.

CHRONOLOGY OF SPEECHES

Maiden speech. House of Representatives, Canberra, 31 May 1994

After serving as press secretary to Liberal Leader John Hewson from 1990 to 1993, Tony Abbott is approached by John Howard to seek preselection for the blue-ribbon seat of Warringah, in Sydney's lower northern beaches. Abbott wins preselection and the subsequent by-election on 26 March 1994. In his maiden speech he says Australia's heritage and traditions inspired him to enter public life and pledges to build on those foundations. Twenty-five years later, he remains true to those principles. Page 1

Victory speech. Sydney, 7 September 2013

The results on election night were an emphatic victory for the Coalition after six years of Labor rule. Abbott arrives at Sydney's Four Seasons Hotel to claim victory as only the fourth Liberal Party leader to win office from opposition, and the first since John Howard in 1996. He declares Australia is now "under new management" and "open for business". Page 11

Taking oath. Canberra, 18 September 2013

Accompanied by his wife and three daughters, Abbott is officially sworn in as Australia's 28th Prime Minister by Governor-General Quentin Bryce in a brief ceremony at Government House. The Prime Minister promises to lead a "problem-solving" government. Page 9

Australia-Indonesia co-operation. Jakarta, Indonesia, 1 October 2013

Following in the footsteps of John Howard, Prime Minister Abbott makes Indonesia his first overseas destination as PM. He attends a bilateral meeting with Indonesian President Susilo Bambang Yudhoyono and assures him that Australia's efforts to stop people smuggling will respect Indonesia's territorial integrity. In an address to the Indonesia-Australia Business Breakfast, he says strengthening and broadening the business ties between the two countries will help Australians and Indonesians "know each other, learn from each other and help each other". Page 56

Address to *Quadrant*'s 500th edition dinner. Fort Denison, Sydney, 16 October 2013

Anti-Communist intellectuals James McAuley and Richard Krygier founded *Quadrant* magazine in 1956 to promote the values of freedom during the Cold War. In October 2013, it celebrated the publication of its 500th edition at a dinner with Abbott as the guest of honour. The Prime Minister praises *Quadrant* as an advocate for Western values and human dignity against the "intellectual pessimism" and "cultural despair" of postmodernism and political correctness. Page 122

negative consequences will make way for new opportunities in a changing world, such as the expansion of the Olympic Dam mine. Page 40

Urging the WEF to promote freer trade. Davos, Switzerland, 23 January 2014

Addressing his first World Economic Forum, Abbott reiterates his faith in open markets and trade as the key to greater global prosperity, co-operation and peace. He urges the G20 to repudiate protectionism in favour of freer markets. Page 255

Welcome to the team. Sydney, 26 January 2014

Presiding over his first Australia Day as Prime Minister, Abbott speaks of Australia's origins and modern sense of "unity in diversity". On Australia Day we should honour our Aboriginal and British heritage while welcoming new citizens from all corners of the earth at citizenship ceremonies. He notes that Australia Day 2014 marks the 65th anniversary of the Australian Citizenship Act, which created the concept of Australian citizenship. He says 4.5 million people have since chosen to make Australia their home, including himself, his parents, his sister and his wife. His Australian citizenship is not something he takes for granted. Page 128

Blood brothers. Sydney, 7 February 2014

Appearing with his New Zealand counterpart John Key at a business lunch in Sydney, Prime Minister Abbott says the cross-Tasman relationship is between "blood brothers". He lauds New Zealand for its recent liberal economic reforms and impressive economic growth, thanks largely to Key. Abbott says Key's approach to smaller government and lower taxes has buoyed New Zealand's economy, setting an example Australia could emulate. Page 68

Closing the gap. House of Representatives, Canberra, 12 February 2014

In 2008, the Council of Australian Governments agreed to set targets for "closing the gap" between indigenous and non-indigenous Australians. Six years later, the Abbott Government releases a progress report, which Prime Minister Abbott presents to Parliament. Its findings are mixed: reductions in child mortality and increased participation in education, but inadequate progress in other areas. He says there should be no conflict between indigenous pride and participation in modern Australia. Page 104

Completing our Constitution. Old Parliament House, Canberra, 12 February 2014

At Reconciliation Australia's annual dinner at Old Parliament House, sponsored by Rio Tinto, the nation's largest private indigenous employer, Prime Minister Abbott announces one of his key ambitions in Government: formal acknowledgement of indigenous Australians in the Constitution. Such a change would need to be passed in a referendum, he says, which is historically difficult in Australia. But he remains optimistic. The acknowledgment would be his "crowning achievement". Page 109

Stronger ties with Canada. Melbourne, 24 February 2014

Attending his first Australia-Canada Economic Leadership Forum since forming Government, Prime Minister Abbott says the alliance is close but underdeveloped. Although geographically remote, the two countries are, in John Howard's words, "kindred-spirits". The Prime Minister says Australia and Canada need to "make more of this friendship", and outlines the nations' common challenges – indigenous recognition, multicultural unity, environmental sustainability and managing a federation. Page 71

Empowering women. House of Representatives, Canberra, 4 March 2014

Addressing his first International Women's Day as Prime Minister, Mr Abbott attributes his evolving views on women to his otherwise all-female household, consisting of wife Margie and three daughters. As an example of his modern views, the Prime Minister points to the paid parental leave scheme that he and his government are planning to introduce. Page 295

Supporting forestry. Canberra, 4 March 2014

ForestWorks is an industry-owned not-for-profit organisation offering skills development and advocacy support for businesses involved in wood, paper, furniture and other timber products. The Prime Minister tells its annual dinner that respect for the natural environment does not necessarily need to be to the detriment of industry. "It is possible to combine respect for the environment and respect for nature with healthy private business," he says. Timber workers are not "environmental bandits", as the Greens believe, but are "the ultimate conservationists". Page 234

Cutting red tape. House of Representatives, Canberra, 19 March 2014

The Prime Minister acts on his long-held belief of reducing the size of government, which has grown prodigiously since Federation, especially during the previous Parliament. He says Australia is now ranked 128th in the world for government regulation. He says red tape is often based on the false premise that governments know best. Instead, citizens should be given more control over their own lives, and announces the first annual "Red Tape Repeal Day". Page 279

Honouring C.E.W. Bean. Australian War Memorial, Canberra, 15 April 2014

Prime Minister Abbott speaks at a dinner to honour Australia's pre-eminent military historian, Charles Edwin Woodrow Bean (1879-1968). At the outbreak of World War I, Bean was appointed official war correspondent, and most famously covered the Gallipoli campaign. Bean's other great legacy is the Australian War Memorial. In this address to an audience of guests from the media, military, politics and industry, Abbott lauds Bean as a "keeper of the Anzac flame". Page 148

Jobs are better than welfare. Canberra, 24 June 2014

Abbott tells the Committee for Economic Development of Australia's annual conference that more jobs need to be created for the sake of both the unemployed and the nation. Quoting Robert Menzies, he says, "the pursuit of happiness lies along a self-made road; seldom along a road made by others no matter how good their intentions". The ageing of the population means more workers will be needed to prop up social welfare. "I want this Government to be the best friend that the workers of Australia have ever had," he says. Page 42

Honouring Monash. Australian War Memorial, Canberra, 25 June 2014

Prime Minister Abbott attends the launch of the digital version of more than 10,000 wartime papers revealing the thoughts and strategies of General Sir John Monash (1865-1931). Born in Melbourne to Jewish parents, Monash is best remembered as one of the greatest Allied generals of World War I and the most famous commander in Australian history. "The more you read Monash, the more you admire him," he says. "And this is why it's so important that his papers be widely available." Page 153

Address to Federal Council. Melbourne, 28 June 2014

Prime Minister Abbott reiterates the guiding philosophy of the Party he has led since December 2009. He invokes the legacies of Menzies, Fraser and Howard, the three longest serving Liberal prime ministers, who upheld the principles of patriotism, families, enterprise, community and freedom. Abbott reminds his audience that the Liberal Party focuses on "getting things done", especially in job creation, infrastructure, trade and national security. Page 13

A firm friendship with Japan. Parliament House, Canberra, 8 July 2014

At the invitation of Prime Minister Abbott, Shinzo Abe becomes the first Japanese leader to address an Australian Parliament, and speaks warmly of the friendship between Japan and Australia. Abbott responds by saying the dark period of World War II was an aberration in the relationship. Japan had been an ally in World War I, when a Japanese cruiser helped escort Anzacs to the Middle East. It is now one of "the world's firmest friendships" and "most practical of partnerships", he says, and announces that the Japan-Australia Economic Partnership will soon begin. Page 76

Fiftieth anniversary of *The Australian*. Sydney, 15 July 2014

Prime Minister Abbott joins media executives, current and former editors and the prominent Australians they have criticised, lampooned and praised to celebrate the first 50 years of Australia's original national newspaper. He tells the party that *The Australian* has served the country well: "It's barracked for causes rather than party, it's promoted issues rather than individuals, and the editorial line has never precluded well-argued dissent." It has also consistently reported on indigenous affairs with more rigour and candour than other newspapers. Abbott says he shares the paper's typical support for smaller government, lower taxes, greater personal freedoms and patriotism. Page 125

MH17 tragedy. House of Representatives, Canberra, 18 July 2014

On 17 July 2014, Malaysia Airlines flight MH17 from Amsterdam to Kuala Lumpur is shot down by a Buk ground-to-air missile over eastern Ukraine and crashes near the village of Hrabove, 40km from the Russian border. All 283 passengers (including 27 Australians, 43 Malaysians and 193 Dutch) and 15 crew are killed. Addressing the House of Representatives on the day after the attack, Prime Minister Abbott expresses condolences to the victims and their families, and says the attack was more likely to be malicious than accidental. Page 202

'Not an accident, it's a crime'. Opinion piece for News Corp Australia, 20 July 2014

The Prime Minister resolves to offer emotional and practical support to the grieving families of the victims and to bring the perpetrators of the attack to justice. He says the Department of Foreign Affairs and Trade has assigned consular officers to the family of each victim, who will provide counselling and help. Regarding an investigation into the incident, Prime Minister Abbott and Foreign Minister Julie Bishop will work with the UN Security Council to procure a through international investigation of the debris at the crash site and the flight's black-box recorder. He says Australia is "united in grief", and both sides of politics will co-operate on the matter. Page 204

MH17 memorial service. St Patrick's Cathedral, Melbourne, 7 August 2014

Prime Minister Abbott declares a national day of mourning for those killed in the MH17 tragedy. An interfaith service at St Patrick's Catholic Cathedral in Melbourne attracts 1,800 mourners, including Governor-General Sir Peter Cosgrove, the Prime Minister himself and Opposition Leader Bill Shorten. Abbott says that the most important response on an occasion like this is empathy for those who have lost love ones. "We who have not been bereaved must reach out to those who have and show, by our love, that love has not abandoned them." Page 206

Address to AIG dinner. Sydney, 8 August 2014

The Australian Industry Group represents more than 60,000 businesses employing a total of more than 1 million staff. It invites Prime Minister Abbott to deliver its inaugural Sir William Tyree Address, in honour of the Sydney engineer, businessman and philanthropist who had died the previous year, aged 91. The Prime Minister addresses the themes of business productivity, innovation, competition and free trade, and resolves to change the culture of regulation in Australia. In short, he will "get the fundamentals right". Page 47

Triumph & Demise launch. Parliament House, Canberra, 26 August 2014

Written by journalist and historian Paul Kelly, *Triumph & Demise: The Broken Promise of a Labor Generation* chronicles the Rudd-Gillard Labor Governments (2007-13). Prime Minister Abbott notes Kelly's evenhanded reporting of both the qualities and flaws of the major players. As a former journalist himself, Abbott says these skills set Kelly apart from most others in the profession. Despite the apparent shortcomings of recent Governments, the Australian system can still deliver excellent Governments as it has done in the past. Page 298

Fighting Islamic State. House of Representatives, Canberra, 1 September 2014

With the conflict in Iraq escalating and Islamic State on the rise, Prime Minister Abbott decides Australia needs to intervene on humanitarian grounds. This announcement to Parliament comes just after Shiite militias and Iraqi government forces, backed by US air power, defeated Islamic State fighters who had been threatening a massacre in a key Shiite town. Australia has no intention of committing ground troops to Iraq, the Prime Minister says, but cannot stand idle while genocide is being threatened. Given the atrocities already perpetrated by Islamic State against Muslims, Christians and Yazidis, it was in Australia's humanitarian instincts to offer protection. Australia will also increase funding to fight terrorism at home. Page 184

Honouring Robert Menzies. Old Parliament House, Canberra, 3 September 2014

The 75th anniversary of Sir Robert Menzies' election as Prime Minister in September 1939 is marked by an exhibition of Menzies' public life at the Museum of Australian Democracy at Old Parliament House. The exhibition showcases personal artefacts, including his dairies and photo albums. Prime Minister Abbott is guest of honour at the opening, which is also attended by his predecessor John Howard and Menzies' daughter Heather Henderson. He pays tribute to Menzies' wartime leadership, for founding the Liberal Party and for shepherding Australia through a long postwar period of growth and prosperity. "All of us, in our own way, are Menzies' children," he says. Page 18

Sending students to Asia. Mumbai, India, 4 September 2014

Prime Minister Abbott chooses Mumbai to launch a signature foreign policy initiative: the New Colombo Plan, a 21st Century version of the original Colombo Plan that was initiated by Sir Robert Menzies' Government. Instead of receiving students from the Indo-Pacific region to study at Australian institutions, the New Colombo Plan will send promising Australian students to universities across South-East Asia and the subcontinent. The initiative will enrich both Australia and the region with a new channel for cultural and linguistic exchange. Page 80

National Press Club anniversary. National Press Club Canberra, 10 September 2014

In the 50 years since Prime Minister Robert Menzies delivered the National Press Club's inaugural address, it has attracted parliamentarians, scientists, diplomats, sport stars and other prominent figures to address its weekly lunches. At the 50th anniversary lunch, Prime Minister Abbott recalls his previous life as a journalist, then acknowledges the role of the media and the National Press Club in Australia's national life, which is not only to report the affairs of the country but to improve them. He reflects on how Australian life has changed during the past half century and credits the Hawke and Howard Governments for being the most effective on each side of politics. Page 130

Safety from terrorism. House of Representatives, Canberra, 22 September 2014

Addressing Parliament after counter-terrorism raids in Sydney and Brisbane, Abbott reminds the House of the importance of national security in an era of increasing terrorism. He expresses gratitude for the bipartisanship on the issue and adds that national security is a complex balance between personal freedom and communal safety. He warns Parliament that more personal restrictions may yet be necessary, but such restrictions and inconveniences are necessary to save lives and maintain Australia's social harmony. He outlines some of the practical measures, including more funding for police and security personnel, the recruitment of more ASIO and ASIS officers, the introduction of biometric screening at international airports and legislation to create new terrorist offences and extend existing powers to handle terror suspects. Page 187

Stopping jihadis. New York, 24 September 2014

Abbott becomes the first Australian Prime Minister to address the United Nations Security Council while Australia is a sitting member. This sitting, chaired by United States President Barack Obama, examines how to compel countries to prosecute citizens who travel abroad to join terrorist organisations. Abbott denounces terrorism as an insult to the ideals of both Islam and liberal democracy. More than 60 Australians have become fighters for foreign terrorist groups, he says, and he vows to swiftly bring them to justice. The Security Council agrees on new binding measures requiring all nations to stem the flow of foreign fighters into jihadist war zones. Page 192

Address to UN General Assembly. New York, 25 September 2014

In his inaugural speech to the United Nations General Assembly, Abbott addresses the challenges besetting the global community and the capacity for international goodwill and co-operation, of which the response to the disappearance of flight MH370 is a prime example. He acknowledges the UN's flaws but praises its promotion of world peace and progress since 1945 saying Australia will continue to play its part as a "good global citizen". Australia's humanitarian aid, fight against terrorism and commitment to economic growth has helped raise the quality of life for hundreds of millions of people in the Asia Pacific. Australia will always work for the betterment of mankind "wherever we can lend a helping hand". Page 82

Food for thought. Canberra, 1 October 2014

In an address to the Australian Food and Grocery Council Forum, Abbott pledges to continue bolstering Australia's agricultural sector after assisting it by abolishing the carbon tax, reducing energy costs and cutting red tape. He promises new infrastructure and the training of job-ready employees through a new apprenticeship system. It will allow export capacity to grow, the creation of jobs and reduce the cost of living. A thriving agricultural sector is not only in Australia's national interest but a boon for the burgeoning markets of Asia. Given the insatiable appetite for food commodities in the region, the Prime Minister says the potential for Australia's agricultural sector is effectively boundless. Page 273

Tribute to Gough Whitlam. House of Representatives, Canberra, 21 October 2014

Abbott speaks at the memorial to Gough Whitlam, the former Labor Prime Minister who died in Sydney on 21 October 2014, aged 98. Abbott says the benefits of Whitlam's reforms remain debatable, but people in public life can still learn much from such a "giant". Page 320

More cuts to red tape. House of Representatives, Canberra, 22 October 2014

After the success of the first Red Tape Repeal Day on 19 March 2014, which saved the economy about $700 million, Abbott announces that the second repeal day will target tax returns and bureaucracy, saving a further $300 million. The end goal, he says, is not only about reducing the size of government but increasing flexibility for people and businesses. With less red tape to contend with, it will be easier for creativity, enterprise and innovation to thrive. Page 284

Sir Henry Parkes Oration. Tenterfield, NSW, 25 October 2014

Abbott travels to the northern NSW town of Tenterfield to deliver an oration named after the "Father of Federation". Sir Henry Parkes' speech in Tenterfield in 1889 is widely credited for igniting the Federation movement. Abbott reflects on the significance of Parkes' oration and suggests ways to improve federal-state relations. He discusses his own journey from being a "philosophical federalist", in common with most traditional Liberals, to a "pragmatic nationalist", favouring neither the abolition of the states nor the further centralisation of power in Canberra but a cohesive Federation in which the Commonwealth and the states can better align revenue with spending. Given the delicate balance between state and Federal responsibilities, he concedes that reform of Australia's Federation will be a challenge, but one the government needs to face if it is to build a "greater nation". Page 310

Advancing medical research. Parliament House, Canberra, 27 October 2014

In this address to Australian Medical Research Institute's annual dinner, Abbott, a former Health Minister, says he likes to regard himself as the "Prime Minister for medical research". Despite having less than 1 per cent of the world's population, Australia has contributed to almost 5 per cent of refereed medical research, he says, and is responsible for such breakthroughs as the bionic ear, a cervical cancer vaccine and the first treatment for influenza. He announces a $20 billion Medical Research Future Fund, partly supported by the $7 co-payment for GP visits. Page 227

PM's Prizes for Science. Great Hall, Parliament House, Canberra, 29 October 2014

The Prime Minister's Prizes for Science reward achievements in scientific research. In this address in the Great Hall, Parliament House, Canberra, Abbott says Australia punches above its weight in published research but needs to do better at translating that research into practical outcomes. His government will help the new Commonwealth Science Council improve connections between science and business, and introduce a new award for the commercial application of science. Page 223

Building infrastructure. House of Representatives, Canberra, 30 October 2014

Abbott says he wants to become Australia's "infrastructure Prime Minister". This is not only about building more roads, bridges and dams but about improving the quality of life for Australians, reducing commute times and increasing business efficiency. He promises his Government will support new infrastructure projects in every Australian state and territory. Page 242

Bradfield Oration. Sydney, 5 November 2014

The Bradfield Oration, in honour of the engineer behind the Sydney Harbour Bridge, is a joint initiative of the *Daily Telegraph*, University of Sydney, Lend Lease and NRMA. Prime Minister Abbott delivers the inaugural address at the Museum of Contemporary Art, Sydney, attended by leaders from industry, business and politics, including NSW Premier Mike Baird. He says the challenge for contemporary policy makers is to follow Bradfield's example of planning far into the future. Page 248

'A relationship of peers'. House of Representatives, Canberra, 14 November 2014

Welcoming his British counterpart David Cameron to Canberra to address a joint sitting of parliament, Abbott reflects on the strong relationship between the two nations. "There's so much that Britain has given to us," he says, not only parliamentary democracy, common law and constitutional monarchy but also Shakespeare, the Beatles, the Industrial Revolution, the humanity of Wilberforce, and the determination of Churchill. But Australia's growth means the nations are now more like peers, pursuing a common agenda of lower taxes, fiscal restraint, private-sector investment, liberal trade and fighting Islamic terror. Page 86

Hosting the G20 summit. Brisbane Convention Centre, Brisbane, 16 November 2014

Australia hosts the ninth G20 Summit in Brisbane, attended by the presidents of the United States, China and Russia, among others. In his address at the conclusion of the summit, Abbott reiterates its three key themes of boosting growth and employment, enhancing global economic resilience and strengthening global institutions. He says the summit has also committed itself to global approaches to infrastructure, reducing the gender gap in workforce participation, developing better approaches to energy efficiency and reforms to the financial sector to avoid another global financial crisis. Page 261

Welcoming Xi Jinping. House or Representatives Canberra, 17 November 2014

The Chinese were among the earliest to migrate to Australia, Abbott says at a function to welcome Xi Jinping to Australia for the first time as President of China. Starting with prospectors in Victoria in the 1850s, Chinese migrants had made a mighty contribution to Australia, helping to build the nation through both war and peace. Now China is Australia's biggest trading partner, more than double the trade Australia has with the United States, as reflected in the recent free-trade deal. Abbott acknowledges the deal could not have been signed without previous PMs cultivating the relationship, especially Gough Whitlam. Page 89

Welcoming Narendra Modi. House of Representatives, Canberra, 18 November 2014

Prime Minister Abbott welcomes his Indian counterpart to the Australian Parliament. As the first Indian Prime Minister to address parliament and the first Indian leader to visit Australia in 28 years, Modi affirms Australia's importance to India, declaring that "Australia will not be at the periphery of our vision but at the centre of our thoughts". Abbott reciprocates, adding that the two nations have common ties of democracy, language, heritage and sport, from which it is possible to build both trade links and, through the New Colombo Plan, a cultural exchange. We "have much to teach each other", he says. Page 92

A friendship forged in trenches. House of Representatives, Canberra, 19 November 2014

François Hollande becomes the first French President to be hosted by an Australian Prime Minister. The visit occurs during the year of the 100th anniversary of the start of World War I. Welcoming Hollande to Australian shores, Prime Minister Abbott speaks warmly of the Franco-Australian friendship forged in the trenches of the Western Front. Despite differences in language and culture, France represents Australia's oldest and arguably closest continental European ally. Although the number of French-Australians is small compared to other immigrant communities, Abbott acknowledges their contribution to Australia life through the arts, the wine industry and the uptake of French as the most popular European language in the classroom. Page 95

Reassuring local pharmacists. Canberra, 24 November 2014

The Pharmacy Guild of Australia, founded in 1928, represents 5,700 community pharmacies, seeking to maintain their place as local health providers. Prime Minister Abbott's dealings with the guild extend back to his time as Health Minister in the Howard Government. At this speech to the guild's annual dinner, Abbott says pharmacists are widely trusted professionals, offering essential community services. They share the same goal as his Government – the health and wellbeing of Australians. "With government support, I am very confident that community pharmacy can do more for the people of Australia," he says. Page 230

Neville Bonner Oration. Sydney, 28 November 2014

Neville Bonnor (1922-1999) was the first indigenous person to be elected to Federal Parliament. An elder of the Jagera people, he joined the Liberal Party in 1967 and became a Senator for Queensland in 1971, where he served until 1983. In the late 1990s, he became a public advocate for the monarchy. In this oration to Australians for a Constitutional Monarchy, who are customarily reluctant to change the Constitution, Abbott channels Bonner's example as both a trailblazer and a traditionalist by advocating for indigenous recognition, which would "complete" the nation's founding document. Page 112

Prime Minister's Literary Awards. National Gallery of Victoria, Melbourne, 8 December 2014

Addressing the Prime Minister's Literary Awards at the National Gallery of Victoria, Melbourne, Abbott remembers how a teacher at his high school would implore his students to spend summer holidays reading with a "voracious appetite" instead of playing. "It's a phrase that I've never forgotten after all these years and have mostly tried to live by," he says. As a former Rhodes Scholar and journalist, his respect for storytellers is strong. He recounts correspondence with Tasmanian writer Richard Flanagan, who had just won the Man Booker, in which the two men lament the assumption that Australian writers only speak for the left side of politics. "Every government should want to encourage all of the voices in Australian life," the Prime Minister says. Page 135

Prayer vigil with Ukranina President for MH17 victims. Ukrainian Greek Eparchy of Saints Peter and Paul, Melbourne, 11 December 2014

Petro Poroshenko becomes the first Ukrainian President to visit Australia when he arrives to discuss the downing of Malaysia Airlines flight MH17 on Ukrainian soil. He accompanies Prime Minister Abbott to an ecumenical prayer vigil for the victims at the Ukrainian Greek Eparchy of Saints Peter and Paul in Melbourne. Abbott officially welcomes Poroshenko and pays tribute to the Ukrainian people who had suffered under the occupation of the Soviet Union, noting their religious faith was irrepressible even during Soviet persecution. As a practicing Catholic himself, Abbott appreciates the importance of faith to both the solace and strength of individuals, and to the flourishing of culture and civilisation, not least in Australia itself. In the wake of tragedies such as MH17, the people of the Ukraine and Australia alike can draw comfort, inspiration and hope from their faith. Page 213

Recognise inaugural dinner. Sydney, 11 December 2014

Recognise, a branch of Reconciliation Australia, holds its inaugural dinner in Redfern, Sydney, with Abbott as guest of honour. In his speech, Abbott says most Australians underestimate the characteristics they have inherited from their indigenous brothers and sisters. Stoicism and laconic humour, which are prominent Australian attributes, did not come ashore with the British settlers, he says. Rather, they developed when the white fellas and black fellas interacted on the frontier. Abbott says those characteristics are typical of the "indigenous people who it has been my privilege and honour to meet over the last 20 years or so of my public life," and reiterates his profound commitment to indigenous recognition in the Constitution. Page 117

Government progress report. National Press Club, Canberra, 2 February 2015

Sixteen months after being elected to Government, the Prime Minister outlines his team's impressive achievements to a lunch at the National Press Club in Canberra - including the release of an Australian journalist from an Egyptian prison, the abolition of two debilitating taxes, a record number of new companies and stopping the boats – and says there is still much to do. "Australia deserves the stable government that you elected us to be just 16 months ago," he says. "You deserve budget repair, no return of the carbon tax, no restart of people smuggling, and no in-fighting. We promised that we would do our best to keep you safe. We promised you hope, reward and opportunity. That's what the Abbott government is working to deliver for you." Page 302

Lindt Café siege. House of Representatives, Canberra, 9 February 2015

On 15 December 2014, lone gunman Man Haron Monis entered the Lindt Cafe at Sydney's Martin Place, took ten customers and eight employees hostage, and was killed 16 hours later when counter-terrorism police stormed the building. Also killed were hostages Tori Johnson and Katrina Dawson. All the other hostages were rescued. On the first Federal sitting day after the attack, and with the hostages and the families of the two victims present, Prime Minister Abbott moves a motion of condolence. He says December 15 was a "testing day for our country", but terrorism can never diminish Australia's yearning for freedom. "Australia is a peaceful country," he says. "We are a beacon of hope and liberty throughout the world… Our differences demonstrate our freedom and our willingness to lend a hand and to get along to make this the best place on earth to live." Page 323

War on terror. AFP Headquarters, Canberra, 23 February 2015

Prime Minister Abbott tells Australia's domestic security agencies, including ASIO, the Federal Police and others, that the war against terrorism is increasingly challenging. "These are testing times for everyone here, and for everyone sworn to protect democratic freedoms," he says. "The terrorist threat is rising at home and abroad – and it's becoming harder to combat." The Prime Minister outlines a comprehensive suite of policies designed to restrict hate preachers, prosecute foreign fighters, proscribe hate groups and screen immigrants. "We cannot allow bad people to use our good nature against us." Page 194

Celebrating Buddhism. Nan Tien Institute, Wollongong, NSW, 1 March 2015

Before an audience of dignitaries and senior members of the Buddhist community at the opening of the Nan Tien Institute in Berkeley, Wollongong, Prime Minister Abbott points out the common characteristics of peaceful religions. He says Buddhism relies on the universal human values of decency, generosity, understanding, integrity and moral rectitude. As such, Nan Tien has much to offer Australia. In a multicultural society, citizens of different faiths can work together to uphold liberal democratic ideals. Page 215

The mystery of MH370. House of Representatives, Canberra, 5 March 2015

A year after Malaysia Airlines flight MH370 from Kuala Lumpur to Beijing mysteriously disappeared with all 227 passengers and 12 crew, Prime Minister Abbott calls a special sitting of Parliament, to which the families of the missing are invited, to express the nation's condolences and praise the search and rescue personnel, despite their lack of success. The missing people include 153 Chinese, 50 Malaysians and six Australians. The search was the most expensive in aviation history, involving teams from Australia, Malaysia, China, South Korea, Japan, New Zealand and the United States. Page 209

Malcolm Fraser's legacy. House of Representatives, Canberra, 23 March 2015

Abbott pays tribute in Parliament to Malcom Fraser, describing him as a "complex and driven man," after his death in Melbourne aged 84 on 20 March 2015. Under Prime Minister Fraser's Government, building of the National Gallery of Australia, High Court and new Parliament House commenced, although credit is rarely attributed to him. He also established the AFP and SBS, and laid the foundations for financial deregulation. He was not as much of a reformer as Whitlam before him or Bob Hawke after him, but he "gave the country what we needed at the time". Abbott expresses gratitude on behalf of the party, which he says had not been said often enough in the past. Page 326

Peace summit, Turkey. Istanbul, Turkey, 23 April 2015

On the eve of the centenary of Anzac Day, Abbott addresses a peace summit in Istanbul attended by leaders from Australia, New Zealand and Turkey. He remarks on the friendship that has developed between Turkey and Australia: "When the battle is over, when the wounds have healed and when the ground has cooled, warriors can see their enemies' virtue." Abbott says the two nations were now working together to fight a common foe, terrorism. Page 156

Anzac Dawn Service centenary. Gallipoli, Turkey, 25 April 2015

Following in the footsteps of his predecessors, Bob Hawke, John Howard and Julia Gillard, Abbott travels to Anzac Cove to address the Dawn Service at Gallipoli, on its centenary, attended by New Zealand PM John Key, Prince Charles, Prince Harry, 8,000 Australians and 2,000 Kiwis. One hundred years have not dimmed the reverence felt for the "founding heroes of modern Australia". Abbott says the Anzacs were from every occupation and rung in society. The standard they set was still relevant during a time of relative peace. "They were as good as they could be in their time; now, let us be as good as we can be in ours," he says. Page 159

The Burkean pact. Lone Pine, Gallipoli, 25 April 2015

Shortly after speaking at the Anzac Cove Dawn Service, Prime Minister Abbott delivers an address at the Lone Pine Australian memorial, the site of a key battle during the Gallipoli campaign. He channels conservative philosopher Edmund Burke's famous dictum that society is a compact between the dead, the living and the yet-to-be-born. That pact, he says, is renewed here for all those who wish to understand what it means to be Australian. Page 162

Repatriation of Vietnam casualties. House of Representatives, Canberra, 25 May 2015

On the 50th anniversary of the departure of the first troops to the Vietnam War, Prime Minister Abbott tells Parliament Australia will offer to repatriate the remains of 25 Australian soldiers who never made it home. The offer will be made to the families of the soldiers. "We do remember all who served in the Vietnam War," he says. "We especially remember those who were faithful, even unto death." Page 174

MCA annual dinner. Parliament House, Canberra, 3 June 2015

At the annual Minerals Council of Australia parliamentary dinner, Abbott lists the achievements under his Government so far: carbon and mining taxes abolished, $1 trillion worth of mining projects initiated, 50,000 pages of red tape repealed and three free trade deals signed. But there is still more to do. "I look forward to working with you to build a strong economy and a clean environment," he says. "Together, we will build the best possible Australia on the shared understanding that a strong economy makes possible the high environmental standards that we all seek." Page 238

The rewards of faith. Old Parliament House, Canberra, 17 June 2015

The Australian Catholic University held its inaugural Parliamentary Interfaith Prayer Breakfast in 2014 at the NSW State Parliament in Sydney. The second breakfast is held in Canberra, featuring Christians, Jews, Muslims, Hindus, Buddhists, Sikhs and Baha'i. All sides of politics are represented. Keynote speaker Stepan Kerkyasharian, Prime Minister Abbott and Opposition Leader Bill Shorten all address the breakfast. Abbott discusses the importance of faith in realising "there is something more than the here and now to which we must aspire". Page 217

FTA with China. Canberra, 17 June 2015

After a decade of negotiations, initiated under John Howard, Abbott signs a watershed Free Trade Deal with China, Austalia's largest trading partner. Under the deal, more than 85 per cent of Australian goods exports will be tariff free, rising to 95 per cent upon full implementation. Tariffs on dairy, beef and seafood are set to be eliminated within years. Tariffs on Australian resources are also eliminated. Trade Minister Andrew Robb says the FTA "will be a catalyst for future growth across goods, services and investment". Addressing the lunch to mark the occasion, Abbott says Australians will now pay less for cars, clothes, electronics and other Chinese goods. "Today is a truly historic step forward in our comprehensive strategic partnership," he says. Page 266

Magna Carta anniversary. Great Hall, Parliament House, Canberra, 24 June 2015

The Magna Carta's proclamation that the King could not arbitrarily impose taxes, and that laws applied equally to citizens and monarchs is one of the founding documents of Western civilisation. Its 800th anniversary is commemorated with a dinner in the Great Hall of Parliament House, hosted by the British High Commission. Abbott says that, much like common law, the charter was born of practical experience rather than abstract theory. Its glorious legacy lives on even on the other side of the world, centuries later. "Security under the law is what our tradition has given people," he says. "It's what the Magna Carta represents. It's hard to imagine any human progress without it." Page 141

A responsibility to be prepared. Canberra, 25 June 2015

Abbott tells the Australian Strategic Policy Institute, a Canberra think tank, that while Australia is a peace-loving nation, it still needs to be able to to defend its citizens, advance its interests and uphold its values around the world. "We owe it to those in uniform, we owe it to our country and to our citizens, we owe it to the wider world in which we are a force for good to ensure that our armed forces are becoming more potent and more capable all the time," he says. Page 167

Building a better Australia. Sofitel, Melbourne, 27 June 2015

Abbott's second address to the Liberal Party Federal Council, after 21 months in office, is both a progress report and a reminder of the values that he and the party represent. He says his Government has stopped the boats, created 290,000 jobs, abolished two unnecessary taxes, cut red tape and signed three FTAs. The future looks bright. "We believe in family, in community and that our nation's greatest achievements come when our people are encouraged to have a go," he says. Page 20

US alliance. United States Embassy, Canberra, 30 June 2015

Hosted at the United States Embassy by US Ambassador John Berry to mark the forthcoming anniversary of the Declaration of Independence, Abbott speaks warmly of the multi-layered alliance between the two nations. "American leadership is as necessary as ever," he says. Page 97

A 'most unusual man'. Sydney, 30 July 2015

B.A. Santamaria, an outspoken Catholic, anti-communist political activist, was Abbott's earliest political mentor. Speaking at the launch of Gerard Henderson's biography of Santamaria, Abbott ponders the paradox of a man who "held no public office and claimed to have failed in all his principal endeavours, yet he has spawned a more extensive literature than most prime ministers". His claim to failure might have been modestly overstated – Abbott says Santamaria saved Labor from being overrun by communists and became the extra-parliamentary conscience of both sides of politics. "If his life was the failure he often protested it was, it was a magnificent failure that changed and improved our country and hundreds if not thousands of its leading citizens." Page 138

Boao Forum for Asia. Sydney, 30 July 2015

Addressing this forum for regional economic co-operation, Prime Minister Abbott is emphatic about the extensive benefits of free trade deals, such as the ones Australia has recently signed with China, South Korea and Japan, which had already stimulated spectacular increases in exports. "Freer trade will strengthen and deepen the relationship between Australia and the nations of our region. Australia has nothing to fear and everything to gain from freer trade. We gain and the world gains as well." Page 269

The benefits of a religious education. Manly, NSW, 7 August 2015

Addressing students at a Catholic school in his electorate, Prime Minister Abbott is effusive about the sense of mission and destiny imbued into a religious education. "I am sure each one of you, looking back on your school days in a few years' time, will be able to say, 'Yes, it was special... It wasn't just an education – it was more than that'." Such schools received some public funding but mostly survived on the communal spirit of parents, and the history of private schools in Australia was a "truly massive effort". Page 220

Thanking World War II veterans. Torrens Parade Ground, Adelaide, 15 August 2015

Abbott quotes Churchill at the the 70th anniversary of Victory in the Pacific: "In defeat defiance, and in war resolution; but in victory magnanimity, and in peace, goodwill." The generations who have enjoyed the decades of prosperity and international co-operation that followed World War II owe it all to those who fought, some of who are present here today, he says. "This is your world," he says. "I hope that you are proud of it; for we could not be more proud of you." Page 177

Helping Liberal women. Adelaide, 15 August 2015

The Liberal Party pioneered most aspects of female political representation in Australia, Abbott tells the 70th anniversary lunch of the party's Federal Women's Committee. Among these are the first quota for women, which was insisted by Dame Elizabeth Couchman as a condition of her Australian Women's National League joining Robert Menzies' new Liberal Party in 1944. Abbott also lists Enid Lyons, Annabelle Rankin, Ivy Wedgwood, Marie Breen, Margaret Guilfoyle, Margaret Reid, Kathy Sullivan and Julie Bishop as trailblazers for both country and party. In order to revive this proud tradition, the party needs not quotas but a "platitude-free conversation" about helping women who are natural Liberals. Page 290

Remembering Long Tan. Canberra, 18 August 2015

At the 49th anniversary of the Vietnam War's Battle of Long Tan, Abbott expresses reverence for the courage, determination, resourcefulness and unflinching loyalty to mates marked both the battle and the Australian experience in Vietnam. Sadly, this was not the feeling at home at the time. "People were entitled to question the war, but they should never have doubted our soldiers," he says. Nevertheless, the magnanimity of Australian personnel had enabled the two nations to become friends in peace. Page 181

Ending the disruption. Mosman, NSW, 28 August 2015

This address to the Mosman branch of the Liberal Party, in his Sydney electorate, is a plea to democratise the party and then to win the next Federal election. All members who have been in the party for 12 months or longer should have a say regarding candidates, he says. He then pledges to prove the disruption of the Labor Rudd-Gillard years are over. "My challenge, our challenge, is to demonstrate that chaos and incompetence is not the new normal in Australian politics," he says. "Our challenge is to prove that the age of meaningful reform is not ended, it was merely interrupted between 2007 and 2013." Page 26

Economic growth in PNG. Port Moresby, Papua New Guinea, 10 September 2015

On the 40th anniversary of Papua New Guinea's independence from Australia, Abbott says the burgeoning nation has proved the pessimists wrong. Trade with Australia is now strong, and aid is now being realigned to bolster business. PNG has just hosted the Pacific Games and will host APEC in 2018. "It's critical that both of us remove the barriers to growth because stronger economic growth is the key to addressing almost every national problem," he says. Page 99

Parting thoughts. Courtyard at Parliament House, Canberra, 15 September 2015

After losing the leadership to Malcolm Turnbull in a party-room ballot, Tony Abbott tells a press conference that it has been an honour to serve in the nation's highest elected office. He thanks his family, party, staff, the armed forces and the people of Australia for the privilege. He again lists his Government's proudest achievements. "I have consistently said – in Opposition and in Government – that being the Prime Minister is not an end in itself," he says. "It is about the people you serve." Page 331

1

What Shall I Render:
The Career Defining Speeches

'There is no limit to what Australia can achieve'
House of Representatives, 31 May 1994

Faith, trust, duty, social cohesion, family, governmental frugality and ambition for Australia – the themes of Abbott's maiden speech would go on to define his political career.

On the corner of Castlereagh and Hunter streets in Sydney stands a monument to mark the site of the first Christian service in Australia. The preacher, the Reverend Richard Johnson, took as his text: `What shall I render unto the Lord for all his benefits towards me?' It is just a small stone obelisk hardly noticed by the thousands of passers-by and dwarfed by skyscrapers, yet its message of faith and hope is fundamental to our nation's success and the key to Australia's future.

The congregation at that first service was poorer, sicker, and less trained than any conceivable group of modern Australians, yet there was nothing small about what they were to achieve. Our challenge, 200 years later, is to have hearts that are just as big. So at this opening of my time in parliament, I place on record my deep conviction that, nourished by the past and inspired by our great ideals, there is no limit to what Australia can achieve.

Also, I want to record my deep conviction that our Australian story should fill our hearts with pride and our eyes with tears. It is a story of the dispossessed and the outcast, redeemed through the innate goodness of humanity—a society challenged by nature, tested by war, enlarged by other cultures and blessed by such peace, prosperity and tolerance that we are now the envy of the earth.

Almost 100 years ago, the founders of our constitution echoed Richard Johnson's sense of gratitude when they instituted this mighty Commonwealth, yet they declared themselves, in the words of our constitution, to be` humbly relying on the blessing of Almighty God'. We have so much, yet almost everything we have we owe to someone else. If I can achieve anything at all in this place, I will owe it to the people of Warringah who have sent me here. If I can amount to anything at all in our national life, I will be indebted to my great predecessors whose shoes I struggle to fill: Michael MacKellar, who stood for the humane and the decent; Edward St John, who never shirked a fight in a good cause; and Sir Percy Spender, one of our greatest statesmen and international public servants.

Bounded by water on three sides, boasting some of Sydney's largest tracts of urban bushland, containing a significant concentration of high technology industries, often set in green and open parks, Warringah is almost a Garden of Eden. Mackellar might be God's own country but Warringah is God's own garden. So it is my job to make more perfect what is already one of the best places in the world to live. In particular, it is my job first to help Warringah's 13,000 families with children who are heavily burdened by government policies and, second, to help find a solution to our transport problems which mean that Warringah is indeed the best place in the world to live, but only until you need to go somewhere else.

When authority first came to the Warringah district, the inhabitants showed what they thought of government policies by spearing Governor Phillip in the shoulder. I hope I can be a similar goad to government, at least until such time as government serves my electorate better. One of the depressing features of modern Australia is the low esteem in which governments and politicians are generally held.

Shortly after the by-election, some kind supporter gave me polling data which ranked the ethics and honesty of various occupations. Lawyers rated 30 per cent for ethics and honesty; stockbrokers ranked 15 per cent; and I was terrified to see that federal parliamentarians ranked just 10 per cent. Notwithstanding this, I feel very honoured to be here because newspaper journalists—my previous trade—scored just eight per cent.

Perhaps we politicians have mostly ourselves to blame because we have neglected what government does well to indulge in what government does badly. The best way to restore politicians' standing is to have governments which meddle less and lead more; to have governments which stick to their traditional job of providing transfer payments and sponsoring national development but which stop playing the busybody in every nook and cranny of society. Above all, we need governments which believe in Australia and Australians as much as in the trappings of office, the dictates of ideology or the minutiae of policy.

Loss of faith is a social problem extending far beyond politics and far beyond Australia. Throughout the Western world we are living through a pandemic of doubt and introspection in which people are questioning their God, their country and even themselves. Nothing is safe from the corrosive cynicism of modern times: neither political goodwill nor institutional benevolence nor even parental love. Our challenge is to answer uncertainty with conviction and to refute doubt with faith.

This is not a matter of logical argument. No-one can be persuaded to believe. People must be inspired to believe; they must be picked up and carried along by other people—people who believe with heart and soul that no defeat is final, no unhappiness permanent and no evil invincible.

Modern Australia is rightly concerned about unemployment, crime, family breakdown and social disintegration. But we are becoming pre-occupied with problems and not answers. We must see each problem in its true setting: unemployment together with the new opportunities of a better trained work force; crime against the background of the greater complexity of modern life; family pressure against the higher expectations of people living longer; and social alienation against greater individual rights. It is absolutely vital that we Australians keep seeking solutions to all the difficulties in our homes, workplaces and neighbourhoods. But the real antidote to fear is hope, and the difference between despair and confidence is often just the very decision to try to make a difference – a decision based on a balanced appreciation of our true position.

For the first 180 years or so of our national life, Australian government was an exercise in nation building. Government directed work gangs, encouraged settlers and rewarded explorers. In more modern times, government has launched the immigration program, which has helped to make our society so diverse and exciting; it has established the Snowy Mountains Scheme, which powers our cities and waters our farms; it has funded the universities, which are the basis of our technological edge; and it has sponsored much of the national development, which is the foundation of our prosperity.

Yet some time in the recent past Australian government developed a strange affliction. Since Labor came to power in 1983, government has become a means for applying bandaids to social problems rather than an instrument for giving cohesion and purpose to our national life. Our government has policies to bring peace to Cambodia and to keep Antarctica clean. It has policies for unemployment and for making the sick well and the lame walk. But it has only bits and pieces of a policy to ensure that our nation will enter the next century in better shape than it is now. The government is like a householder who keeps fixing walls and mending floors, in a medley of styles often entirely at odds with the original design, plastering up the cracks without working out how the foundations are constantly shifting.

In the quest to solve social problems, government reaches into our schools, our workplaces and even our bedrooms. Government tells us what we should think, whom we should like and how we should feel. But it has by and large given up trying to touch our hearts and make us realise that we Australians are a great people with a great destiny. The best that this government can do to lift people's gaze above the humdrum is tear a corner off the flag, undermine the Crown and attack the very constitution itself. This is the opposite, the absolute opposite of nation building, because it is guaranteed to tear Australians apart rather than bring us together.

Yet there is no mystery in Australia's needs or voters' wants. There is no secret about what governments should do. As Edmund Burke said, governments are human contrivances to satisfy human wants. People expect governments to work—and I hope honourable members opposite recognise these lines—'for the betterment of mankind, not just here but wherever we can lend a helping hand', as Ben Chifley said in his 'light on the hill' speech. There are some things which only individuals can do; there are other things which only governments can do; and there are many things which people can do better, provided governments help. So let people run their own lives and let government do what individuals cannot.

I stand for active government, not big government. I stand for government which gets off people's backs, not government which opts out of the future because it cannot face hard decisions. I stand for government which backs Australia's families with real policies and not just platitudes.

This government says that it is in favour of the family, all the time pursuing policies which make family life harder to sustain. At present, for instance, a single taxpayer on $30,000 a year after tax has about $445 a week to live on. A taxpayer on the same $30,000 a year but with a dependent spouse and two dependent children has just $495 a week to live on—and that is after tax, after the dependent spouse rebate and after family allowance. In other words, three extra people to clothe, feed, house, educate and transport and just $50 a week extra with which to do it.

Family policy needs to begin with a recognition that our existing tax and welfare system turns middle income families with children into Australia's new poor. Families are best helped not by argument over definitions but by policies which help the children—the children who are this country's greatest asset and our most golden hope.

One way to help families with children is to change the tax system to take account of taxpayers' responsibilities as well as their income. A family-friendly tax system stresses self-help and individual responsibility. But the problem with income splitting, at least in its simplest form between husband and wife, is that it helps high income earners more than low income earners and couples without dependants as much as those with the responsibility for children. While voters have shown an innate mistrust of radical change to the tax system, everyone understands and hardly anyone objects to a cash payment. So one alternative to income splitting is to raise the current level of family allowances to such an extent that they become, in reality, a family wage; in other words, to pay the principal carers of children a substantial sum far in excess of current family allowance, a sum which acknowledges the real cost of raising children.

Paying the principal carer a family wage of, for argument's sake, $100 a week for the first child would virtually cover the cost of child care, if the principal carer wanted to continue in the paid work force. Alternatively, if the principal carer preferred to be a full-time mother or father, $100 a week would make a big difference to the family budget and quite possibly eliminate the need for both parents to work just to make ends meet.

Many have a philosophical preference for tax splitting rather than a cash payment. But a family wage is quite different from welfare. It is a recognition of responsibilities, not need. It is a payment for services, not a handout. It means that personal choice could replace economic necessity as a rationale for family decisions. One beauty of a family wage system, unlike a tax rebate, is that it would take one public servant, just one, and a computer to administer. Payments would start the moment a birth is recorded on the Registrar of Births, Deaths and Marriages database and finish 16 years later.

The budgetary cost of introducing a family wage of $100 a week for the first child and $30 a week for each subsequent child would be about $7.5 billion a year. It is worth remembering that this was the approximate size of Labor's One Nation personal income tax cuts, which were to be funded entirely out of economic growth. The cost of not providing more help for families is more family breakdown, greater call on the welfare system, increased crime and further social instability.

The vast majority of families would be much better off under a family wage policy. For instance, a family with three children on $30,000 a year now receives just $30 a week in family allowance. Under a family wage policy, this family would receive $160 a week. The vast majority of families, those with two or fewer children, would be more than $90 a week better off. It is possible to help families in ways which involve no radical surgery to our system, ways which are financially responsible and ways which avoid debilitating debate about definitions. But it takes a government that is committed to the long-term welfare of society to do so rather than a government which is preoccupied with the short-term management of pressure groups.

Governments that live in fear of tomorrow's headlines are incapable of change — even change that gives their constituents what they want. It is clear, for instance, that the people of Warringah are sick of clogged roads. So I congratulate the New South Wales transport minister, Bruce Baird, for establishing a committee to investigate alternatives and to recommend a solution. It seems that a road tunnel under Military Road with a better crossing at The Spit can be built with just $30 million of taxpayers' money. By contrast, the most publicised mass transit system is estimated to require a taxpayer subsidy of some $600 million and is predicated on higher population densities in the peninsula.

It would be a tragedy for the people of Warringah if an anti-car mentality stopped development which would help all Warringah commuters, including those who travel on public transport, especially if that development does not require any extension of medium or high density housing to be financially viable and does not preclude the construction of a mass transit system. The government's job is not to lay rails, shift earth and pour concrete. The government's job is to make necessary development happen. Say the word and private enterprise will do the job and very possibly build and operate huge infrastructure projects at no cost to the taxpayer.

Australians rightly object to higher taxes because they observe that most government spending disappears down a bottomless well. Government often seems like an evening out—it costs a fortune and in the morning there is little to show for all the expense. But it is my hunch that people would be less hostile to paying tax if they were more confident they were investing in lasting assets rather than $200,000 carports, $170,000 barbecues and $63,000 bicycle accidents. For most of Labor's decade, we have enjoyed the day by mortgaging the morrow. The $6.5 billion currently spent servicing the Commonwealth government's own debt could pay for a host of national development projects, including a Warringah mass transit system.

Mr Speaker, standing before you in this chamber, which is heir to 700 years of parliamentary tradition, I feel like a very small boy in a very big school. To my parents and to my grandparents; to my sisters, who have made me what I am; to my wife, my mainstay; to my priceless friends; to my party, which has given me the privilege to serve, I give my heartfelt thanks. To the Jesuits who first encouraged an ideal of public service; to Bob Santamaria, who sparked my interest in politics; to several editors, who honed my way with words; to John Hewson, who introduced me to this place; and to John Howard, who has been the contemporary politician I admire most, I hope I can be true to the principles you taught. May God and the ghosts of great men give me strength. May those who have laboured greatly to build this nation fortify my resolve to make a worthy contribution in this House.

'We pledge ourselves to serve'

Government House, Canberra, 18 September 2013

Abbott presents his ministry to be sworn in by Governor-General Quentin Bryce, promising a "problem-solving" Government.

Your Excellency, I present your new ministers and, through you, I present the people of Australia their new government.

We are all conscious of the honour of serving our country as ministers of the Crown and members of your Executive Council.

We pledge ourselves to serve the people of Australia for their benefit to the very best of our ability.

We are determined to honour our commitments: to scrap the carbon tax, to stop the boats, to get the Budget under control, and to build the roads of the 21st century. We will be a problem-solving government based on values, not ideology. We will strive to govern for all Australians, including those who didn't vote for us.

We won't forget those who are often marginalised: people with disabilities, indigenous people and women struggling to combine career and family. We will do our best not to leave anyone behind.

We aim to be a calm, measured, steady and purposeful government that says what it means and does what it says.

We hope to be judged by what we have done rather than by what we have said we would do.

We are conscious of the ideals of duty and service exemplified by our Queen whom you have so graciously represented here in Australia.

And we will not spare ourselves; we will not spare ourselves in order to deserve the trust placed in us this day.

2

THE LIBERAL PARTY

Election night victory speech
Sydney, 7 September 2013

The prime minister-elect declares Australia "under new management" and "open for business".

My friends, thank you. Thank you so much.

I can inform you that the government of Australia has changed for just the seventh time. You obviously enjoyed hearing it, so let me say it again, the government of Australia has changed. For just the seventh time in 60 years the government of Australia has changed.

The Coalition has won 13 seats clearly, with 10 seats still in play and I can inform you that the Australian Labor Party's vote is at the lowest level in more than one hundred years.

So, tonight, for the last time in this campaign it is my honour to address you, the people of Australia.

Mr Rudd has conceded defeat. He has been the prime minister of this country, not once, but twice, so I acknowledge his service to the people of our nation.

I now look forward to forming a government that is competent, that is trustworthy and which purposefully and steadfastly and methodically sets about delivering on our commitments to you, the Australian people.

Something very significant has happened today. Today, the people of Australia have declared that the right to govern this country does not belong to Mr Rudd, or to me, or to his party, or to ours, but it belongs to you, the people of Australia.

It is the people of Australia who determine the government and the prime ministership of this country and you will punish anyone who takes you for granted. That is how it should be in a great democracy such as ours.

So, my friends, in a week or so the Governor-General will swear in a new government. A government that says what it means, and means what it says. A government of no surprises and no excuses. A government that understands the limits of power as well as its potential. And a government that accepts that it will be judged more by its deeds than by its mere words.

In three years' time the carbon tax will be gone, the boats will be stopped, the budget will be on track for a believable surplus and the roads of the 21st century will finally be well underway.

From today I declare that Australia is under new management and that Australia is once more open for business.

Today, hundreds of thousands of people would have voted for the Liberal and National Parties for the first time in their lives. I give you all this assurance – we will not let you down.

A good government is one that governs for all Australians, including those who haven't voted for it. A good government is one with a duty to help everyone to maximise his or her potential, indigenous people, people with disabilities, and our forgotten families, as well as those who Menzies described as 'lifters, not leaners.' We will not leave anyone behind.

I want to thank my strong and united Liberal and National Party Coalition team. I thank Julie Bishop, Warren Truss, Joe Hockey. I thank the Members of the Shadow Cabinet. I thank my parliamentary team. I thank all our candidates, those who have succeeded and those who haven't, for the faith that you have placed in me.

I thank the Coalition Premiers, all of them, who have stood shoulder to shoulder with their federal colleagues throughout this campaign.

I thank the Liberal Party organisation, President Alan Stockdale and Federal Director Brian Loughnane – and, yes, it is right that you should show such enthusiasm for Brian Loughnane because he has run our most professional campaign ever.

I thank my personal staff led by Peta Credlin, who is the smartest and the fiercest political warrior I have ever worked with.

I thank my family who have given me so much and supported me throughout public life.

I thank the people of Warringah for returning me as their member of parliament for the eighth successive time.

Most of all, I thank you, the people of Australia, who have just given me the greatest honour and the heaviest responsibility that any member of parliament can have.

I am both proud and humbled as I shoulder the duties of government. The time for campaigning has passed. The time for governing has arrived. I pledge myself to the service of our country.

I have many friends in this audience. I say thank you to each one. We have been on a journey together – a long, long journey. May it continue and may it help to bring better times to this great country of which we are all so very, very proud.

Thank you so much.

'The family over everything'
Melbourne, 28 June 2014

Address to the Liberal Party Federal Council, Abbott's first as Prime Minister.

On this the 70th anniversary of our party, my colleagues and I stand before you proud of our history, humbled and honoured by the responsibility of government and determined to keep faith with our values that have shaped modern Australia.

We are the party of Menzies and Fraser and Howard – determined to do the right thing by the forgotten people, by the battlers and by everyone who is making a contribution – or who is yearning to make a contribution to our great country.

As Liberals, we stand for the people who work hard, pay their taxes, volunteer in their local community and save for their retirement. Because you embody what's best in our national character; helping neighbours, giving people the benefit of the doubt, welcoming strangers, and "having a go" at making everyone's life better.

As Liberals, we stand for you: the citizen over the official, the community over the state and the family over everything. As Liberals, we trust the citizens of Australia to get most things right, most of the time – and mostly, you do because you understand your best interests, at least as well as officials.

No one owns the Liberal Party except its members who are drawn from every nook and cranny of modern Australia. And because no one owns us, we can govern in the national interest – for all Australians.

On this, our 70th anniversary, we can be proud of what we have achieved. It is the Liberal Party that always has to clean up the mess our opponents create: to end the waste, pay back the debt, scrap the big new taxes and stop the boats. And because people turn to us to clean up the messes we did not create, we can take credit for our country's best years, under Howard and under Menzies, when millions of jobs were created and wages went up and up.

It is the Liberal Party that oversaw the post-war explosion of home ownership – putting the keys of a home within the grasp of most families.

It is the Liberal Party that rejected sectarianism and backed parents – providing funding for independent schools.

It is the Liberal Party that created the modern university system and built our national capital.

It is the Liberal Party that has always supported small business with lower tax, less regulation, and a hand up rather than a hand out.

It is the Liberal Party that delivered child endowment, family allowances and the baby bonus.

It is the Liberal Party that drove the post war migration programme and ended the white Australia policy – and it's the Liberal Party that welcomes immigrants from the four corners of the Earth eager to join our Australian team.

It is the Liberal Party that doesn't just announce the infrastructure of the future – we build it! We built the Snowy Mountains Scheme, completed the Alice Springs to Darwin railway, created national highways and are now building the roads of the 21st century:

- East West Link stages one and two here in Melbourne
- WestConnex and NorthConnex in Sydney
- the Gateway upgrade in Brisbane
- the North-South Road in Adelaide
- the Swan bypass in Perth, and
- the Midland Highway in Tasmania.

It is the Liberal Party that put forward the 1967 Referendum; that selected the first Indigenous members of the Senate and the House of Representatives – and that will sponsor a referendum acknowledging the first Australians in the Constitution.

It is the Liberal Party that kept Australia strong by signing the ANZUS Treaty, by properly funding our defence force and by stopping the boats – not once but twice!

But we don't do this on our own: we have had the National Party by our side and I honour them today. As John Howard has often reminded us, we succeed in Coalition – and only in Coalition.

He also reminded us that our party is the political custodian in Australia of the liberal and the conservative traditions. As Liberals we support lower taxes, smaller government and greater freedom. As conservatives we support the family and values that have stood the test of time. And as patriots we assess our actions not against ideology but against common sense – does this make our people and our country stronger?

While much has changed since 1944, our yearning is undimmed: to leave our children richer than ourselves, to come closer to our best selves individually and collectively and to leave our country a better place. A better Australia needs a government that values long-term respect ahead of short-term popularity. That's why we are taking action now to repair the Budget.

The Australian people know that we inherited porous borders and a broken Budget. You know that our country faces difficult choices and you expect us, as your government, to deal honestly with them. You know that the Commonwealth Government can't keep spending $1 billion every month on interest alone. You know that economic drift is not a policy – because we had six years of that. You know that problems don't automatically go away and that tough decisions today are needed to avoid even tougher ones tomorrow. That's why this Government has faced up to the challenges before our country, not put them off for another day.

This Budget cuts almost $300 billion from our projected debt over the next decade and brings the Budget back to balance within four years. It shifts the focus from short-term spending to long-term investment. It saves and it builds; it lives within our means and it plays to our strengths, with the Commonwealth's biggest ever road program and perhaps the world's biggest medical research future fund. The Budget is purposeful, thoughtful and effective.

We are asking young Australians to earn or learn – because no one should start adult life without a clear purpose. We are changing the way social security benefits are indexed - to make the system sustainable – because what's fair for some payments is fair for others. We are deregulating higher education – because universities, of all institutions - should be capable of running themselves. And we're spreading Commonwealth support to more institutions of higher learning and to diploma courses.

We are charging a modest co-payment for visits to the doctor – to make Medicare sustainable - because what's fair for the PBS is fair for Medicare.

The Budget is not about what's easy or popular in the short-term. It's about what's right for the long-term. It's about clear principle and sound practice – the clear principle and sound practice that has marked the nine months since the election.

There is still work to do but there has not been one single successful people smuggling venture this year.

Handouts to shaky business have stopped because you can't subsidise your way to prosperity.

Infrastructure projects are starting. After 50 years of procrastination, Sydney's second airport is finally going ahead.

I've led business delegations to China, Korea, Japan, Indonesia, Papua New Guinea, the United States and Canada – because the world should know that when we say that Australia is under new management and open for business – we mean business!

By the end of this term you will see real changes across every area of our country – to give you more choice, more freedom and more control over your future. Families won't pay the carbon tax – saving about $550 a year. Pensioners will keep the carbon tax compensation – but lose the carbon tax. Bulldozers will be at work on new roads up and down the eastern seaboard. Exporters will be reaping the benefits of free trade agreements with Korea and Japan – and, we hope, with China. Young unemployed people will have their dignity restored with expanded Work for the Dole. Businesses and community groups will see less red and green tape – with 50,000 pages of red tape, costing $700 million a year to administer, already identified and on the way out. Investors will be more confident – because of a one-stop shop for environmental approvals; the construction cop back on the beat; and the Mining Tax gone. More Indigenous kids will be in school, adults at work and communities safe. Apprentices will have access to $20,000 in low interest loans to finish their training. Australian university students and researchers will be fanning out through our region under the New Colombo Plan. The Green Army will be marching to the rescue of degraded land and polluted streams. Refugees will be coming safely to our country through the front door, not unsafely through the back door. Our armed forces and security agencies will be better funded and more capable. We will be a better friend to our neighbours because our foreign policy will be "Jakarta before Geneva" - with a practical approach to problem solving. And the people smugglers will stay out of business – because this government will never return to the failed policies of the recent past.

I wish I could say that at the end of this term, our farmers will be experiencing more rain – I can't promise that. Still, our $320 million drought package is a sign that we will respond to whatever challenges are ahead.

And we will be on the path to reforming our federation. We all know that our federation has great strengths – combined with buck passing, duplication, waste and inefficiency. With Liberal-National governments in Canberra and most of the states and territories, now is the time to make each level of government sovereign in its own sphere.

Today, I announce that the Government has released the Federation Reform White Paper terms of reference. This White Paper will be developed with the states and territories, released by the end of 2015, and inform the policies we take to the next election.

Next week, there will be a new Senate – and our invitation to the new senators is to help us build the better country that our people want. Work with us to reduce families' power bills. Work with us to restore confidence in our mining sector. Work with us to return the rule of law to building sites. Work with us to establish one of the world's biggest medical research funds. Work with us to give working mums a fair go.

I say to the new senators – we won't hector you and we won't lecture you. We respect your election as we ask you to respect ours. We simply ask that you acknowledge the trust placed in us by the Australian people to be their government.

At our 70th anniversary our party is strong. It is united. It is delivering the leadership and policies that our country needs.

We are guarding and guiding the destiny of a nation that's as free, fair and prosperous as any on earth and may God guide us as we go about this task.

Finally, I say to the Australian people that we will strive to be worthy of the faith you have placed in us and to give you ever more reason to be proud of our country.

Standing on the shoulders of giants
Old Parliament House, Canberra,
3 September 2014

Launching an exhibition of memorabilia to Sir Robert Menzies, the Liberal Party's founder and longest-serving leader.

This is a most fitting day to launch the *Menzies: By Howard* exhibition because it is 75 years ago this day that Sir Robert Menzies declared war.

It is the job of history to revisit every conflict, to search for reasons, to question assumptions and to pass judgment on the actions of the protagonists. History's verdict is close to unanimous – that World War II was a battle between good and evil, it was a conflict where civilisation itself hung in the balance.

The role of our wartime leaders should be remembered and today through this exhibition we remember Sir Robert Menzies and his prime ministership from 1939 to 1941.

When Menzies first visited the then Governor General, Lord Gowrie, the Governor General asked him, "If I commission you, how long do you think you will last?" Menzies thought for a moment and replied, "Six weeks, your excellency." The Governor General smiled and said, "That will do for a start." And as we know Menzies lasted for much longer than six weeks and accomplished much.

He is a figure worthy of remembrance for his wartime leadership, for founding the Liberal Party and for presiding over our long golden age of postwar expansion. When Menzies took over the prime ministership in April 1939 he found himself as Anne Henderson puts it, "leading an unwilling nation towards the second global conflict in the space of just two decades and at the helm of a fractious political team."

Preparing a country still scarred by World War I to deal with a world sliding toward war, not confined this time to distant shores but with danger on our doorstop preoccupied Menzies at the expense of political management and - yes - it did cost him his prime ministership.

Yet, as he himself later acknowledged, it was the lessons of his first prime ministership that laid the foundations for his second. These lessons resulted in him honing his political philosophy and developing his political skills.

As he wrote about that time, a quarter of a century later, "I was still in a state of mind in which to be logical is to be right and to be right is its own justification. I had yet to learn that human beings are delightfully illogical but mostly honest and to realise that all black and all white are not the only hues in the spectrum." And certainly his political exile paved the way for his subsequent success.

Sir Robert Menzies did not simply govern Australia for a long time. He shaped it according to an enduring set of values and principles; support for the family and small business and respect for traditional values and institutions.

All of us, in our own way, are Menzies children.

In this exhibition, John Howard expertly chronicles his first prime ministerial term. I want to congratulate the Museum of Australian Democracy for inviting our second longest serving prime minister to bring his unique perspective to our longest serving one. Giants, both, in whose extraordinary foot prints I am proud to follow. Both touched by political adversity and both triumphing magnificently over it.

Included in the exhibition is the correspondence between John Curtin and Robert Menzies; men with different world views but with a bond founded in genuine respect for each other and deep love of our country.

The life and times of Sir Robert Menzies warrant constant study because from his life and times we better understand our own.

I am honoured to declare *Menzies: By Howard* open and I hope it enjoys the largest possible patronage.

'Our plan is working'
Melbourne, 27 June 2015

Address to the Liberal Party Federal Council, his second
as Prime Minister.

Our party went to the last election with a plan to build a strong, prosperous economy and a safe, secure Australia. Today, my job is to report to you on our progress and to set out our next steps in achieving this goal.

Our plan means backing hard working Australians to get ahead and to fulfil their dreams. Our plan is not about us; it's about you.

It's about you having more control over your pay packet, more control over your bills and more choice over child care, health care and planning for your own retirement. It's about keeping you safe: because that's more important than anything.

From Menzies' forgotten people, to the Howard battlers and "Tony's tradies" – we have always been the party that "turned on the lights"; that stood "for all of us"; and that seeks "hope, reward and opportunity" for everyone.

Today, I can report to you that our plan is working. Our plan to grow the economy with lower tax, less red tape, more trade, better infrastructure and stronger borders is working. Since you elected this government, almost 290,000 new jobs have been created. Economic growth is now stronger than in most developed nations – and stronger than during the last year of the Rudd-Gillard Government. Company registrations are at record highs because people are ready to have a go when they know that government is on their side. Export volumes are up, as is residential housing construction and retail sales. And business confidence continues to strengthen. Our economy and our country are stronger – despite economic headwinds from the end of the mining investment boom and the low iron ore price.

People might have been a little bit uncertain about us; they always are about new governments – but now they know that we are serious: that our country really is under new management and that Australia really is open for business. The carbon tax is gone – and everyone is benefiting from lower power prices. The mining tax is gone – and Australia is once again seen as a good place to invest. New projects worth over a trillion dollars have received environmental approval – and there is no longer a green veto on development.

50,000 pages of regulation have been scrapped – saving businesses and individuals over $2 billion a year – with much more to come in the months ahead.

Free Trade Agreements with China, Japan and Korea are already creating opportunities for tens of thousands of Australian businesses – and new markets mean new jobs.

Projected long-term debt and deficits have been halved because of the difficult, but necessary decisions we made in Joe Hockey's first Budget.

The largest Commonwealth-funded infrastructure programme in Australian history is now underway. We are delivering WestConnex, the Pacific Highway duplication, the Bruce Highway upgrade, the North-South spine in Adelaide, the Midland Highway in Tasmania and major roads throughout Western Australia. Here in Victoria, there is $3 billion in a locked box waiting for a state government that wants to build the East West Link.

The NBN has passed one million premises and Malcolm Turnbull is turning, another Labor disaster into an asset for Australia.

Most importantly, the Budget is finally on a credible path back to surplus – with the deficit projected to fall by half a per cent of GDP every year. Already, we have made over $50 billion in savings to help repair the Budget – and the last sitting fortnight has been the most productive since the election. The parliament has passed legislation to make the age pension more sustainable – with more assistance to 170,000 pensioners with modest assets. The parliament has passed the instant asset write-off for small business. The parliament has passed changes to renewable energy to make power more affordable and investment more secure. The parliament has passed changes to fuel excise and the parliament has passed changes to the PBS.

We're making the hard decisions so we can make the necessary investments in our country's future. For the first time, Northern Australia has a plan for its economic development – including for new dams – because we can't make the most of Australia unless we make the most of our Great North.

We aren't just improving Australia's economic security – we are improving our national security as well because a nation's economic security and its national security go hand in hand.

This government has steadfastly met the challenges of the past 22 months. We've been resolute, determined and have kept the faith. We've stopped the boats – a task that Labor said couldn't be done – and secured our borders for the first time since the Howard Government.

When 39 Australians were shot out of the sky over Ukraine, our police and armed forces brought our dead home from a war zone. Our people were superb – and I couldn't be more proud. Today, I single out one – my deputy and Foreign Minister, Julie Bishop who criss-crossed the world in the name of justice.

Overnight, we saw again horrors in France, Tunisia and Kuwait. We are meeting the challenge of the Daesh death cult and the Australians it brainwashes. Abroad, Australian armed forces are working with a worldwide coalition against a group as evil as any in human history.

At home, we have provided more resources and more powers to our security and intelligence agencies – because they need whatever it takes to keep you safe.

This week, we sent a clear message to those Australians who think they can fight overseas with impunity. Think again. We will strip Australian citizenship from terrorists who are dual nationals – because terrorists shouldn't be walking our streets looking to make our citizens their trophies.

Our country is confronting the evil of terrorism – and we are also facing up to the evil of domestic violence. If there is any place that should be a safe haven – it's the family home. There are no excuses for domestic violence. Former Police Commissioner Ken Lay, and Rosie Batty, are heading up our advisory panel and you'll soon hear more about how we'll tackle this national scourge.

Let's start by making domestic violence orders national, so violent men can't chase their families across the country. And let's expect the perpetrators – and not the victims – to be the ones to leave home.

Ken Lay is also helping us to beat the scourge of ice – the most dangerous drug of addiction yet seen. No one should be lost in a world of fear and fantasy in the best country on earth.

In just a few days' time, Australia will have completed 24 consecutive years of economic growth – only the Netherlands has had a longer run of economic growth. But we cannot be a country that lives off yesterday's achievements; we can't take growth for granted. The foundation of the next quarter century of prosperity won't be bigger government, higher taxes or more debt and deficits. It will be unleashing the entrepreneurs of our country, particularly our small businesses to have a go.

Since the days of the early settlers, through the gold rushes, the wars and successive waves of immigration, Australians have always been willing to work hard, lend a hand to neighbours, make sacrifices for children and look over the horizon to a better future. That's the Australian way and they're the Australians that we want to back.

Every day we are making further progress. We are working to re-establish a tough cop on the beat in the construction industry to deliver billions of dollars in productivity benefits.

We'll soon release the Agriculture White Paper and – again – there'll be more money for dams because you can't grow things without water.

We'll soon respond to the Harper Competition Review and the Murray Review into the Financial System – because we want all parts of our economy growing strongly.

By the end of the year, we'll release Australia's first ever 15-year plan for infrastructure to get more bulldozers on the ground and cranes in the sky.

Work is underway eliminating thousands of mobile phone black spots in regional areas.

Thousands of young people have already been in the Green Army in hundreds of projects to clean up our lands and waterways – and there'll be tens of thousands more.

We want to support hard working Australians – especially parents who want work or who want more work.

Our Budget childcare measures should encourage more than 240,000 families to earn more, including almost 38,000 jobless families.

Low and middle-income families using childcare will be $1,500 a year better off even before they earn more. I have said what we will do – let me also tell you what we won't do. We won't increase taxes on superannuation or increase the restrictions on superannuation because your retirement savings belong to you and not the government. We won't change the rules on negative gearing because Australians have made decisions based on the rules as they stand – and the last time a government fiddled with negative gearing it caused a crisis in the rental market. And we won't be putting a tax on electricity because there are smarter ways of reducing emissions than whacking everyone with a new carbon tax.

For over seventy years, the Liberal Party has built modern Australia – not on ideology, but on backing hard working Australians – people prepared to have a go.

If you're a young Australian looking for a good job and working for a deposit on your first home – we're for you. If you're a small business person who wants to employ people – we're for you. If you're a young parent trying to balance work and family – we're for you. If you're a migrant who came the right way to build a better life for your children – we're for you. If you want to spend less time stuck in traffic to get to work or to pick up your kids – we're for you. If you're working more to get ahead and to provide the best opportunities for your children – we're for you. If you believe superannuation is your money and want certainty in retirement – we're for you. If you're on the land despite the ravages of drought – we're for you.

I should ask: who's Labor for these days? I guess *The Killing Season* answered that: they're for themselves. They're the party that promised to be like John Howard, but weren't. They're the party that promised us they wouldn't restart the boats, but did. They're the party that promised surpluses, but delivered record debt and deficits. They're the party that said no carbon tax, but gave us one anyway.

The guilty party has not changed. Almost two years into this term, they still want a carbon tax; they still have no policies to stop the boats and they're still addicted to taxes and spending. The choice is clear: They're for boats, we're for none. They're for a carbon tax, we're for lower tax. They're for taxes, we're for jobs. They do union bidding. We stand for all of us.

Now I have to confess, I did sneak a peak at that ABC series *The Killing Season*. The one thing that Kevin Rudd and Julia Gillard could agree on was: you can't trust Bill Shorten. If Julia Gillard and Kevin Rudd don't trust Bill Shorten, why should you? If the workers of the AWU couldn't trust Bill Shorten, why should you?

Only the Liberal party and our National Party colleagues can be trusted to build a strong, prosperous economy and a safe, secure Australia. It's built by people who believe in our country and who believe that our best days are ahead of us.

When the history books are written, they will recognise my friend, and our Deputy Prime Minister, Warren Truss as one of the great leaders of this government. I can report to you that our Coalition is strong. I can report to you that our party organisation, so well led by President Richard Alston is strong. Our secretariat, led by Brian Loughnane and supported by our state directors, is the most professional political organisation in the country.

But our greatest strength is not our leadership, it's our membership. Our party has been built by hundreds of thousands of men and women from all walks of life, from every nook and cranny under the Southern Cross. We believe in family, in community and that our nation's greatest achievements come when our people are encouraged to have a go. We reflect the length and breadth of Australian life: young and old, rich and poor, farmer and suburbanite, indigenous and immigrant, tradies and nurses. Our party does not demand blind obedience. We respect differences – because discussing them is how we come closer to wisdom. We are a party that honours our history – it's the foundation we build on. It's why we are proud to be the heirs of Menzies, Holt, Gorton, McMahon, Fraser and Howard. In honouring our history, we remember the good government that Malcolm Fraser led. He turned on the lights and we're grateful.

But, today we're focused on the future. We're making our country safer and more prosperous for everyone. We're the optimists of Australian life. We're yearning and striving to build a better Australia, leaving our children more than we ever hoped for. That's our task; that's our mission and, for our country's sake, we will succeed.

'Carry the torch of freedom'
Mosman, NSW, 28 August 2015

Address to the Mosman branch of the Liberal Party, in his Sydney electorate, regarding two upcoming challenges: democratise the party and win the next federal election in 2016.

It is a tremendous honour to be here to help celebrate the 70th anniversary of the first Liberal Party branch.

I suspect that the first Liberal Party branch might be a bit like the first surf club – a rather contested title... a bit like the oldest pub in Australia. There are a number of claimants, but we think that the first Liberal Party branch was established subsequent to the meeting here at the Mosman Town Hall on 12 February 1945.

Back in October of 1944, Sir Robert Menzies or R.G. Menzies as he then was brought together the disparate strands of Liberal conservative thinking in our country. He recreated the conservative side of politics as the Liberal Party of Australia. And subsequent to that, he embarked on a series of tours around our country to establish the branches that would give life to the party that he had created a few months earlier.

My understanding is that on 12 February there were hundreds of people in the Mosman town hall. The attendance was so large that loud speakers had to be set up in the street outside to accommodate all the people who wanted to attend this inaugural meeting of the Liberal Party of Australia here in Mosman.

It was chaired by Pat Morton who went on to become the youngest ever mayor of Mosman, a long serving member for Mosman and the leader of the state opposition in the late 1950s and Trish McPhee – Pat's daughter – is with us tonight. My understanding is that some 560 membership forms were taken on that particular evening.

So it is great to be here with the Mosman branch. I was preselected on a Sunday back in 1994 and at my preselection I said that the Liberal Party could not afford to be a closed shop. We could not be like a castle with the drawbridge up and the defenders gone to sleep.

I said that we needed to have more fighting spirit in the Liberal Party. And the following night I was at the Mosman branch and there was such a fighting spirit that night that security had to be called. I see a few here that were at that particular meeting. But from that day to this, the Mosman branch has normally been the largest branch in the Warringah conference and it's always been the most lively branch.

I also pay tribute to the Warringah conference. The Warringah conference has worked with me for 21 years now. It's been a tremendously strong and close partnership. I hope every member of our party in this electorate does feel a strong sense of pride because I was looking back over the records and there are only six electorates in the country that have produced a Liberal prime minister.

Now, I don't say that that is my doing. It is our doing because I could not be the Prime Minister of this country without you and your support. I could not be the Prime Minister of this country without the sustainment, the counsel, the guidance, the encouragement that you have given me over 21 years.

The important thing, even on an evening such as this is not just to look back. It is also to look forward.

When Bob Menzies address the meeting at the Mosman Town Hall on 12 February 1945, he had this to say: "So far the Liberal Party has resulted from the activity of a few people, but if it is to be a great national party, it must come from the people of Australia themselves".

That was what Bob Menzies said all those years ago at the meeting which launched the Liberal Party here in Mosman. If it is to be a great national party, it must come from the people of Australia themselves.

Let's ask ourselves, what does a political party do? A political party is quality control in the system. When someone carries the label of a great political party, people can vote for that person with a great deal of confidence that he or she has been subjected to close scrutiny and found not to be wanting. People can vote for that person with a great deal of confidence that there is a system of beliefs, a set of values, a coherent set of policies that that person believes in and will support in the Parliament.

In order to give our people confidence in the candidates that we Liberals put up, it is important that our party is as representative as possible of modern Australian society. The key problem we have right now is that we simply don't have enough members. If we want to attract more people to our Party, we have got to have good candidates and we have got to have good policies. When we are in government we have got to do a good job – we have got to be competent we have got to be trustworthy.

But there has got to be something in party membership for its members. That is the difficulty. Right now, we expect rank and file Liberals to do everything except that which is at the heart of a political Party's existence – directly select the candidates.

Surely, if there is one thing that Liberal Party members ought to be empowered to do, it's all of them, certainly, those who have been members for 12 months or more – who have proven themselves to be serious about membership – it's giving each and every one of them a say in who wears the Liberal badge in their seat. This is the great challenge for us: to democratise our party. That is the first great challenge before us, as Liberals: to carry the torch of freedom – to hold it high – when we have our state council meeting in a month or so to consider Party democratisation.

The second great challenge is to win the next federal election. My vision, as your Prime Minister, is to prove that the Rudd/Gillard/Rudd era is not the new normal in Australian politics – simply an aberration, simply a peculiar result of the unpreparedness of the Labor Party at that time.

My challenge, our challenge, is to demonstrate that chaos and incompetence is not the new normal in Australian politics. Our challenge is to prove that the age of meaningful reform is not ended, it was merely interrupted between 2007 and 2013.

We must, first, democratise our party as far as we humanly can, and second, to win the election and send a signal to the world that stability and competence and trustworthiness in government is recognised by the Australian people and rewarded with a second term of office.

Now, I don't say that everything that my Government has done has been without blemish. I don't say that we haven't made mistakes. We are a Government of men and women – not a Government of Gods walking upon the earth. Nevertheless, we have done the things that we said we would do: the carbon tax, the mining tax – they're gone; the boats – they have been stopped; the roads – they're being built; the Budget – it's coming back under control; and as well things like the Free Trade Agreements with Korea, Japan and China are setting up our country for the future.

We will go to the next election with a program of further solid reform focused on tax cuts because as Liberals we believe that people should be trusted to get on with their own lives. As Liberals we want to liberate people from the dead hand of government and the most tangible way we can do that is to get their taxes down.

So we will go to the election with a strong record and with a good platform. In the end the people will make their decisions and they will make their decision based on whom they most trust to keep their country safe and secure.

When people go to the ballot box on polling day next year, they will ask themselves who do they trust with national security? Do they trust the Party which in Government cut $16 billion from our defence Budget; the Party that didn't place a single naval shipbuilding order in six years; or the Party which is restoring defence to 2 per cent of gross domestic product? Who will they trust on national security? The Party that started the boats and the drownings at sea or the Party who stopped the boats and drownings at sea? Who will they trust on the economy? The Party that ran up $250 billion worth of accumulated deficits or the Party which has put our country back in the path of sustainable surplus and has actually made painful decisions when it comes to spending. Who will they trust as their Prime Minister? Someone who has been faithful to the commitments that were made pre-election? Or someone who backstabbed two Prime Ministers?

There will be struggles ahead – politics is a business of struggle. Nothing comes easy in public life. Nothing comes easy for Governments, particularly in the modern 24/7 media cycle. But I am absolutely confident that when the time comes for the people to vote they will make, as they always do, the best decision for our country. I am absolutely confident in placing myself – and our Government – in the hands of the people come polling day.

Can I say finally: none of this would be possible without you. I am sustained, every day, by the work, the encouragement and sometimes the prayers of some outstanding people. I am sustained – every day – by the encouragement of so many good people but particularly by the people in this room. I know you won't let me down and I pledge not to let you down.

3

THE ECONOMY

A Cornerstone for a Stronger Economy

House of Representatives, Canberra,
13 November 2013

Abolishing the carbon tax was a centerpiece of Abbott's election platform in 2013. Two months after winning that election, Abbott introduces the Clean Energy Legislation (Carbon Tax Repeal) Bill to the House of Representatives, saying it will remove a $9 billion burden from the economy.

I introduce the *Clean Energy Legislation (Carbon Tax Repeal) Bill 2013*.

The Australian people have already voted upon this Bill. Now, the Parliament gets its chance. The election was a referendum on the carbon Tax. The people have spoken. Now, it's up to this Parliament to show that it's listened. The Australian people have pronounced their judgment against the carbon tax: they want it gone and this bill delivers. It delivers on the Coalition's commitment to the Australian people to scrap this toxic tax. It is also a cornerstone of the Government's plan for a stronger economy built on lower taxes, less regulation and stronger businesses.

Repealing the carbon tax should be the first economic reform of this Parliament and it will be followed by further economic reforms: bills to repeal the mining tax, to restore the Australian Building and Construction Commission and to deal with Labor's debt legacy.

The first impact of this bill will be on households whose overall costs will fall $550 a year on average. Thanks to this bill, household electricity bills will be $200 lower next financial year without the carbon tax. Household gas bills will be $70 lower next financial year without the carbon tax. Prices for groceries, for household items and for services will also fall because the price of power is embedded in every price in our economy. This is our bill to reduce your bills, to reduce the bills of the people of Australia.

When the price of power comes down, the Australian Competition and Consumer Commission will be ready to ensure these price reductions are passed on to households and businesses. But families and pensioners will keep the tax cuts and benefit increases already provided. The carbon tax will go, but the carbon tax compensation will stay so that every Australian should be better off. Repealing the carbon tax will reduce costs for all Australian businesses, every single one of them.

The previous Government said and argued that only big business paid the carbon tax. That simply wasn't true. Every small business paid the carbon tax through higher electricity and gas bills and higher costs for supplies.

As well, the carbon tax acts as a reverse tariff. Not only does the carbon tax make it more difficult for Australian businesses to compete abroad, it makes it more difficult for domestic businesses to compete at home – because there is no carbon tax on imports.

Repealing the carbon tax removes over 1,000 pages of primary and subordinate legislation. Repealing the carbon tax cuts the size of the climate change bureaucracy. So, repealing the carbon tax will reduce the cost of living, make jobs more secure and improve the competitive position of our country. That's what it does: it reduces the cost of living, it makes jobs more secure and improves the competitive position of our country. Why would anyone be against that, particularly when it's what the Australian people have just voted for?

Repealing the carbon tax is what the employers and what the jobs providers of our country want now. The Business Council of Australia "supports the wind-up of the current carbon pricing mechanism because it places excessive costs on business and households and because (our) carbon charge…is now one of the highest in the world".

The carbon tax has ripped through the economy, hitting schools, hospitals, nursing homes, charities, churches, council swimming pools and community centres. It has hit each and every group and each and every individual that uses power – and that was always its goal: to make electricity more expensive. That was the intention of the previous government, to put power prices up because that was their way of reducing carbon emissions.

The intention of the new government is to put power prices down by axing this toxic tax and by using other means to reduce emissions. By reducing the cost of electricity and gas, we will help to make households better off, workers more secure and our economy stronger.

No one should be in any doubt – the Government is repealing the carbon tax in full. We are not playing word games. We are not playing tactical political games. We are doing what we were elected to do.

Others have said they would terminate the carbon tax, but they were only renaming it. Well, we are not renaming it. We are not floating it. We are not keeping the machinery in place so we can dust it off in the future. We are abolishing the carbon tax in full. We have said what we mean and we will do what we say – the carbon tax goes. It goes.

Repealing the carbon tax at the end of the financial year provides certainty for business and it simplifies the transition. It means that this Government will not be proceeding with the previous Government's legislated carbon tax increase that would have taken effect from the 1st of July next year.

As well, Labor's carbon tax changes for the on-road fuel costs of heavy vehicles that were going to commence on the 1st of July 2014 will not happen. That saves consumers the previous Government's planned increase in the price of everything that had to be trucked around the country.

Unfortunately, the new Government cannot undo the past, we can only make the future better – and that is what we intend to do.

Under this Government, the carbon tax will not apply from 1 July so there will be no need for further compensation packages. We will end the merry-go-round of carbon tax industry assistance that takes from one pocket and puts less back in the other. We will ensure that the benefits of repealing the carbon tax are passed on to consumers. The ACCC will have further powers to take action against any business that engages in price exploitation in relation to the carbon tax repeal. Penalties of up to $1.1 million for corporations and $220,000 for individuals will apply.

The Government is repealing the carbon tax because there is a less complicated and less costly way to reduce greenhouse gas emissions – a way that will actually reduce emissions and won't damage the economy.

The Government will scrap the carbon tax and then proceed with its Direct Action Plan. The centrepiece of the Direct Action Plan will be the Emissions Reduction Fund – a market-based mechanism for reducing carbon dioxide emissions; a Fund which provides a powerful and direct additional incentive for businesses to reduce their greenhouse gas emissions. The Fund will use positive incentives to reduce Australia's emissions. Direct Action through the Fund means more trees, better soils and smarter technology and this is the right way to get emissions down.

The carbon tax is a $9 billion hit on the economy this year alone. It is a $9 billion burden on jobs, a $9 billion burden on investment and a $9 billion burden on Australia that we just don't need. So, this bill gets rid of it. This bill is the Government's bill to reduce people's bills and I so commend this bill to the House.

'Making it easier for business'
National Gallery of Australia, Canberra, 20 November 2013

Just two months after declaring that Australia was again "open for business" on the night of his election victory, Prime Minister Abbott outlines his agenda to Australia's peak business association: freer enterprise, smaller government and greater respect for entrepreneurs and innovators.

When I said on election night that Australia was under new management and, once more, open for business, I was acknowledging an iron law of public policy. You cannot have strong communities without strong economies to sustain them and you can't have a strong economy without profitable private businesses.

Making it easier for businesses to start, to grow, to employ and to invest is at the heart of this Government's policy to build a stronger and better Australia. Without successful businesses, invariably private businesses, no goods can be produced, no services can be delivered, no wealth can be created and – ultimately – no other fine ideals can be realised. That's why I salute the businesses of Australia: those who start them, those who work in them, those who invest in them, and those who run them.

I particularly salute the small businesses of Australia and everyone who puts his or her house on the line to start a small business: to serve our community and to employ our fellow Australians.

The people who start businesses and who keep them going are the largely unsung heroes of our society – especially as the obstacles they must overcome and the burdens they must carry have become harder and harder.

There's the notorious case of the major resource development project in Gladstone that required 4,000 meetings and 12,000 pages of environmental reporting before it was finally approved – only with 1,200 state and 300 Commonwealth conditions, plus 8,000 sub-conditions.

Now, delay and expense on such a scale ill becomes even a $15 billion project, lest those investing such astronomical sums choose to go where their money is more welcome and their good intentions less suspect.

But it's not just massive new projects that are subject to regulatory strangulation. Opening and running a child care centre should hardly be a bureaucratic ordeal. Yet the national childcare law introduced by the previous government is almost 180 pages long and is accompanied by 345 pages of regulation and several hundred more pages of guidelines. No one could reasonably be expected to keep abreast of this.

So what's the point of such prescription other than to give officials a permanent stick with which to beat entrepreneurs or, to put it bluntly, to give wealth consumers a permanent upper hand over wealth creators?

So, the job of the new government is to ensure that Australia really is open for business because that is the only way that Australians can have the jobs, the services, the prosperity and the financial freedom that is at the heart of a good life.

That means getting taxes down, getting regulation down, and getting productivity up. It means ensuring that government lives within its means so that there is scope for sensible tax reform. Above all, it means a preference for smaller government over bigger government and for freer citizens over more regulated ones. And, yes, it means keeping our commitments: the tough ones like ending the schoolkids bonus as well as the easier ones like abolishing the carbon tax.

The new government, I believe, has made a good start. We've saved the car industry from Labor's $1.8 billion fringe benefits tax hit. We've saved teachers, nurses and salespeople from Labor's tax on self-education expenses. We've declared that most of the nearly 100 announced-but-not-enacted tax changes won't go ahead. We've established a once-in-a-generation Commission of Audit to consider the size, scope and efficiency of government. And we are passing legislation to abolish the carbon tax and to abolish the mining tax.

As things stand, the mining tax forces 145 miners to keep books for a tax that only 20 of them actually pay and forces the ATO to spend $100 million to collect a tax that's raised just $400 million!

But there's good news because tonight, the mining tax repeal bill is passing the House of Representatives. Tomorrow, the House of Representatives is likely to pass the carbon tax repeal legislation, thus forcing the Labor Party in the Senate to decide whether it really does, like the Greens, want electricity bills to be $200 a year higher than they should be.

We are fully restoring the Australian Building and Construction Commission to be a strong cop-on-the-beat in a tough industry.

We've closed some 21 non-statutory boards and committees as a down payment on the substantial reduction in the size of government that is yet to come.

We've signed Memoranda of Understanding with New South Wales and Queensland to establish one-stop shops for environmental approvals.

More importantly and crucially, in the eight weeks since the Government was sworn in, Environment Minister Greg Hunt has given the environmental go ahead for projects worth $160 billion. This is a very, very substantial down payment on cutting businesses' red and green tape costs by $1 billion a year, every year.

Tonight, I announce that the former Commonwealth Bank boss and Future Fund chairman David Murray will chair our financial sector inquiry. This is designed to make financial services more competitive and ultimately more fair – with lower costs, lesser fees and greater efficiency in the use of capital.

Almost everything this government does is directed towards making doing business easier – because that leads to more jobs, higher wages and greater prosperity. Abolishing the carbon tax will remove a $9 billion a year hit on the economy. Abolishing the mining tax will not only remove the sovereign risk cloud over resources investment but will also remove $13 billion in unfunded expenditure from the budget.

These are just the first big steps towards reforming our economy. Tax reform, for instance, begins with abolishing the carbon tax and the mining tax, but it doesn't end there. The White Paper on tax reform, due within two years, will canvass all of the credible options for lower, simpler, fairer taxes and will shape the further tax mandate that the Government will seek at the next election.

The Productivity Commission inquiry into workplace relations will consider how Australia can have the world's best paid workers by also having the world's most productive workers; and, again, will inform the further workplace relations mandate that the government will seek at the next election.

Our objective is to maximise productivity and to maximise participation so that we can maximise pay and maximise the number of jobs. Because, especially with an ageing population, we just can't afford to lose 200,000 people from our workforce – as we have over the past three years. That's why we are introducing a fair dinkum paid parental leave scheme so that women can better combine having a family with maintaining a career. That's why we're establishing a Productivity Commission inquiry into childcare so that parents can maximise their participation in a 24/7 economy.

One of the issues we will have to tackle is the steady build-up of working age people on the disability pension, most of whom only leave it to go onto the old aged pension. So early in the New Year, the Government will be considering proposals to get back into the workforce people with conditions which are not always long-term: such as many types of mental illness; or not always incapacitating, such as muscular skeletal deterioration.

Another issue that an infrastructure prime minister will have to tackle is the extraordinarily long lead times for vital infrastructure projects. The official advice, for instance, is that normal planning for the Gateway Motorway upgrade in Brisbane could take up to two years – even though this is simply widening an existing road!

So one of the issues I will be asking premiers to consider at the Council of Australian Government meeting in December is special legislation for vital projects: so that WestConnex in Sydney and the East West Link in Melbourne are not indefinitely delayed by professional objectors.

I am determined to ensure that we are a country that builds things. The argument about Sydney's second airport that's raged since Gough Whitlam first proposed Galston, should fully and finally be resolved well within this term of government. Of course, this will require new habits of mind from everyone. It will be necessary to reconsider the need for 130-plus national regulators and some 350 state and territory regulators that tend to justify their existence by finding ways to say "no" or "maybe" rather than "yes".

With such a regulatory superstructure, it's hardly surprising that Australia's ranking in the World Economic Forum's global competitiveness index has fallen from 12th to 21st; and that Australia's ranking for government regulation has fallen, would you believe it, from 68th to 128th – that's 128th in the world – over the past six years.

No one wants to see corners being cut in environmental best practice or anywhere else. Still, we need to remember that projects' proponents are citizens as well as builders who normally have to live in the communities they want to develop. They would hardly imperil their own futures or trash their own reputations. We need to remember that eliminating risk normally means eliminating initiative, too, and to resist the urge to regulate every time something goes wrong.

Freedom can never be untrammelled but the urge to create, to build and to innovate should never be suppressed if our people are to enjoy the prosperity that we all want and deserve.

If Australia really is to be open for business, people have to be trusted to get on with their own jobs. People have to be trusted to get on with doing what only they can do.

Looking at business, indeed looking at the people here tonight, the new government not for a second sees people who are naturally inclined to rip off customers, to persecute workers or to despoil the environment. That, I'm afraid, is how the former government tended to look at people in this room.

The new government looks at this room and we see people whose intention is to serve the community, to employ millions of Australians and to build a better and more beautiful world. We see people like you – who deserve to be encouraged and admired.

'A dark day but better days ahead'
House of Representatives, Canberra,
11 December 2013

Marking the end of Holden manufacturing in Australia with a promise to foster new ventures and opportunities, especially in South Australia, the state hardest hit by the closure.

On indulgence: I do not want to mince my words and I do not want to pretend to the parliament that this is anything other than a dark day for manufacturing in this country.

We have today received the very bad news – but not entirely unexpected news – that Holden is to cease manufacturing in this country in 2017. Twenty-nine hundred jobs will be gone by 2017 and thousands of jobs are at risk in up to 150 suppliers. This follows the withdrawal from motor manufacturing in our country of Mitsubishi some years ago and Ford's announced 2016 close-down.

This was part of a world-wide restructure that, amongst other things, involved the closure of General Motors' plants in Korea and the withdrawal of Chevrolet from Europe. So we should not think that motor manufacturing in this country alone has suffered bad news this day. But as the managing director of Holden has said, and I thank him for his sober statement today on what must have been a sad and bitter day for him, Holden has been hit by a perfect storm: high costs, the high dollar and low volumes, and that explains the decision that they have made.

Now is the time for a strategic response to the difficulties in manufacturing and particularly to the difficulties in our motor industry. It is not the time to play politics. It is not the time to indulge in the blame game. It is not the time to peddle false hope. It is time for a candid and constructive conversation with the Australian people and it is time for a considered and constructive response from government. That is exactly what this government will be providing in coming days. That strategic response starts with a review of the fundamental strengths of our country.

It starts with a review of the fundamental strengths of the areas which will be most impacted by the Holden close-down in three years time. We do have strengths in component manufacturing. We do have strengths in manufacturing, particularly for the mining sector. We have enormous strengths in research and development, in higher education and in biomedical science. The government will be announcing measures in coming days that will build on the strengths that we have and which will offer hope for the people of the regions impacted. It will be a considered package of measures, designed to rebuild confidence in the long-term economic future of those regions, in the long-term future of manufacturing of this country.

As part of that, we will be talking to Toyota. They have long been the strongest motor manufacturer in this country and I want to say that it is the government's strong wish that Toyota continue to manufacture in this country. It is the government's strong wish that Toyota continue to export from this country and we will be talking to them about the best ways of ensuring that that happens.

I accept that this is a sad, bad day for everyone involved in the motor industry. It is a particularly sad, bad day for the workers of Holden, for the families of the workers of Holden and for the communities which are home to Holden's major facilities in this country. There is no way that I can gloss over that, and there is no way that I should gloss over that.

But the people of this country – the people of our industrial centres – have been through hard times before, and they have come through hard times. They have flourished through hard times. When BHP withdrew from steel-making in Newcastle, many people thought that it was the end of an era – and, yes, it was the end of one era. It was the end of a grimy, industrial era for Newcastle. But it certainly was not the end of economic dynamism for Newcastle, which has gone from strength to strength in the decade or so since the announcement.

I accept that the economy of South Australia is fragile, and I accept that Adelaide in particular has suffered a series of knocks. It lost Mitsubishi just a few years ago, but it did come through. There is much that we can be hopeful and optimistic about in the resistance of the South Australian economy, particularly if government can do all that is necessary to see that the Olympic Dam mine expansion goes ahead.

So this is a dark day. But there will be better days ahead, and it is my determination and the determination of everyone in the government to work with the people of Australia – to work with the creative people of this country – to ensure that the great strengths of our society and the great strengths of our economy continue to be built on in the days and weeks and months ahead.

'The era of something for nothing is no more'
Parliament House, Canberra, 24 June 2014

At the Committee for Economic Development of Australia's annual conference in Canberra, Prime Minister Abbott outlines a plan to lift the nation's workforce participation, saying a job is the best form of welfare for all people, regardless of age or ability.

For over 50 years, CEDA has helped to drive debate about our country's social and economic development. Most people have an opinion about what's best for our country – unsurprisingly, it's often whatever's best for the person expressing the opinion but because CEDA has no institutional self-interest to push, it's been better than most at taking a long-term view focused on what's genuinely in the national interest, so congratulations.

The decisions that we now acknowledge have shaped our country and have set up our prosperity have often been unpopular in the short-term and initially difficult for the governments that made them.

Prime Minister Menzies for instance opened up trade with Japan at a time when Japanese cars were still banned from RSL club car parks. Prime Minister Whitlam opened the door to China when many Australians thought that communism and trade could not mix. Prime Minister Hawke's opening to foreign banks, privatisation and tariff cuts were deeply unpopular inside the Labor Party. Prime Minister Howard's tax reforms, waterfront reforms and welfare reforms were ferociously opposed by the then-opposition.

It's always easy to pander to fear and short-term self-interest but Australia has succeeded because at least some governments have been better than that. Especially between 1983 and 2007, a golden quarter century of political courage and economic reform, good governments from both sides of the political fence made Australia more competitive, more innovative and more productive. As this *State of the Nation* Conference meets, we again face tough choices that will lay the foundation for a stronger Australia. What must surely be clear is that doing nothing is not an option.

In 2007, the Commonwealth government had a $20 billion surplus and $50 billion in the bank. But by 2013, consistent surpluses had turned into the six biggest deficits ever with no end in sight under the policies of the former government despite the best terms of trade in our history.

The former government was addicted to borrowing and spending. In real terms, spending grew almost twice as fast as the economy and debt was forecast to grow to $667 billion. So the task for this government has been to get spending down while maintaining and even increasing economic growth. We need to boost the three "Ps"- population, productivity and participation without taking the soft option of pretending to do so just by spending more.

Today, I want to focus on the Government's measures to encourage more people to join the workforce or to stay in the workforce. But first, we need to be clear about the scale of the challenge: Longer lives are a cause for celebration – I am celebrating more the older I get! But all these extra retirees have to be paid for. The ratio of working age people to people over 65 will decline from five to one to under three to one by 2050.

To preserve generous social security benefits and good health and education services, we need relatively more tax payers. We have to find ways of increasing the proportion of workers in our economy. We need more people who are "having a go" in order to preserve the "fair go" that has always been such a crucial part of the Australian way of life and we need to start addressing these issues now, and changing policy now, rather than later when change will be even harder.

Policy drift is the refuge of the political opportunist who has forgotten the purpose of public life.

Now almost everything that this Government does is designed to ensure that more people have jobs. But there's a right way and a wrong way to boost the number of jobs: more government spending might boost employment in the short term but, in the long-term, more government spending usually makes it harder to sustain the profitable private businesses that are the real engine of jobs growth.

Lower tax, less red and green tape, and freer trade are the best and most successful means to higher economic growth and more jobs. But in particular, we need to make it easier for young people, for older people and for women to enter or to re-enter the workforce because these are the groups with the most potential to boost employment participation. Lifting participation among these three groups is an important economic outcome that would help offset the pressures of an ageing population.

Over sixty years ago, Sir Robert Menzies put the case for greater workforce participation. He said: a job "is much more than source of income...it is also a source of personal satisfaction and individual dignity … The pursuit of happiness lies along a self-made road; seldom along a road made by others no matter how good their intentions". "The sense of individual dignity", he said, "which comes from doing a job gives to the doer the personal satisfaction of helping one's self, rather than having to rely on a social security benefit". So the policies of this Government are very much in the tradition established by our distinguished forbear.

You'll note that Menzies wasn't just referring to more self-reliant people; he was celebrating more self-fulfilled people. This Government is not promoting more jobs because that's what economic theory tells us to do. We are promoting more jobs because that is most likely to lead to happier, more-self-fulfilled people. We are building a stronger economy because that will lead to a happier society. Empowered citizens can do more for themselves than government will ever do for them, and the best form of empowerment is a job.

My friends, work is so much more than just a way to gain a living. Work gives people's lives meaning and purpose. Work gives individuals the satisfaction of providing for themselves and their families. Work helps to give people the practical, intellectual and social skills needed for a full and rewarding life. Indeed, the camaraderie of workmates is something we don't often appreciate fully, until we don't have it anymore.

To be without work is a disaster, especially for young people. It locks them out of the economic and social mainstream of our community. It stops them achieving their potential. That's why there's no compassion in having people start their adult lives on unemployment benefits. Even in difficult times, there's little that's more satisfying than finding a job, making a success of it, and providing for yourself. That's why all fit young people should be earning or learning – and be expected to persevere for six months to find a job or to choose a further training programme before accessing welfare payments. That's why all young people who do find themselves on unemployment benefits should be working for the dole. Fit young people should be working, preferably for a wage but, if not, for the dole.

From 1 January next year, new jobseekers up to the age of 30 will have to look for a job for six months before receiving unemployment benefits. Young people who have been working will wait a shorter time because they have been having a go and making a contribution. Of course, there's no change to access to income support for young people in education or training; or for young people with a significant disability or parenting responsibilities.

These changes do mean, though, that the days of doing nothing on the taxpayer are over. Gone. The era of something for nothing is no more. Being an adult means taking responsibility for the choices you make and making the best possible choices in the circumstances you face. Only after six months will young jobseekers receive income support and then there will be a requirement to participate in at least 25 hours a week of Work for the Dole. Work for the Dole is giving as well as receiving; that's why there's a dignity to work for the dole that's not there for people who simply receive unemployment benefit, especially long-term recipients. Given a choice between being useful in the community and taxpayer-funded idleness, governments, parents and society at large should prefer purposeful activity every time.

As Employment Minister, I spent a lot of time with people on Work for the Dole projects. I never saw anyone demeaned by it; I never saw anyone who hadn't benefitted from participation. Most unemployed people are yearning to show the world what they can do – not what they can't do – and work for the dole gives them that chance.

Because there is no time to waste, next week, Work for the Dole will commence in 18 areas across Australia for all job seekers between 18 and 30 years old. Work for the Dole will move to a full national scheme from 1 July next year. Under these reforms, young jobseekers, at any time, may commence eligible study or training and receive Youth Allowance for students until this is completed.

Australia's training completion rates are too low – only about 50 per cent of the people who commence an apprenticeship actually finish it. One of the reasons young apprentices don't complete their training is because they can't afford the costs of being an apprentice – especially when their workmates are earning more in less skilled jobs. So from 1 July this year, we will support those learning a trade by providing concessional Trade Support Loans of up to $20,000 over a four-year apprenticeship – with the loans structured to encourage completion. And from 1 July 2016, the Government will remove the 25 per cent loan fee that applies to VET FEE-HELP for eligible full-fee paying students in higher level vocational education and training courses.

Along with support for younger Australians seeking training, this Government is determined to make employment more attractive for mothers. First, we'll make the existing child care system more flexible and accessible than it already is – and the Productivity Commission will report shortly to the Government with its recommendations. Second, we're implementing a Paid Parental Leave scheme that's based on people's actual wage rather than the minimum wage.

It's important to remember that of the 34 nations of the OECD, 33 offer paid parental leave schemes – and, of these 33 countries, Australia is one of only two that fails to pay leave based on a replacement wage. Paid parental leave isn't a gift. It isn't welfare. It's a workplace entitlement – and to ensure it doesn't make it more expensive to employ a woman, it's administered by government and paid for by a levy on big business.

As well as boost youth participation and female participation in the workforce, this Government is determined to boost seniors' participation too. Ability, not age, should be the test for employment – but all too often older workers face prejudice when they apply for jobs. Older workers have the experience, wisdom and stability to be the very best of employees. So from 1 July this year, the Government will introduce a new wage subsidy, Restart, for businesses that take people over 50 off welfare and into sustained work. Employers who hire an eligible older job seeker for full-time work will receive $10,000 over 2 years. This should be sufficient incentive for employers to step outside their comfort zone, and give mature jobseekers a fair go.

As well, we want to ensure that disabled people with some work capacity are supported to seek employment, especially those under 35. So the Government will strengthen the measure introduced by our predecessor to create participation plans for disability support pensioners under the age of 35 with some capacity to work.

I want to stress that Australia has always been the land of the fair go; but part of giving people a fair go is encouraging them to be their best selves; making it easier for them to have a go too.

The new Government wants more Australians to be economic contributors as well as social and cultural contributors and the best way for that to happen is through work. I want more Australians to be workers; I want our people to be more productive because, that way, our country will be stronger and our citizens will be more fulfilled. I want this Government to be the best friend that the workers of Australia have ever had and making it more likely that more Australians will join the workforce is part of that.

A climate in which free enterprise can flourish
Sydney, 8 August 2014

Prime Minister Abbott delivers the Australian Industry Group's inaugural Sir William Tyree Address, saying his Government would reduce regulatory overreach.

It is a great pleasure to be here to celebrate the life and work of Sir William Tyree. It was said of him that he had "always been a thinker". His ingenuity started as an 8 year-old with the famous toaster made from a kerosene container and it continued throughout his long and productive life.

His legacy includes a laboratory in power engineering at Sydney University and an energy technologies building at the University of New South Wales, both of which bear his name. He was an industrialist, a philanthropist, a brilliant engineer and, of course, a dedicated supporter of the Australian Industry Group. He was an inventor who turned ideas into reality; he turned concepts, into plans, into products; he built businesses and he created jobs.

In doing so, he grasped the interaction – the essential interaction – between ideas, policy, competitiveness, success in business and ultimately our nation's economic strength. He understood that economic reform not only required direction from government but also advocacy from business. His involvement in the AI Group was recognition that business, as the beneficiaries of economic reform, also had a responsibility to be advocates too – to be compelling, frank and fearless advocates of the policies our country needs.

Sir William Tyree's companies, specialising in transformer manufacturing, are indeed a niche manufacturing success story. What could be more fitting, in this inaugural Sir William Tyree address, than to focus on our nation's competitiveness? As he often said, "My companies have never stood still." It's the same with countries – we can't sit still – because if we do, we lose.

John Howard often said that national competitiveness is like a race with an ever-receding finishing line. That race is a race that you run, not so much governments, for it is businesses that create wealth, not governments.

It is business that innovates, invests, takes risks and employs people. Our job – the job of Government – is to take the weights off you so that it is easier for you to compete here and in the wider world.

The Government's Economic Action Strategy is about building a strong and prosperous economy for a safe and secure Australia. We do that by creating the conditions under which businesses can best prosper. After all, you can't have strong communities without a strong economy to sustain them and you can't have a strong economy without strong and profitable private businesses. A strong economy makes everything else so much easier.

Building a strong economy, therefore, has to be at the heart of everything we do. We know that Australia has now experienced some 23 years of continuous economic growth – most likely the longest economic expansion in our history. This owes much to the economic reforms of the Hawke and Howard governments. But you can't take growth for granted, especially when government pursues policies that make growth harder.

I want to assure you that after a six-year interruption, Australia is returning to the path of economic reform, for countries, like businesses must not stand still.

The key elements of our plan to improve the competitiveness of Australian business are very clear: lower tax, less red tape, better infrastructure, freer trade, higher participation and stronger productivity. As already pointed out, we have reduced costs for households and businesses alike by scrapping the carbon tax.

Labor's carbon tax, which the Opposition still supports and very much wants to bring back, was a reverse tariff. It made our exports more expensive. It gave imports an advantage over locally made goods because locally made goods attracted the carbon tax while imports did not. In fact, the more energy used to produce something, the heavier the burden. It was a tax whose creators actually boasted of the jobs it would destroy as prices went up and up. The aluminium industry was forecast to shrink by 60 per cent, the iron and steel industry was forecast to shrink by 20 per cent and gross national income per person was forecast to be $4,000 a year less by 2050 because of the carbon tax. It was a $9 billion a year hit on the Australian economy and scrapping it will save the average Australian household $550 a year. It is gone, but it could come back. It could come back if the people were to make the wrong choice at a subsequent election.

As well as scrapping the carbon tax and keeping it scrapped, this Government is absolutely committed to abolishing the mining tax – a tax that has raised next to nothing yet has robbed an important industry, and all the other businesses dependent upon that industry, of confidence while harming our country's reputation.

As well, from the 1st July next year, the company tax rate will be reduced by 1.5 percentage points to 28.5 per cent. At the same time as we are lowering the tax burden, we are also tackling the costs of compliance that plague every business, because every regulation has a cost, to government and to the wider community. For example, the Australian Taxation Office has spent over $50 million administering the mining tax, the tax that raises hardly any revenue; just 3 per cent in fact of initial revenue forecast.

The Clean Energy Regulator that administered the carbon tax was provided with $60 million a year to monitor the world's biggest and most complex carbon tax.

The Australian Charities and Not-for-profits Commission, responsible for administering the red tape that charities are required to comply with, costs $15 million a year. These are just the costs to government on top of the costs to you.

All this regulation is well-intentioned. The problem is that there has been this massive accumulation of good intentions. This continual encroachment of regulation at Commonwealth, state and local level is not strengthening our country, it's weakening it. It's stifling creativity and progress and robbing us of the risk-taking that drives successful economies.

The fault lies with governments that all too often respond to every risk, accident or mistake with the promise of yet more regulation. Occasionally, more regulation does mitigate risk, but often it does not. More regulation has become the default option for governments eager to be seen to be "doing something" even though knee-jerk reactions rarely provide long-term public policy benefits.

This Government is determined to change the culture of regulation in this country. Engaging in due diligence need not mean procrastination, clearer standards do not mean lesser standards and certainty in decision making is nearly always less costly than hand-wringing and delay.

One area that's been marked by a culture of delay, obfuscation and reluctance to say "yes" or "no" has been the provision of environmental approvals. But that's changing. Since the election, Environment Minister Greg Hunt has been clearing the backlog of stalled project applications. All up, he has made 310 decisions to approve or progress projects resulting in approvals to projects worth over $800 billion. The end result of clearer standards and more timely decision making is more investment, more construction, more trade and more jobs. In this area, the Government is tackling red tape by establishing one-stop shops with the states and territories for environmental approvals.

Right across government, we are cutting unnecessary red tape and changing the way we do things to guard against its regrowth. We had the first Repeal Day in March which saw 9,500 unnecessary or counter-productive regulations and 1,000 redundant Acts of Parliament thrown out. Part of that means that businesses will no longer be required to administer the former government's paid parental leave scheme, saving them an estimated $48 million. National businesses will soon be allowed to operate under one workers' compensation scheme right around our country rather than have to operate in up to eight. Businesses, for instance, will no longer have to re-apply to use agricultural chemicals and veterinary medicines because one approval should be enough.

But these repeal days are the start of what the Government wants to be a real and lasting change of culture – a real and lasting change of culture that we are determined to bring to every aspect of administration and program delivery. Every Government portfolio is auditing its regulations and estimating the compliance costs those regulations impose on businesses, community organisations and individuals. Ministerial advisory committees are now providing a real-world assessment of what to cut and what to keep and to ensure that the balance is as right as it can be.

I would say to your senior leadership that if the AIG has more kindling for the next bonfire of red tape later on this year, please let me know, because our commitment is to reduce red tape costs by $1 billion, not just once, not just twice, but every single year. To date, there's

50,000 pages of regulation to go, and that will save hundreds of millions of dollars. But this is the low hanging fruit; this is the start, not the finish.

I want to make it clear that regulatory overreach has not only harmed business, it's harmed government too. Government, to be effective, must know its limits. Also, it must live within its means. The best way to protect Australia from the higher taxes which do damage our competitiveness is to get government spending under control. As I hope most of you know, without policy change, Australia was on track to $667 billion in debt with interest costs rising to almost $3 billion every single month.

This Budget – the Budget that we are now negotiating through the Senate – reduces peak debt by almost $300 billion and that means more capacity, over time, to make long-term investments and more capacity, over time, to reduce tax.

Investment in infrastructure is an essential part of improving our national competitiveness, because the opportunity cost of poor infrastructure is not paid by government, it's paid by you – it's paid by business. To give you perhaps the most obvious example, for 50 years, governments have procrastinated on building an airport in Western Sydney. Sydney's airport is the gateway to Australia's largest city; it accounts for 40 per cent of international arrivals and 50 per cent of international air freight every year and it's rapidly approaching full capacity. If no action is taken on a second airport, Australia would lose 80,000 additional jobs and $34 billion in economic activity by the middle of the century. So the Government is building a second airport for Sydney, or as I prefer to say, we are building a first airport for Western Sydney. Western Sydney is already Australia's third largest economy and, in its own right, would be our fourth largest city.

You here at the AIG recognise that inadequate infrastructure is one of businesses' top frustrations. As you know, poor infrastructure means delay, higher costs and a wider gap between business and its customers.

Transport and logistics companies and their customers pay every day for the indecision of successive state and Commonwealth governments. But in our first Budget, this Government has committed a record $50 billion to the infrastructure of the 21st century. New roads will cut the wait for freight and speed the movement of people and goods around and between our big cities. It is, in fact, the biggest road building program in our country's history and we all know that our country really needs it.

Every infrastructure project will benefit from re-establishing the Australian Building and Construction Commission because our building and construction industry does need a tough cop on the beat to tackle lawlessness.

While it is business' job to grasp the opportunities that markets provide, it is government's job to improve the environment in which businesses operate. To support businesses as you respond to market opportunities and challenges, in the Budget, the Government announced the establishment of an Industry Skills Fund. This will be a $476 million investment to support the training needs of small to medium enterprises and it will provide up to 200,000 training places over the next four years. It's a fund that will prioritise small and medium enterprises, because every large business started as a small business.

Sir William Tyree started his business by scraping together £5,000 and then getting a loan for another £5,000.

This Government is working to lift apprenticeship completion rates because those dependent on skilled labour are finding it harder and harder to attract and to keep trained staff. Only about 50 per cent, as you well know, of the people who commence an apprenticeship actually finish it. One of the reasons young apprentices don't complete their training is because they can't afford the costs, especially when their workmates are earning more in less skilled jobs. The Government will reinvigorate vocational training with a focus on the needs of industry rather than the preferences of government and bureaucrats.

We need a whole gamut of skilled tradespeople – bakers, electricians, panel beaters, locksmiths, sheet and metal workers. We need skilled workers across the whole range of Australian businesses. They are all first-class occupations and all of them are needed to underpin our future growth. That is why the Government is now providing concessional Trade Support Loans of up to $20,000 over a four-year apprenticeship with the loans structured to encourage the completion of the apprenticeship. And from 1 July 2016, we will remove the 20 per cent loan fee that's applied to VET FEE-HELP for eligible full-fee paying students in higher level vocational education and training courses.

So let me go back to the basics. On election night, I said that Australia was under new management and once more open for business.

Freer trade is central to growing a stronger economy with more jobs and more profitable businesses. As some of you know, because some of you were on them, I have led business delegations to Korea, China, Japan, Canada, the United States and PNG over the last 11 months. We have new free trade agreements with Korea and with Japan to further open the door to these important markets. Once the FTA is ratified, Korea will provide duty-free access to 84 per cent of Australia's current exports by value, increasing to over 95 per cent within 10 years.

To illustrate what this means in 2013 – last year – Australian auto manufacturers exported $101 million worth of gear boxes and $51 million worth of engine parts to Korea and under the FTA they will do so without the burden of an 8 per cent tariff. Korea is Australia's second largest market for pharmaceutical products with significant potential to grow now that the tariffs on almost 90 per cent of our pharmaceutical products will be eliminated, with the remainder to be phased out within three years.

With Japan, the door to trade has also further opened and this is our second largest trading partner with two way trade of over $70 billion a year. The Japan-Australia Economic Partnership Agreement, signed last month, is the most liberalising bilateral trade agreement that Japan has ever concluded. It will benefit agriculture, financial services, education, telecommunications, legal services, and yes, manufacturing.

We now have free trade agreements with seven of our top ten trading partners. And, as you know, we have accelerated talks with China which is already our largest trading partner, which I hope can be concluded later this year.

In addition, we are working to free up trade in our region, through the Trans Pacific Partnership, the Regional Comprehensive Economic Partnership Agreement and the Pacific Agreement on Closer Economic Relations.

All of these measures, lowering tax, cutting regulation, concluding free trade agreements and investing in Australian skills are part of our desire, as Government, to make it easier for you to grow your businesses. We are opening the door so that you can walk through it. We aren't providing you with corporate welfare and that's not what you want. What we're giving is business a 'fair go' so that all of you can 'have a go' to run your businesses to exploit your opportunities better.

I have long said that government should be at least as interested in the creation of wealth as in its redistribution. Governments should make it as easy as possible for people like Bill Tyree to take a chance and to create a business.

We are all on a journey; a journey to make our country stronger by doing our jobs better. Government's job is to get the fundamentals right so that business can do its job of being more competitive and more successful, not just here, but right around the world, because the world doesn't stay still – and none of us can stay still either.

4

FOREIGN AFFAIRS

'So much we can do together'

Jakarta, Indonesia, 1 October 2013

In an address to an Indonesia-Australia Business Breakfast, Prime Minister Abbott says the two nations can "know each other, learn from each other and help each other" through better business ties.

I'm here in Jakarta within two weeks of being sworn in as Prime Minister because of the importance I place on the relationship between two great neighbours and two major economies.

Australia currently has more significant economic relationships – but we have no more important overall relationship because of Indonesia's size, proximity and potential. Indonesia is a member of the G20 and a leader of ASEAN as well Australia's most important neighbour. It's the world's most populous Muslim nation. It's the world's third largest democracy. And along with India, it's the emerging democratic superpower of Asia.

At present, Indonesia's annual GDP per person is less than $4000 – or a tenth of Australia's – but it's growing at about 6 per cent a year. It may be many years before individual Indonesians' standard of living equals that of Australians but it probably won't be very long before Indonesia's total GDP dwarfs ours. From Australia's perspective there should be an urgency to building this relationship while there's still so much that Australia has to give and that Indonesia is keen to receive.

There's been trade of one sort or another between Australia and Indonesia at least since the 17th century and it's now 80 years since the first trade commissioner was appointed to what was then Batavia. Despite these connections and despite the annual pilgrimage that hundreds of thousands of Australian tourists make to Bali and elsewhere in the archipelago; and that tens of thousands of Indonesian students make to our universities and colleges, a fully mature economic relationship is yet to be achieved.

Annual two-way trade between Australia and Indonesia is still only about $15 billion. In fact, our two way trade with New Zealand, with just four million people, exceeds our current two way trade with Indonesia with its 250 million people.

Obviously, there's plenty of room to improve. That improvement should start today with me and my ministers and with the business leaders in this room. Australia and Indonesia have so much we can do together. The global centre of economic gravity is shifting to Asia and on present trends, Indonesia will be the number four economy in the world by mid-century. Fifty per cent of Indonesians are aged under 30, ready to play their part in this economic miracle. Even now, they make up a technologically literate workforce, enjoying a standard of living their parents or grandparents could not have imagined. There are more billionaires in Indonesia today than in Japan and, here in Jakarta, the minimum wage has risen by 44 per cent in the past year. There are still 100 million Indonesians, though, living on less than $1000 a year.

Within two decades, there will be 135 million middle class Indonesians whose demand for goods and services – including financial services, health services, educational services, infrastructure and food – will be backed by purchasing power.

Protein is becoming a more important part of the Indonesian diet, particularly among prosperous urban communities and, within two years, beef consumption in Indonesia is expected to exceed domestic production by about 21,000 tonnes a year.

There is a chance here for each of us to play to our strengths: Indonesia, an acknowledged world leader in fattening and finishing, with some of the world's finest intensive feedlots; and Australia, with our vast grazing lands and our long pastoral history, skilled at breeding beef cattle at a globally competitive price. We can work together – but it will take some effort, especially after the shock of the former Australian government cancelling the live cattle export trade in panic at a TV program. Nothing like this can ever be allowed to happen again.

Last year, I visited abattoirs in Indonesia which were quite comparable to those in Australia and reject any notion that Indonesian standards are lower than Australia's. The new Australian government is determined to put this episode behind us and to build on the joint Red Meat and Cattle Forum established in July to foster partnership between the meat industries here and in Australia.

Australian business has rarely been keener to explore investment opportunities and build partnerships that transfer skills and build local industries – here and at home.

I also welcome Indonesia's desire to invest in Australia – including in agriculture. As I said on election night, Australia is under new management and is once more open for business. We are open to investments that will help to build the prosperity of both nations.

Food security is just one area of opportunity – another is the rapidly expanding demand for services. Educational services are a good example. Indonesia is already home to 100,000 former students from Australian universities. Of those Indonesian students who choose to study abroad, roughly one in four make Australia their destination.

While tens of thousands of Indonesian students are studying in Australian universities and colleges, only a few hundred Australians are returning the compliment by studying in Indonesia. Starting next year, the new Australian government will establish a new Colombo Plan that doesn't just bring the best and the brightest students from the wider Asia-Pacific region to Australia but takes Australia's best and brightest to the region.

The Colombo Plan, operating from the 1950s to the 1980s, saw tens of thousands of the future leaders of our region educated at Australian universities. A contemporary, two way street version of the Colombo Plan, would acknowledge how much the region can teach us as well as how much we can offer our region. Operating at different levels and for different periods of time, and often with a business internship component, this new Colombo Plan could provide us with a new and more contemporary version of Rhodes scholars and Fulbright fellows, this time with a strong Asia-Pacific orientation.

As well, within a decade, working with the Australian states and territories, the new government aims to have 40 per cent of high school students studying a foreign language – as was the case in the 1960s – only this time the emphasis will be on Asian languages as well as European ones. This New Colombo Plan aims to ensure that we are a more Asia literate country, more able to play our part in the Asian Century. Specific policies like these will have an impact, over time.

Still, deepening and broadening the Australia-Indonesia relationship means millions of human interactions, tens of thousands of business deals and hundreds of institutional arrangements in which Australians and Indonesians get to know each other, learn from each other and help each other.

National leaders can do so much – but only so much. That's why Foreign Minister, Julie Bishop, Trade Minister, Andrew Robb and I are accompanied by a strong business delegation of leaders from Australia's financial services, health, agriculture, resources, infrastructure, telecommunications, office management and manufacturing sectors.

I thank each of you for taking the time and trouble to make this trip and to build these links. Government initiatives mean little if they are not backed by dozens, hundreds, and ultimately tens of thousands of individual contacts between Australians and the people in other countries that we deal with.

As befits a country that's under new management and once more open for business, it's my intention to take a trade delegation with me on all significant overseas trips to showcase Australia and to let our partners know more about how we can work together to mutual advantage. We're establishing a register in the Department of Foreign Affairs and Trade for businesses that want to be part of trade delegations accompanying ministerial visits.

I also thank the organisations working tirelessly to promote Australia-Indonesia business links such as the business partnership group, Kadin, and the Indonesian-Australian Business Council. Such organisations are indispensable because they know their way around the local scene.

At another level, governments come together bilaterally to forge formal arrangements like the Indonesia-Australia Comprehensive Economic Partnership Agreement. One of my first acts as prime minister was to ask the Minister for Trade and Investment, Andrew Robb, to accelerate the work with his Indonesian counterparts towards this new deal. The new government's approach is very straightforward: we will take a respectful, consultative, no-surprises approach to relations with Indonesia.

Our aim is to rebuild confidence so that both sides respect each other and trust other to keep commitments. Trust is essential to the future success of the businesses represented here today.

There's the hard grind of establishing regulatory certainty. There's the patient negotiation that helps to eliminate barriers to trade and investment and facilitate market access. Then there's the further engagement that takes place in the regional and global forums – such as ASEAN, the East Asia Summit, APEC, and the G20. Forums like these are critical to the long-term prosperity of every country – and Australia hosting the G20 in a year's time; and Indonesia, hosting APEC in a week's time, will both be pushing for regional and global strategies to promote economic growth. The new Australian Government intends to showcase fiscal restraint, deregulation, tax cuts and investment in economic infrastructure.

Another example is the Regional Comprehensive Economic Partnership, currently being negotiated under the auspices of ASEAN. Australia and Indonesia have much to gain from a regional free trade area encompassing ASEAN member states and the nations with which they have existing free trade agreements. The 16 nations that this would cover account for roughly half of the world's population, about a third of world GDP and a quarter of global exports. This further agreement would not just cover trade in goods and services, but such matters as competition, dispute resolution, intellectual property and technical cooperation.

It's negotiations like these – hard, open, with no surprises – that deliver the transparent and stable regulatory regimes that give companies the confidence to make the long-term investment decisions that boost economic growth and ultimately deliver a safer and freer world.

Early next year, right across Indonesia, Australia will present a major cultural festival to strengthen our engagement here, beyond the cabinet room and beyond the boardroom. The aim is to showcase Australian creativity and innovation and to foster creative collaborations between Indonesians and Australians. A business program operating in parallel with this cultural festival will help promote trade and investment. Then there's the new Australia Indonesia studies centre at Monash University to be jointly funded by government and the private sector to build business, cultural, educational, research and community links and to promote greater understanding of Indonesia and its growing importance to Australia.

A more culturally aware Australia and an economically stronger Indonesia would mean more Australian students in Indonesia and more Indonesian tourists in Australia. More and more Australians now see Indonesia as a place to do business and to embark on joint ventures, as well as to have a holiday, as the business leaders' presence here testifies. Our challenge is to ensure that more and more Indonesians see Australia as a good place to invest and do business: in short, as a trusted partner.

I am proud to be here in Jakarta with such a group of business leaders acting as ambassadors for our country. I'm confident you can engender the trust in Australia that's essential for our future.

A better, richer world
2013 Sir Edward "Weary" Dunlop Lecture
Melbourne, 5 December 2013

In his Sir Edward "Weary" Dunlop Asialink Lecture, Prime Minister Abbott outlines his "Jakarta not Geneva" plan.

It is an honour to deliver this Sir Edward "Weary" Dunlop Asialink Lecture. As a prisoner on the Burma Railway, he could hardly have had a worse introduction to Asia. Yet, as a medical specialist, he returned repeatedly to Asia to help train surgeons under the post-war Colombo Plan.

Weary Dunlop was a surgeon, prisoner of war, philanthropist and Victoria's first ever rugby union international. He could inspire hope when all seemed lost and he could forgive those who had been his implacable enemies.

Instead of disappearing into the prosperity of comfortable, postwar Australia, he reached back into Asia. On trip after trip, he helped to hone the skills of his medical colleagues across our region and helped to forge some of the connections that have transformed the way we see our neighbours and the way they see us.

Weary Dunlop wasn't the only Australian of the war time generation to transcend magnificently any bitterness towards the Japanese. My former constituent and local Liberal Party branch president, the late Captain Norman White, another POW, was the much loved convenor of a monthly Japanese business lunch in Sydney.

The suggestion that Australians of that era regarded Asia as a place to fly over (or to sail past) on the way to England is just dead wrong. Our society has not been entirely free of misunderstanding, prejudice, and perhaps even racism in its darker corners. It has also been marked by curiosity about the wider world, impatience with received truth, and a willingness to give almost anything and anyone the benefit of the doubt.

The easy-going disposition of most Australians plus the beginning of backpacker tourism in the 1950s and the rise of the global village has made Asia an exhilarating place for us to visit and to make friends so much more than somewhere exotic and sometimes strange.

The parties I lead have long been more alive to Asia's opportunities than its challenges. It was, after all, Sir Robert Menzies who first called the "far east" the "near north". It was Sir Percy Spender who established the Colombo Plan which educated the leaders of our region here in Australia – perhaps our greatest ever exercise in soft power. It was Menzies and Sir John McEwen who negotiated the 1957 trade treaty with Japan. Japan's then-prime minister Kishi, the grandfather of today's prime minister Abe, observed that the trade treaty and the Colombo Plan were proof of Australia's "awakened Asia-mindedness". It was Harold Holt who ended the White Australia policy. It was Malcolm Fraser who began large scale Asian immigration. And it was John Howard who signed the deals which led to China becoming our largest trading partner.

As John Howard observed in his 1997 Weary Dunlop Lecture, "history that is written with a chip on the shoulder tends to be very poorly balanced". Like Prime Minister Howard, I acknowledge the achievements of all previous governments, not just Liberal ones. Australia's deepening relationship with Asia started with Menzies and has continued without substantial interruption ever since.

Under my leadership, the Coalition has emphasised the need for our foreign policy to have a "Jakarta not Geneva" focus. At some level, Australia is engaged wherever there is a citizen to protect, a value to uphold, or an interest to advance. Australia does have global interests, so developments in America, Europe and the Middle East often concern us. That said, we need to focus our efforts where we can make the most difference.

For some years now, the centre of world economic power has been shifting decisively and dramatically to Asia and to our part of the world. Today, seven of Australia's top ten trading partners are in Asia. Together, they account for just over 50 per cent of our trade. On current trends, China is on track to become the world's largest economy within a couple of decades.

There is much to welcome in this. As with Japan, Australia has played a part in the rise of China. Our iron ore furnishes much of the steel that's building its cities; our coal and gas powers much of its booming industry; and our universities and colleges have opened their doors to many of its people.

Yes, our friendship with China is more recent than that with Japan and less developed than that with the United States. Nevertheless, it is more and more important to us. Our relationship with China has come further in the past 40 years than that with any other country: from a country with which we did not even have diplomatic relations to our biggest trading partner and largest source of immigrants.

China's rising economic power has lifted hundreds of millions of people out of poverty. Indeed, the emergence of the Chinese middle class in little more than a generation may qualify as the most remarkable transformation in human history. Inevitably, economic success means more integration with other countries as well as more competition with them.

We accept the modernisation of China's armed forces because that is what all countries want for their military. Of course, the more successful the country is, the more capacity it has to throw its weight around; but it also has less reason to do so and more to lose from the attempt. Growing power is accompanied by increased responsibility.

In Australia's experience so far, a stronger and more confident China has been a better friend and there is no reason why this shouldn't be the experience of other countries too. We already have a strong relationship with China based on shared interests and I would hope that, over time, it might be based more on shared values.

The rise of China, of course, is just one part of the more general rise of Asia. Within 50 years, another Asian giant – India – is likely to be among the three largest economies in the world.

With India, Australia has democracy, the rule of law and the English language in common – not to mention cricket! India is also a source of our migrants to rival China and the United Kingdom. Partly because of India's long preoccupation with the non-aligned movement and statist economics; and partly because of Australia's historical amnesia and fascination with China, this relationship has been neglected.

There was the Rudd-Gillard Government's off-again/on-again attitude to uranium sales on our side; and on theirs, the fact that no Indian Prime Minister has visited – even for a Commonwealth Heads of Government Meeting – since Rajiv Gandhi. Still, no one should underestimate India now; nor its potential to be a global superpower in this century.

Although Japan has hardly grown economically in the past three decades, it remains the world's third largest economy, a mature liberal democracy, Australia's second largest trading partner, and an important military partner. Japan is understandably anxious about China's ambitions in the China Sea. Australia, for its part, takes no sides in territorial disputes but insists that they be addressed peacefully and in accordance with international law. Whatever the historical rights and wrongs, no one's current best interests would be advanced by threats of force, let alone use of it.

Then there's Indonesia, Australia's nearest large neighbour, a country whose size, proximity and potential makes it, perhaps, our most important overall relationship. Although one hundred million Indonesians still earn less than $2 a day, its GDP already matches ours (at least in purchasing power terms) and, most likely, will be several times ours in a few decades. With India, Indonesia is the emerging, democratic superpower of Asia.

Being Indonesia's "trusted partner" is easier said than done, given the media's tendency to play to stereotypes and past disagreements over East Timor. Still, there is already a very wide range of military and academic interaction plus the affinity born from hundreds of thousands of Australian tourists in Indonesia each year and tens of thousands of Indonesian students here in Australia.

Over time, I hope to see more Australian students in Indonesia and more Indonesian tourists in Australia as Indonesia's economy grows and our mutual understanding expands. In the meantime, the new government is working on structures that can absorb the passions unleashed when Australia could be made to seem oblivious to Indonesia's good will or when Indonesia could seem hard on an Australian citizen.

Challenged over whether he was pro-Asia or pro-America, John Howard famously observed that Australia did not have to choose between its history and its geography - particularly as America remains deeply engaged in the Asia-Pacific region.

Almost uniquely for a great power, America has used its strength not to weaken others but to strengthen them. That's why a strong America is good for Australia and for our friends and neighbours in the region.

More or less openly, almost every Asian country wants to retain a strong American presence. Even China understands how much it has benefited from the global stability and economic freedom that US power has largely brought about. Any significant decline in the United States' influence and interest in our region would be significantly destabilising and therefore bad for everyone.

The growing economic strength in our region gives Australia more opportunities but, if not matched by commensurate strengthening of our own economy, it also makes us more vulnerable. A stronger economy is the foundation of successful foreign policy as well as of successful domestic policy. Cutting taxes and reducing red tape to boost productivity is ultimately as relevant to our international standing as it is to our domestic prosperity. The Coalition's economic reforms are not at odds with any aspect of our foreign policy but are necessary to make all our policies work to their best.

Redirecting flagged future increases in spending from foreign aid to domestic infrastructure should actually boost our influence in the region when it helps to bring about the stronger economy on which our international standing rests. After all, Australia's international clout does not rest on the size of our aid budget but on the size of our economy and the weight it gives us in the wider world.

Regardless of the relative size of the aid budget, during disasters and emergencies Australia will always be there to lend a helping hand. John Howard's swift gift of $1 billion to help Indonesia recover from the Indian Ocean tsunami was an important element in the growing rapport between our countries.

Indonesia is Australia's largest recipient of foreign aid. At some point, Indonesia's overall economic strength will make further Australian aid unnecessary – as has already become the case with China and India.

As far as possible, Australian aid should be designed to enable other countries to stand on their own two feet as quickly as possible. It is good that Australian citizens contribute to a range of charities dedicated to improving the individual lives of poor families in poor countries. The Australian Government's aid, however, should be directed towards improving other countries' governance and strengthening their economies.

Reducing the rate of increase in the aid budget over the next few years will enable the new government to ensure that our aid really is best targeted and most effective. Aid must mean doing good for donees rather than merely feeling good for donors. The government retains the Millennium Development Goal aspiration of spending 0.5 per cent of gross national income on aid but is concerned that it not reinforce stereotypes of a rich first-world and a poor third-world that are already rapidly being overtaken by events.

In any event, trade rather than aid is the best way to sustainably boost poor countries' prosperity – as the extraordinary success of Singapore, Hong Kong, Taiwan, Korea, Thailand, Malaysia, and more recently, China and India demonstrate. The more quickly countries can integrate with global markets, the better for their citizens.

Australia generally allows the products of our Pacific island neighbours freely to enter our markets. We support freer trade on a multilateral, plurilateral and bilateral basis. We already have free trade agreements with New Zealand, the United States, Singapore, Thailand, Chile and Malaysia, and are working on them with Japan, China, India and Indonesia. Then there's the Trans-Pacific Partnership free trade negotiation that's making good progress.

Tonight, I can confirm that a free trade deal has been negotiated with South Korea, subject to detailed consideration by the Cabinet and by the Parliament. This is a significant breakthrough towards a deal that started in 2009 but has been stalled for eighteen months. Better access to Korea for Australian agricultural produce will help Australian farmers and Korean consumers; while better access to Australia for Korean manufactured products will help Korean workers and Australian consumers.

As the history of the world abundantly demonstrates, wealth can't be enjoyed without being shared. In this way, the desire for a better life can drive the kind of interactions which ultimately change human hearts and build a better world as well as a richer one.

The universal dream of a more peaceful, harmonious world will only be achieved if people everywhere are more aware that what unites us all is more important than anything that divides us. It means encouraging people to put themselves in others' shoes so that everyone is more drawn to the golden rule of ethics: to treat others as you would yourself be treated.

In our own region, this means more Australians who can speak Asian languages, catch cultural meanings and navigate local networks. It means starting with children at school. The decline in the study of foreign languages is a worrying erosion of Australia's broader international literacy. In 1960, for instance, 40 per cent of year 12 students studied a second language compared to just 12 per cent today. Asian language take-up has been steadily declining over the past decade such that barely 1000 year 12 students across our country are enrolled to study Indonesian. The new Government will work with the states to reverse this trend.

Last year in Bali, I was part of a high-level meeting between Indonesia and Australia. Of the seven people in the room, six had been educated in Australian universities. Over the past couple of decades, Australian universities have built a $15 billion a year export industry around fee-paying students. The number of Asian students in Australian educational institutions has grown from 170,000 a decade ago to 320,000 now. Of the two and a half million international students in Australia over the past decade, 1.9 million have been from Asia. It is a largely market-based version of the old Colombo Plan.

The new government wants international education to be a two-way street. Our New Colombo Plan will be different and better than the original, adding an outward-bound component to the original inward one. Yes, our region has much to learn from us, but we also have much to learn from our region. So, under the New Colombo Plan, thousands of Australian undergraduates will study at the universities of Asia and the Pacific, complementing the thousands who come to Australia to study each year. We will return the compliment that the region has paid to us by learning as much in their countries as they have learnt in ours.

Over time, a period of study in the Asia Pacific should become a "rite of passage" for Australian undergraduates. Over the next five years, the Government will invest $100 million in the New Colombo Plan. A pilot scheme involving Hong Kong, Indonesia, Japan and Singapore will operate in the coming academic year with a full roll-out in 2015. Another important element of the New Colombo Plan will be an internship program involving the business community. It's all part of restoring our focus and reinforcing our mindset to reflect our geographic reality and our economic future by deepening our links with our neighbours.

This is hardly news to the supporters of Asialink. You have worked for many years to deepen relationships with our region. I thank you and congratulate for all you have done; and hope that the work of the new government might complement yours.

This is always the challenge: to keep faith with the best values of our forebears, and to build on them to face the challenges of today and tomorrow. Weary Dunlop was a great teacher for his time and an inspiration for ours and would, I'm sure, be pleased with what we have in mind.

'We are blood brothers'
Sydney, 7 February 2014

Appearing with his New Zealand counterpart, John Key, at a business lunch in Sydney, Prime Minister Abbott applauds economic reform across the Tasman, saying he hopes to emulate the Kiwis' phenomenal success.

It is a real honour for me to be sharing the podium today with my friend and brother Prime Minister, John Key.

John Key has done mighty things in New Zealand. I am happy to bask in his reflected glory today and I salute him as someone who, with yet I hope many years to go in New Zealand's top job, has already marked himself out as one of New Zealand's most accomplished prime ministers.

The size and the enthusiasm of this gathering testifies to an economic relationship which is strong and getting stronger. New Zealand is our sixth largest export destination. It's our ninth largest source of imports. It's our third largest destination for exports and 16,500 Australian businesses also call New Zealand home.

It isn't just an economic relationship. We were blood brothers, beginning on the battlefields of Gallipoli and France. We have since served together in so many theatres of conflict, most recently Afghanistan. We are not two foreign countries; we are two somewhat different countries, but we are two countries united by an abundance of family ties. New Zealand and Australia are family. We are brother countries. We are sibling countries.

My wife – as many of you would know – was born in New Zealand. In fact, Prime Minister Key was one of my constituents for several years. He couldn't vote for me, but nevertheless, he was a constituent for several years.

Our challenge is to turn the personal bonds, the cultural bonds, the historic bonds into ever stronger economic bonds. Our challenge is to try to ensure that while we remain two countries, increasingly, we are one seamless market economy.

I really am thrilled that Australia has been able to invite New Zealand to participate in the full range of this year's G20 activities. This year, thanks to New Zealand's presence, it will be not so much the G20 as the G21.

The G20 year will see the most significant international gathering ever held in this country. It kicks off with Finance Ministers coming here in a couple of weeks' time. It culminates with the Heads of Government of the world's 20 largest and most representative economies coming to Brisbane in November.

There are many countries that we could have invited but we decided that the country that we must invite was our brother country, our sibling country across the Tasman – New Zealand. It's an opportunity to showcase not just Australia but to showcase Australasia.

In the week leading up to the B20 – or as now I prefer to say the B21 gathering in mid-July – we will have an Australasian business week which will be an opportunity to showcase the capacities and the capabilities of the businesses of both our two countries.

We are both countries which need investment. We are both countries that are dedicated to exports and this will be our opportunity to show to the leaders of the world's largest businesses just what we can do for them.

When I look at New Zealand I see a country which currently has much to teach us. There was a period in the 1980s – the era of Rogernomics – when we rightly looked across the Tasman for lessons. Over the last five years we have again rightly looked across the Tasman for lessons.

When I said on election night last year that Australia was under new management and open for business, I had New Zealand in mind. I had in mind many of the policies and programs which have been pursued by the Key Government.

Thanks to the fiscal discipline of the Key Government, government as a percentage of New Zealand's economy will drop from 35 per cent to 30 per cent. As government gets smaller, citizens get bigger and that is what this government wants to achieve in this country – empowered citizens. New Zealand is on track for a surplus next year and strong sustainable surpluses in the years ahead.

I was delighted to hear the New Zealand Health Minister explain to me and my colleagues this morning that health spending in New Zealand has grown by just three per cent over the last five years yet, by all reasonable indicators, the quality of health services and health outcomes have actually improved.

The policies of the New Zealand Government, under John Key, are not just about fiscal rigor; they are about providing a better life for citizens. The point of being economically responsible is not to keep the 300 smartest economists in the country happy. The point of being economically responsible is to provide a better life for people.

In New Zealand, inflation is down, mortgage interest rates are down very substantially from over five per cent to under two per cent. These are good results for the people of New Zealand. Real wages are up 13 per cent; there's been 53,000 new jobs in just the last 12 months. This is why the New Zealand lessons have such resonance for us on this side of the Tasman. Not for nothing has Forbes Magazine recently described New Zealand as the world's number one place to do business.

I do welcome Prime Minister Key, not just as a brother, but as soul mate. I do welcome him, not just as a friend, but in very significant ways already a political mentor. As the Australians in this audience know only too well, this new Government here in Australia is determined to get taxes down, to get red tape down and to get productivity up because that means you get prosperity up. This is not just textbook learning because across the Tasman in New Zealand we have seen precisely that happen.

So in welcoming John Key to the microphone I say that he has been a truly exemplary leader of his country, he has been a fine leader for New Zealand, but his inspiration and his example is very, very powerful on this side of the Tasman and I am very grateful indeed to be in the company of my brother Prime Minister John Key.

'Together as comrades'
Melbourne, 24 February 2014

Attending his first Australia-Canada Economic Leadership Forum since winning Government, Prime Minister Abbott says the two countries have much to learn from each other regarding indigenous recognition, the balance between unity and multicultural diversity, sustaining the environment, supporting industry and manufacturing, and managing a federation. As with his New Zealand counterpart, Abbott is full of praise for Canadian Prime Minister Stephen Harper.

On a wall in my offices, hangs a painting of a World War I battlefield near Vimy Ridge where Canadian and Australian soldiers had been comrades-in-arms. In those days, it would have been taken for granted that Canadians and Australians should have gone into action together, as part of the British Empire's armies in France.

These days, despite a language in common, a shared Westminster parliamentary tradition, and a Queen of Canada who is also the Queen of Australia, we are not so often in each other's thoughts. That should change.

With two-way investment at over $70 billion – and with Australian companies such as BHP playing an active role in Canada – the commercial relationship is in reasonable shape; but there should be more to our friendship than money.

Although John Howard perceptively described Australians and Canadians as kindred spirits, we haven't talked to each other as often as we should. The relationship is strong but under-developed even though we are as like-minded as any two countries can be. So, I want to make more of this friendship: for our own good and for the good of the wider world.

As the world's tenth and twelfth largest economies, our two countries carry considerable clout but normally prefer, in Teddy Roosevelt's words, to talk softly rather than carry a big stick. That's why, as nations, we tend to have more friends than critics. But despite inhabiting a very similar intellectual and cultural space, we are rarely as conscious as we should be of each other's presence. In part, this is because Australia and Canada are amongst the happiest and the most tranquil societies on earth.

We have our issues, of course – many of them issues in common:

- How do we ensure that our first peoples are not second-class citizens in their own country?
- How do we best promote sophisticated manufacturing in economies dominated by resources and agriculture?
- How much stress, as immigrant societies, should we place on diversity and how much on unity?
- How in a federation, do you ensure that particular problems can be sheeted properly home to particular levels of government?
- And how do we best manage vast wilderness areas consistent with creating jobs and prosperity?

Canada and Australia don't often figure in each other's news bulletins because, to give due credit, none of these issues have been disastrously mismanaged. Our comparative success at managing comparable problems means that we have more to learn from each other, not less.

Australians and Canadians should be more conscious not only of all that we have in common but of all the good that we might do together. So, my intention is to broaden and deepen the relationship between our two kindred countries.

Just as my office rescued the Vimy Ridge painting from a public service storeroom where it had been languishing until just a couple of months ago!

Later this year, I hope to visit Canada as Prime Minister. Scarcely less than Washington or London, Ottawa should be a destination for Australian officials because there are few big issues where we don't have a similar outlook. And there are few economic issues here in Australia that Canada hasn't grappled with too. Like its distinguished counterparts in the United Kingdom and New Zealand, the Harper Government has cut taxes, fought against cheque-book government, de-regulated the economy and brought a robust common sense to the consideration of international problems. Like New Zealand, Canada is on track to balance the budget in the coming financial year. Like the UK, Canada's economic growth is strengthening.

Unlike those governments, though, but like Australia's, the Canadian government won an election campaigning against a carbon tax that would kill jobs without helping the environment. So Australia has much to learn from Canada, especially as this new government prepares its first Budget and begins its year chairing the world's most important international economic forum.

In Canada, it's worth noting, the deficit has been all-but-eliminated as much through restraining the growth of spending programs and through cutting government itself – than through big cuts to existing government programs. New Zealand has followed an almost identical path back to surplus.

Like our counterparts in these comparable countries, the Australian Government is determined to get the economic fundamentals right. Because you can't give what you haven't got; no country has ever taxed or subsidised its way to prosperity; you don't solve a problem of debt and deficit with yet more debt and deficit; and profit is not a dirty word because profitable private businesses create jobs and prosperity.

In the marrow of our bones, we understand that you can't have strong communities without a strong economy to sustain them; and you can't have a strong economy without profitable private businesses.

Lower taxes, less red tape and higher productivity mean higher economic growth, more jobs, more prosperity and, ultimately, more ability to pay for government services. But you can't spend money until you've earned it or until you've created the means to pay it back.

Governments, no less than families and businesses, have to live within their means. So, repairing the budget, is an essential element to building a stronger economy. It is in fact part of keeping faith with the public.

As this Government said pre-election, within three years, Australia will be on track for a sustainable surplus. As we said pre-election, within a decade – hopefully well within a decade – Australia will again enjoy sustainable surpluses in the order of one per cent of GDP.

That way, debt will be falling and interest repayments can instead be directed to lower taxes, better services and stronger infrastructure. But we have to get there – and this year's budget will put us back on the right track. It will start the process needed to avoid the $123 billion of prospective deficits and the $667 billion of gross debt that this Government inherited. We will abolish the carbon tax and the mining tax and make the sustainable savings that we committed to before the election. We will build the infrastructure that we committed to before the election and invest the proceeds of further privatisations in more economic infrastructure that passes cost-benefit tests. The public sector will be trimmed and new bureaucracies abolished because more government doesn't create more wealth. The growth of overseas aid will be substantially reduced because largesse with borrowed money loads up our children with debts they don't need. We will keep our pre-election commitments to maintain health spending and school spending but we must reduce the rate of spending growth in the longer term if debt is to be paid off and good schools and hospitals are to be sustainable.

Across every area of government, our duty is to reduce less productive spending in favour of more productive spending so that taxpayers are always receiving the best possible value for their money. After all, government does not spend a single dollar that it doesn't take from you in taxes or borrowings. Governments' duty to you is to spend your money as responsibly as you would. Government's duty is to do all we reasonably can to help all our people to be their best selves; and to maximise everyone's potential to be economic as well as social and cultural contributors to the life of our country. That's why all new spending in this budget will be fully funded, invariably from savings, and will be directed to making our economy more productive and our people more fulfilled through more engagement in the economy.

Let's face it, the best form of welfare is a job; and keeping people on welfare who could otherwise be active is no lasting favour.

This year, as most of you would know, the world is especially watching Australia because of our role with the G20. Our objective is to do what we can to promote higher growth, freer trade, better infrastructure, resilient-but-not-entirely-risk-averse financial institutions and less leaky tax systems.

I want to thank Joe Hockey for the magnificent way in which he chaired the Finance Ministers' meeting in Sydney. Australia has made a good start to its G20 presidency. Joe has made crystal clear our focus on a few key areas where each country can make change for the better for its own people and for the wider world.

Soon, each G20 member will submit its national plan for higher economic growth. We all know that each country is entirely free to choose the plan that suits it best. But this does amount to a kind of peer-review process for each government's economic policies. I'm confident that Australia and Canada will bring a shared perspective to the G20's talks and we'll both do what we can to persuade other governments to get taxes down, regulation down and productivity and participation up. If the G20 is to be more than a talk-fest, at least some countries will need to show that their actions match their words.

As G20 chair, Australia will lead by example. By the time of the G20 leaders' meeting in November in Brisbane, the carbon and mining taxes should be gone, the company tax cut should be legislated, the parliament will have dedicated time to repeal and deregulate, and the annual infrastructure statement will have been made.

It's likely that at least two of the three major free trade agreements that are Australia's priority would be concluded and that some of the $400 billion in projects that have received environmental approval since the election will be underway.

Australia will be well and truly open for business because the new management team will have well and truly taken charge. At home and abroad, the Australian Government will say what we mean and do what we say. We mean to put in place the lower taxes and the smaller government that makes our citizens strong and self-reliant and makes our country more prosperous. Without over-stating our importance, or exaggerating our success, our aim is to show the world that there is a better way: a clear alternative to the government-knows-best mentality that's persisted right around the world since the Global Financial Crisis.

In all this, Canada has been a reassuring exemplar of how to improve an economy while also strengthening a society. Canada and Australia have a history of supporting each other in times of need. It's good that so many of you are here to deliberate on the problems we have in common, on the opportunities we have in common, on the challenges facing the wider world that would be so better met if we faced them together as comrades.

Refusing to let the past blight the future
Canberra, 8 July 2014

At the invitation of Prime Minister Abbott, Japanese counterpart Shinzo Abe becomes the first Japanese leader to address thr Australian Parliament, speaking of his nation's warm friendship with Australia. Abbott then rises to announce what would become one of his signature foreign policy achievements.

On this historic occasion, today we welcome to this Parliament a great friend of Australia, the Prime Minister of Japan, Shinzo Abe.

Leaders from the United States, China, the United Kingdom, Canada, Indonesia and New Zealand have addressed both houses of the Australian Parliament. It is fitting that we should now hear from the Prime Minister of Japan, in recognition of our special relationship – built on shared interests and common values: democracy, human rights, the rule of law, more open markets and freer trade.

During one of our parliament's early debates, Prime Minister Deakin noted the "high ability…inexhaustible energy…(and) endurance" of the Japanese people that he said "made them such competitors". At some times, it's true, Australians have not felt as kindly towards Japan as we now do but we have never ever underestimated the quality and capacity of the Japanese people.

Even at the height of World War II, Australia gave the Japanese submariners killed in the attack on Sydney full military honours. Admiral Muirhead-Gould said of them: "theirs was a courage which is not the property or the tradition or the heritage of any one nation…but was patriotism of a very high order". We admired the skill and the sense of honour that they brought to their task although we disagreed with what they did. Perhaps we grasped, even then, that with a change of heart the fiercest of opponents could be the best of friends.

Because just 12 years after World War II, Japan's Prime Minister Kishi, Prime Minister Abe's grandfather, visited Australia, and paid his respects to Australia's war dead at the War Memorial in Canberra as you, Prime Minister, have done yourself today. Prime Minister Kishi also signed the commerce treaty between Australia and Japan which helped to spawn the iron ore and coal industries that have done so much for both our countries.

Prime Ministers Menzies and Kishi, allowed history to be their teacher not their master; and, in so doing, provided a lesson in magnanimity for all times and for all peoples.

Since 1957, Australian coal, iron ore and gas has powered Japan's prosperity; and Japanese cars, consumer goods and electronics have transformed Australians' lives. Australians are grateful for the Japanese trade and Japanese investment that has helped to build our modern prosperity. Above all, we appreciate the mutual respect and trust that has underpinned the commercial relationship.

Later today, Prime Minister Abe and I will sign the Japan-Australia Economic Partnership Agreement, a new and perhaps equally historic agreement to further liberalise trade between our countries. This is the first free trade agreement that Japan has made with a major developed economy. For Japan, it means even better access for its manufactured goods. For Australia, it means better access for our beef, dairy, wine, horticulture, and grain products. For everyone, everywhere, it means that two significant countries are prepared to put their hopes above their fears and declare their confidence in the future.

Freer trade means more efficiency; more efficiency means more wealth; and more wealth means more jobs. This is the message that both Japan and Australia will bring to the G20 leaders' meeting in Brisbane in November: Freer trade means more economic growth and more economic growth means more prosperous people and fairer societies.

Both Australia and Japan are serious about boosting economic growth: Australia through lower taxes, less regulation and through shifting spending from short-term consumption to long-term investment; Japan, with the third arrow of Abe-nomics, through less regulated health care, greater female participation, openness to foreign investment and better corporate governance.

Because it takes rare courage to challenge entrenched ideas, even ideas that are holding your country back, Prime Minister Abe is making his mark on history.

Also on this visit, our two countries will conclude an agreement on the transfer of defence equipment and technology, similar to the agreements that Japan already has with the United States and the United Kingdom.

For decades now, Japan has been an exemplary international citizen. So Australia welcomes Japan's recent decision to be a more capable strategic partner in our region. I stress, ours is not a partnership against anyone; it's a partnership for peace, for prosperity and for the rule of law.

Our objective is engagement and we both welcome the greater trust and openness in our region that's exemplified by China's participation in this year's RimPac naval exercises.

Australia and Japan are approaching the 100th anniversary of the first significant occasion when our two counties worked together. The Japanese cruiser, Ibuki, helped to escort the 1914 ANZAC convoy to the Middle East and I am grateful that a Japanese warship will be present for the centenary event in Albany later this year.

More recently, Australian soldiers worked together with Japanese engineers to rebuild war-torn Iraq and I'm pleased to say that the Australian commander in that mission, former Brigadier Andrew Nikolic, is now the Member for Bass in this Parliament!

Under Prime Minister Gillard, Australia was one of the first countries to dispatch assistance to Japan after the devastating 2011 earthquake and tsunami. This is the Australian way. We are true to our word; we threaten no one; we are an utterly reliable partner; and we go out of our way to help when trouble strikes: We helped Indonesia after the Indian Ocean tsunami, the Philippines after typhoon Haiyan and the search for flight MH370 which saw Japanese, Korean and Chinese aviators operating together from an Australian base to try to solve the greatest mystery of our time.

It was Prime Minister Chifley who spoke of a "light on the hill": to work for the betterment of mankind, not just here but wherever we can lend a helping hand. Australia is at the service of the wider world: as an affordable energy superpower, as a plentiful supplier of good food, and as a safe place to get the best and most affordable education. We hope that all the countries of our region will look to us to provide the energy security, the resources security and the food security that all seek.

Over the past two generations, Australian resources have helped to drive the economic miracles of Japan, of Korea and, most spectacularly of all, China.

What's happened in Asia over the past 50 years is a transformation unparalleled in human history. Hundreds of millions of people have been lifted from poverty into the middle class. It is the greatest and the swiftest advance in human welfare of all time.

Great credit belongs to the people and the governments of Asia but Australia is proud to have played our part. We should also be grateful to the United States for its work to guarantee the peace and stability that has made this progress possible. Now the rest of the world has watched these marvels with awe and admiration. It's the reason these times have already been dubbed the "Asian century".

But we can't take a better future for granted; for all the opportunities we have, success still has to be earned. It would be a tragedy for everyone and a disaster for us were these achievements to be put at risk and history teaches us that issues between nations should be resolved peacefully in accordance with international law because the alternative is in no one's best long term interests. The lesson of the last century is that the countries of our region will all advance together or none of us will advance at all.

Prime Minister Howard frequently said that Australia did not have to choose between our history and our geography. My version of this has been to say that you don't win new friends by losing old ones. This Government is determined to improve all Australia's friendships by focusing on the things we have in common.

Australia and Japan have forged one of the world's firmest friendships and most practical of partnerships. But it wasn't always thus. Our partnership began from the ashes of the most destructive war in history because our peoples and our leaders have consistently refused to let the past blight the future. Every country's situation is different, of course, but what a compelling example our two nations have provided of what is possible when we are all our best selves.

We are honoured to have Prime Minister Abe in our Parliament today – thrilled and honoured, and we all look forward to his address.

'The world has much to offer us'
Mumbai, India, 4 September 2014

Prime Minister Abbott chooses the Indian city of Mumbai to launch the New Colombo Plan, which will encourage cultural and linguistic exchanges between the two countries.

It is lovely to be back here in India some 33 years after, as a student between a stint at the University of Sydney and a stint at the University of Oxford I spent three months here in India, including a fortnight in the great city of Mumbai.

I do feel very honoured to be in this great hall of learning to help launch in India the New Colombo Plan. I say this great hall of learning because there are very few institutions of learning anywhere in the world which have done as much to spread the light of knowledge as this great University of Mumbai.

As I said a moment ago, I was a student at the University of Sydney – some 20,000 students in those days. I then went to the University of Oxford – some 8,000 students in those days. Well, 700,000 students here at the University of Mumbai – what a mighty institution. It is my hope that in a small, but significant way those numbers can be augmented in the years ahead by more students from Australia.

Some of you may be aware that back in 1950 the then Australian Government instituted what became known as the Colombo Plan. It was a scheme under which the best and the brightest of the students of our region came to universities in Australia to live, to learn, and then to return to their home countries with the benefits of that education and that life that they'd had in Australia.

It was a marvelous scheme and between 1950 and 1985 some 40,000 people came from the subcontinent, from South-East Asia, from the Pacific, to the universities of Australia, and they returned to their countries the better for that experience.

But I want to say this to you: it was a one-way street and what we now want in Australia is a two-way street. We want to return the compliment to our region by sending our best and brightest to the great universities of our region so that they can live, can learn, can speak the local languages, and come back to our country enriched by that experience.

We have much to offer the world; the world has much to offer us. Australia has much to offer India; India has at least as much to offer Australia. Indian people have been coming to Australia for many years. There are now some half a million people of Indian background living in Australia.

In any one year, there are some 40,000 Indian students studying in Australia. Regrettably, right now, there are just a few tens of Australian students studying in India. That must change and that will change as a result of the New Colombo Plan that I launch this day, here at the University of Mumbai.

From next year, there will be hundreds of Australian students in India. In the years to come, those numbers will mount and mount and mount so that there will be thousands of Australian students here in India, experiencing the richness and the depth of the learning and the culture that this great country has to contribute to us and to the wider world.

There is so much that we can learn from each other. The motto of my first university, Sydney University – *sidere mens eadem mutato* – different skies, the same learning.

And I want to pay tribute to this university for preserving the universal wisdom of mankind, for doing what it can to spread the knowledge, the truth, the wisdom, and the decency, which is at the heart of our common humanity. You have been doing that since 1857. The candle that we lit at the start of this ceremony stands for that light of learning – the light of learning that we want to shine bright, right around the world and that will shine all the brighter because of the New Colombo Plan that we launch today.

Thank you so much. It is a real honour to be here.

'Every country counts'
New York, 25 September 2014

In his inaugural speech to the United Nations General Assembly in New York, Prime Minister Abbott endorses the UN's peaceful objectives and recommits Australia to the cause.

Mr President, in what can seem darkening times, I want to begin with a message of hope. Amidst all our problems: the murderous rage of ISIL in Syria and Iraq, Russian aggression in Ukraine, the spread of Ebola in West Africa and the stubborn sluggishness of many economies, let me start with a small but telling illustration of nations working together to serve our common humanity.

Last March, at the height of the search for missing Flight MH 370, I went to the Pearce airbase in Western Australia to thank all the aviators involved. There were personnel from Australia, New Zealand, Malaysia and the United States, countries that are accustomed to working together; and there were also personnel from China, Japan and Korea, countries whose relations sometimes labour under the weight of historical grievance. On this occasion though, tragedy and a daunting challenge had drawn out the best in everyone.

This organisation, this United Nations, is founded on the principle that we should work together for the common good; and that, over time, talking together and working together will improve our capacity for living together.

Like any institution, the United Nations is an imperfect instrument. Still, it's better than might-is-right and it gives good arguments the best chance to prevail. Despite faults and failures, the UN has worked for peace and progress for nearly 70 years and Australia has been proud to play its part – starting in 1946 when we held the first presidency of the Security Council and helped to draft the Universal Declaration of Human Rights. At the heart of this body is the principle that we should act towards others as we'd have them act towards us.

For almost seven decades now, Australia has believed in the United Nations' potential and supported its work. Keeping commitments, valuing human life, protecting property and extending freedom are universal aspirations, not just Australian ones. Since 1947, Australia has provided more than 65,000 personnel to more than 50 multilateral peace and security operations. We are not a country accustomed to turning back once we've put our hand to the plough; we've had blue beret personnel in the Middle East since 1956 and in Cyprus since 1964.

When leadership is needed, we step up, as we did in Bougainville, in Timor-Leste and in Solomon Islands. In Korea, Cambodia, Kuwait and Afghanistan; in Somalia and Sierra Leone and in other troubled places, Australians have lent a hand under the UN's banner. We have only 21 personnel in South Sudan now but have conducted an airlift of equipment that has supported a much larger force.

With just 24 million people, Australia is a relatively small country but we are the world's 12th largest economy with global interests and with some global reach. We're strong enough to be useful but pragmatic enough to know our limits.

Under successive governments, for more than 100 years, Australia's determination has been to advance our interests, protect our citizens and uphold our values. We have never believed that we can save the world single-handedly; nor have we shrunk from shouldering our responsibilities. After the 2004 East Asian tsunami, we committed $1 billion to Indonesia. We were one of the first countries to arrive with help in Japan after the 2011 earthquake; and in the Philippines after the 2013 typhoon. So far, we've pledged $8 million towards combatting the Ebola outbreak and dozens of Australian health professionals are working with international agencies in the region. To us, this is all part of being a good global citizen.

This July, we were pleased to sponsor Security Council resolution 2166 and to work with the Dutch and the Malaysians to investigate the site and to return our dead after Flight MH17 was shot down by Russian backed rebels over eastern Ukraine. We're grateful for the help that Ukraine gave us and are naturally sympathetic to a country struggling to preserve its independence and territorial integrity against a bully. With the Dutch and the Malaysians, we will do everything we can to ensure that the investigation is not undermined and that the crime is not covered up because that's our duty to the 38 Australians murdered in this atrocity.

Right now, an Australian force has been deployed to the Middle East so that we might join a coalition to disrupt and degrade the ISIL terrorist movement at the request of the Iraqi government.

One of our prime ministers once talked about a great objective, our "light on the hill" as he put it, to work for the betterment of mankind, not just at home but wherever we can lend a helping hand.

To build this better world, we need to respond sensibly to the problems before us (whether through bodies such as the UN or in coalition with like-minded countries); and as well we need to work purposefully to create stronger and more resilient people and communities.

A stronger economy won't solve every problem; but it will make almost every problem easier to tackle. Richer people aren't necessarily better people; but the problems of plenty are invariably easier to deal with than those of want. As this year's chair of the G20, Australia is determined to promote private-sector-led growth: growth, because this is the best way to generate jobs and improve everyone's quality of life; private sector-led, because profitable private businesses are the best source of real, sustainable wealth.

Freer trade, more investment in infrastructure, a modern and fair international tax system, stronger global economic institutions and a more resilient financial sector are all parts of our G20 agenda to strengthen the world economy.

Rather than preaching, we're trying to lead by example. Australia has abolished the carbon tax, abolished the mining tax, provided environmental approvals for $800 billion worth of new projects and begun the task of eliminating our budget deficit within four years. We've finalised a series of trade deals because every time a country trades with another, wealth increases, and when wealth increases countries grow stronger. Our G20 goal is to boost output by an extra two per cent over the next five years to create millions of jobs and to generate trillions in wealth right around the world.

Likewise, the post-2015 Development Agenda should also focus on economic growth because growth makes every other social goal, even tackling climate change, easier to accomplish.

To people who don't know where their next meal is coming from, talk of economic growth can sometimes seem ignorant or indulgent. But economic growth is really just economists' shorthand for more jobs, higher pay, new industries and the better life that only greater wealth can provide. Economic growth might seem a mundane vision but it's what allows millions more people to create for themselves their own vision of how their lives can be better.

To anyone who doubts that stronger economic growth can be achieved, I say look at the countries of East Asia. In scarcely two generations, the rise of Asia has driven the greatest social and economic transformation in history. People live longer; they're better educated, are wealthier and, yes, enjoy freedom and stability that their parents could only dream of. In Japan, Korea and now China; in India and increasingly in Indonesia; many hundreds of millions of people have been lifted from poverty to the middle class. Almost certainly, this is the greatest and fastest advance in human welfare of all time.

While all governments, Australia's included, could always be better, smarter and more compassionate, no one should be blind to the great progress that's occurred. We live in the most remarkable age in human history. For all that remains to be done, we have seen more change for the better than at any other time.

As this General Assembly meets, with such pressing issues before it, our challenge – as always – is to realise our best hopes and to be our best selves. Australians have two defining characteristics: we believe in a "fair go" because innate decency demands that every person have a chance to contribute. We also believe in "having a go" because rolling up your sleeves will always produce a better result than standing on the sidelines complaining. This readiness to make an effort for a good cause is why Australia feels so comfortable in this body and is so ready to contribute to its work.

We should put no limits on what we can achieve, especially when we work together, trust people and are faithful to our deepest values. Every country counts. Every argument must be weighed. Every person has equal rights and dignity. Every person deserves respect. All people are entitled to make their own choices – provided these don't infringe the rights of others. These are the principles which this organisation embodies, on which the future of humanity rests.

'Now a relationship of peers'
House of Representatives, Canberra,
14 November 2014

Welcoming his British counterpart David Cameron to Canberra to address a joint-sitting of Parliament, Prime Minister Abbott describes the contribution Britain has made to Australian society, and how the two nations have grown into peers with common domestic and international goals.

The arrival of the first Britons here in Australia could hardly have been less auspicious.

They'd just sailed half way round the world. Remarkably, thanks to Governor Phillip's good management, only 48 of 1,400 had died on a journey that was an 18th century version of travelling to the moon or landing on a comet.

Of those on the First Fleet, the very best that could be said of them was that they had been chosen by the finest judges in England. Even the soldiers were guards, not warriors.

Yet over the ensuing two centuries, the descendants of convicts have helped to create a society that's as free, fair and prosperous as any on earth, so that to be born Australian is to have won the lottery of life.

The first Christian sermon preached in this country took as its text: "What shall I render unto the Lord for all his blessings towards me". This, indeed, has always characterised us: gratitude for what we have and a fierce determination to build on it. Modern Australia has an Aboriginal heritage, a British foundation and a multicultural character.

There's so much that Britain has given to us. There's so much, indeed, that Britain has given to everyone: parliamentary democracy, the common law, constitutional monarchy, and English – the world's first or second language.

What would the world be without the plays of Shakespeare, the music of the Beatles, the advances of the first Industrial Revolution, the humanity of Wilberforce and the determination of Churchill? What would the world be without the British democratic ethos which took hold in Australia, Canada and New Zealand, as well as in the countries that broke away such as the United States and India? What would the world be if Britain hadn't stood against militarism and fascism? And what would this world be if Britain had not settled the territory that Captain Cook had earlier called New South Wales?

Long ago now, Australians ceased to regard Britain as the mother country – but we're still family. The relationship between Britain and Australia has changed beyond recognition but it's still important and we still matter to each other. Britain is by far our largest trading partner in Europe which remains the world's largest economic bloc. Britain is the second largest overseas investor in Australia, the source of our largest migrant community, and our oldest military ally. Britain is the world's sixth largest economy, the fastest growing big economy in Europe and America's principal military partner.

So, today, we remember the 9000 Australians who died at Gallipoli; and we also remember our British brothers-in-arms who lost 21,000 in the same campaign. We remember the 15,000 Australians who passed into captivity at Singapore; and we remember their 30,000 British comrades who were also taken prisoner. We remember the airmen in the skies over England and Europe from 1940 to 1945 – that few to whom so many owed so much – including the tens of thousands of Australians who helped to win that battle for civilisation. Some of you are with us in the Gallery today. Gentlemen, we honour your deeds and we honour your comrades who did not return.

History matters because it helps us to know who we are and where we're going. It helps us to know what's important and who can be relied upon. It shapes us but it should never control us.

Inscribed on the Australian War Memorial in London are Sir Robert Menzies' words from his time as a member of the British war cabinet: "Whatever burden you are to carry, we also will shoulder that burden."

Today, Britain and Australia are working together to disrupt and degrade the ISIL death cult which has declared war upon the world.

In the Middle East, and now with a new and different crisis in West Africa, Australia and Britain are asking: not "what's in it for us" but "how can we be helpful to people in trouble?"

I can think of no two countries on earth readier to put into international practice the parable of the Good Samaritan. We are like-minded in all the forums we share – the Commonwealth, the United Nations and now the G20 and even NATO – on practical and decent solutions to all the problems facing the world.

At home, both Britain and Australia are committed to lower tax, less red tape, freer trade, bringing budgets under control and creating more private-sector jobs. I have to say, I admire what Prime Minister Cameron has achieved. He has cut the deficit by one third. He has cut taxes for 26 million people. He is creating the best corporate tax system in Europe. A further 1.7 million Britons are in work since 2010. And thanks to his leadership, Britain counts for more than it did five years ago.

Some time ago in this country, we had a largely sterile debate about Australia's place in the world – which John Howard settled with the famous declaration that we don't need to choose between our history and our geography.

Of course, Australia is located in the Indo-Pacific, but our place is wherever there is an interest to advance, a citizen to protect, a value to uphold, or a friend to encourage. To a similar debate in Britain, Prime Minister Cameron has brought the same robust common sense: Britain is a European country with a global role. Like people, countries don't make new friends by losing old ones and they don't deepen some relationships by diminishing others. Britain and Australia are both vibrant multi-cultural democracies determined to make the most of our advantages: of our shared history, of our different geography and, more important still, of our common characteristic curiosity and innate sense that however much you have already done there is always more that is yet to do.

After two centuries in which both of us have constantly adapted to our own changing and different circumstances, it's remarkable how similar we've become. Culturally, intellectually, even economically, it's now a relationship of peers.

In volume one of his memoirs, Clive James has described the gravitational pull of the country of his birth in the country of his choice: As I begin this last paragraph, "a misty afternoon drizzle" he writes. "…soaks the city of London. Down…in the street I can see umbrellas commiserating with each other. In Sydney Harbour twelve thousand miles away and ten hours from now, the yachts will be racing on the crushed diamond water under a sky…of powdered sapphires…Pulsing like a beacon through the days and nights, the birthplace of the fortunate sends out its invisible waves of recollection. It always has and it always will until even the last of us come home."

We will always be conscious of the part that Britain has played in the life of our nation and the friendship between our two countries that will never be taken for granted.

'A wise man seeks harmony, not conformity'
Canberra, 17 November 2014

At a function for Chinese President Xi Jinping, Prime Minister Abbott commends the long and productive relationship between the two nations, which is now more important than ever.

It is a joy to have friends come from afar. With free trade negotiations concluded and with a comprehensive strategic partnership established, this is an historic and memorable day. On behalf of the Government and the people of Australia, I welcome His Excellency Xi Jinping, on his first visit to Australia as President of China, but on his fifth visit to our country.

No Chinese president has ever known more about Australia than President Xi. Tomorrow, when he completes his visit to Tasmania, he will have visited every single one of our states and territories. This President of China, in fact, is more widely travelled in our own country than most Australians. But it runs in his family. Thirty five years ago, the President's father, Xi Zhongxun visited New South Wales as Party Secretary of Guangdong Province.

The President's father visited markets, farms, ports, docks, factories, schools and research institutes and along with then-New South Wales Premier Neville Wran, he signed a joint declaration on Guangdong-NSW friendship and cooperation – it was the first official sister-state relationship between Australia and China and it was so successful that 80 sister-state and sister-city relationships have subsequently been concluded.

Just as the friendships between our cities and states have flourished, our national friendship and cooperation has grown and prospered. Xi Zhongxun saw the potential of our two peoples working with each other and learning from each other.

Today, we should also remember the foresight of the father of Australia's modern relationship with China: Prime Minister Whitlam. When he established diplomatic relations with China, our two way trade was one fifteen hundredth of what it is today. So we acknowledge Prime Minister Whitlam, and all the leaders of our countries who have put aside ideology to see Australians and Chinese as people with common interests and shared aspirations to a better life.

Yes, Australia and China have different systems of government; one is a young country, and the other an ancient one being renewed; but we have become a model of how two peoples and two countries can complement each other. We are testament to the saying that a wise man seeks harmony, not conformity.

In April this year, I saw first-hand Chinese ships and planes working together with Australians (and with Japanese, Koreans and Malaysians), on the sea and in the sky, searching for the missing Malaysian Airlines Flight MH370. In the saddest of circumstances, our people worked side-by-side to seek resolution to this baffling mystery. We mourn the loss of the 154 Chinese passengers along with the six Australians and 79 others on board. To the Chinese families of those who were lost, I promise we will not rest until we have done everything we can to solve this mystery.

Two of those on Flight MH370 were Chinese-Australians: two among almost a million Australians of Chinese background. Chinese people first came to Australia in large numbers during the gold rushes of the 1850s and 1860s and not all of them returned home once the diggings were exhausted. Even before the Great War, there were more than 20,000 Chinese Australians, and at least 198 of them enlisted to fight for King and Country: four won the Distinguished Conduct Medal and 14 won the Military Medal as members of the first Australian Imperial Force. In every part of our national life, Australians of Chinese ancestry have helped to build our modern nation. Around this Parliament today, there are Members and Senators of Chinese ancestry. Professor John Yu is a former Australian of the Year. Dr Victor Chang was our foremost heart surgeon. His school report card said: "Victor conquered language difficulty to obtain matriculation, he gave us all an example of persistence and is now doing medicine at the university". This is the story of the Chinese in Australia.

All of them form a human arch connecting us to what Prime Minister Menzies first called our "near north".

Earlier this year, I led the largest and most high-powered delegation ever to leave this country for the inaugural Australia Week in China: with me were two Ministers, five Premiers and a Chief Minister, the Chairmen or CEOs of companies worth 50 per cent of the value of our stock exchange and hundreds more business people.

Chinese direct investment in Australia (with just 23 million people) is only a little less (on some data) than Chinese direct investment in the United States (with more than 300 million). This is very significant: we trade with people when we need them; but we invest with people when we trust them. A relationship might begin with commerce but it rarely ends there, once trust has been established as I believe it has between Australia and China.

Trade and investment have made China wealthy. The advance of hundreds of millions of Chinese from subsistence to the middle class in just 40 years is probably the greatest material advance in all of human history. China is richer and stronger and the whole world is richer and stronger as a result.

China is by far Australia's largest trading partner. Indeed, China is now the largest trading partner for more than 100 countries. But trade and investment are just one part of how we help each other. For at least a decade, over 100,000 Chinese students a year have been learning in our universities and from our experts. From next year, under the New Colombo Plan, Australia will start to return the compliment with thousands of young Australians soon to be studying in China. They are our new ambassadors to China and to the region.

The success of Australia's G20 presidency owes a very great deal to China's like-minded leadership of APEC over the past year. Australia was only able to mobilise G20 members to make specific policy commitments to deliver inclusive growth and jobs and freer trade because China was already pursuing similar goals.

On behalf of Australia, I thank President Xi for his personal contribution in Brisbane. I congratulate China for hosting the G20 in 2016 and I am sure that, under China's presidency, the world will build on the Brisbane action plan for growth and jobs.

As President Xi told the G20 just two days ago, "if you want to walk fast, walk alone" but "if you want to walk far, walk together". This is true of Australia and China; it's true of Australia and the world because all of us have a long journey to make and only one planet to share. Our challenge is always to seek the best in each other.

We are all walking into the future and, provided we stay together, there is no limit to how far we might go.

'Above all, we share a history'
Canberra, 18 November 2014

Prime Minister Abbott welcomes his Indian counterpart, Narendra Modi, to the Australian Parliament, saying the two countries' common ties of democracy, language, heritage and sport were foundations on which to build both trade and cultural links.

It is long overdue for an Indian Prime Minister to address this Parliament – given that the leaders of the United States, China, Indonesia, Britain, Canada, Japan and New Zealand have already done so. But I am personally delighted that this omission is at last corrected. It is fitting that – in the home of our democracy – we should be addressed by the leader of the world's largest democracy.

There is so much that we can learn from a prime minister who must try to reach some 830 million voters and whose mastery of electioneering has meant that in India's recent election he was literally beamed into dozens of different rallies simultaneously all-round the country.

Prime Minister Modi is the first in decades with an absolute majority in the lower house, the Lok Sabha – because he imbued his fellow citizens with the sure hope that tomorrow can be better than today.

He gave credit for India's success to those who really deserved it; he told voters that their country belonged to them, not to their rulers or to their officials and even here in Australia, the Modi campaign and victory inspired hope because Australians, too, believe in work, family and community; in doing things for love, not just for money; and in living our ideals.

Our two nations have much in common. We share an ocean. We share a language. We share a heritage, as Westminster democracies enjoying freedom under the law. We even share the same national day: the 26th of January.

Above all, we share a history. Way back in 1795, the very first cargo to be shipped out of New South Wales was mahogany and cedar bound for India. In the Gallipoli campaign that forged our nation, 5000 Indians fought by our side and Prime Minister Modi made a splendid presentation to me at the War Memorial this morning in their memory. The

Australian army and the Indian army were brothers in arms at the siege of Tobruk. As part of British Empire forces, our soldiers shared the tragedy of Singapore and the triumph at El Alamein.

Australians admired the way India won independence – not by rejecting the values learned from Britain, but by appealing to them; not by fighting the colonisers, but by working on their conscience.

Through all the troubles of partition and all the subsequent dashed hopes, India has magnificently maintained its democracy. And although India's GDP per person is still only about half of China's, its growth is strong, its economic prospects are bright and its population is likely to overtake China's in the next couple of decades. This is why people now speak of the Indo-Pacific as the focus of the world's economic dynamism.

With China, India is the emerging superpower of Asia – the emerging superpower that is already a democracy. Gandhi taught that the most powerful force is not weapons but good example. I remember as a student in India reading Gandhi's autobiography where he quotes a Gujarati poet: "for a bowl of water give a goodly meal; for a kindly greeting bow thou down with zeal; but the truly noble know all men as one and return with gladness good for evil done."

Mother Teresa taught that good words are next-to-nothing without good deeds. The religions of India taught inner peace in the face of adversity. This land of the most ancient spirituality, of the exotic and of the familiar has always made an impression on me. That's why 30 years ago, I spent three months backpacking from Mumbai to Rajasthan, to Delhi, to Kashmir, around much of Bihar and back to Mumbai.

Australia's second Prime Minister, Alfred Deakin, had also travelled to India and he wrote way back in 1893 that: "India is truly a land of wonders and extremes .... a country of contrasts and contradictions, of splendour and poverty, profusion and barrenness, vicissitude and adventure...." One hundred years ago Deakin wanted Indian students to study in Australia – writing that Australia and India "have much to teach each other." And that's exactly what's now happening.

For over a decade, up to 40,000 Indian students have been in Australia at any one time. And from next year, under the New Colombo Plan, Australia will be returning the compliment by sending thousands of our own best and brightest to study at the universities of India. This is a sign that we are finally grasping the opportunities that India presents.

It was Prime Minister Howard who once said that Australia and India had so much in common but so little to do with each other! That must change.

Australia welcomes India's strength in the Indian Ocean. Australia admires Prime Minister Modi's invitation to "Come, make in India"; which echoes our own determination that Australia is "open for business". But despite that, regrettably, Australia only did $15 billion worth of business with India last year – and that hardly does justice to our two countries' potential. We want to be a dependable source of energy security, of resource security and of food security for India.

If all goes to plan, next year, an Indian company will begin Australia's largest ever coal development which will light the lives of 100 million Indians for the next half century.

If all goes to plan – and no one, if I may say so, has ever made the Indian bureaucracy perform as Prime Minister Modi did in Gujurat – by the end of next year, we will have a free trade deal with what is potentially the world's largest market. And I want to make this declaration here in this Parliament: there are two can-do Prime Minister's in this Chamber today and we will make it happen. And if all goes to plan, Australia will export uranium to India – under suitable safeguards of course – because cleaner energy is one of the most important contributions that Australia can make to the wider world.

Geologists believe that somewhere between 130 and 300 million years ago, Australia and India actually shared the same land mass – we were so to speak joined at the geological hip. We cannot change continental drift, but we can ensure that we are closer friends and partners in the future than we have been in the recent past.

I have never seen any leader as rapturously received in this country as Prime Minister Modi has been – and that's not just by the half a million Australians of Indian descent and not just because the former chief minister of Gujurat has never been a stranger to us. At least this should mean that it never again will be 28 years till the next prime ministerial visit! The cheering crowds sense that there is a natural affinity between Australia and India, a natural partnership for peace and prosperity, and they want us, they want both of us, they want all of us to make the most of it.

'We have defended freedom in France'
Canberra, 19 November 2014

On the 100th anniversary of the start of World War I, Prime Minister Abbott welcomes French President Francois Hollande to Australia, saying the friendship forged in the trenches of the Western Front made France Australia's oldest and arguably closest continental European ally.

It is, for me, a deep honour to be the first Australian Prime Minister to welcome to this country a President of France. A few moments ago the President and I were at the Australian War Memorial; a fitting place to be with the French President given that our friendship was first forged one hundred years ago in the crucible of war.

The friendship between Australia and France has stood the test of time and I should observe Mr President that the Great War touched your own family – it touched, of course, all the families of France with both your grandfathers serving their country in uniform.

Your grandfather, Gustav, might have imagined that his regimental commander, Charles de Gaulle, would one day be President of the Fifth Republic, but I suspect he would not have imagined that one day his own grandson would be the President of the Fifth Republic.

I mention this because Australia does feel a deep connection to France. We have defended freedom in France not once, but twice, as I'm sure the Australians here all know. We lost 46,000 on the Western Front and some of them still lie in the cemetery of St Sever in your own hometown of Rouen.

I hope one of the consequences of the centenary of the Great War now coming up is that we Australians will be as familiar with the story of the Western Front in the years to come as we have long been with that of Gallipoli. We will be as familiar, in part, because of the John Monash commemorative centre that our two countries are resolved to build at the village of Villers-Bretonneux which Australia did so much to defend in 1918. This is France's story and it is Australia's story too. In the Rouen Municipal Library there is a document that might have changed both our stories – the plan and the itinerary co-drafted by King Louis XIV of Lapérouse voyage, a journey which would eventually bring the French explorer to Botany Bay just a few days after Governor

Arthur Phillip. The suburb of La Perouse in Sydney reminds us that but for this near miss of history, Australia might have been a French colony rather than a British one.

Still, France has been an important presence in our culture. From the days of wool buyers setting up businesses in Sydney to the impact of French viticulturalists on our wine industry, there has been a French dimension to the Australian story.

Here today, in the National Gallery of Australia, we are surrounded by the works of the greatest French artists – Rodan, Monet and so many others – because to Australians, France is the epitome of culture, of beauty, of elegance. Traditionally, the numbers of French people migrating to this country have been small, but recently there has been an increase of French travellers to our shores, many of them young people taking advantage of our working holiday arrangements and this has added a new vitality to our relationship.

During your stay, Mr President, you have spoken with French students, researchers and business people who have told you of the potential for great links between our countries. One of the French people here in Australia who you will meet later today is Mr Jacques Adler, who joined the Resistance at 15, became the youngest sergeant in the French army, then came to this country and his daughter Louise manages and runs our most distinguished academic publisher, *The Melbourne University Press*.

I'm pleased that today the President and I have been able to discuss building on our strong $6 billion a year trading relationship, including through an Australia-EU free trade agreement. Because we do need to boost the $78 billion two-way trade between Australia and what is still the world's largest economic bloc.

But our friendship is based on values as well as on interests. We are partners in the Pacific; indeed we are neighbours with New Caledonia. Australia deeply respects France for its work in Africa, particularly against the threat of instability and extremism. I was proud to work with you and with France in the UN Security Council Chamber as we voted recently to take action on the threat of foreign fighters. Today, our Air Forces are working together against the ISIL death cult in the skies over Iraq.

Thank you, Sir, for being the first French President to visit Australia. Ours is a true friendship and I look forward to building on it. It is founded on the memories of the past but it flourishes on our hopes for the future.

Merci beaucoup.

'God bless America'

United States Embassy, Canberra, 30 June 2015

At a function at the United States Embassy attended by Ambassador John Berry, Prime Minister Abbott says the the US is a benevolent standard-bearer for liberty, democracy and human dignity.

It is marvellous to be here in such a throng with the Diplomatic Corps, with my parliamentary colleagues and with many friends of America. It is an honour to mark the Declaration of Independence 239 years ago and to cherish the friendship between the United States of America and Australia.

Almost from the beginning, the destinies of our two countries have been intertwined. They were intertwined in the 1770s when the English government sought a new penal colony because America was no longer available. They were intertwined when the fathers of our Federation looked at the deliberations of America's founding fathers, and they have been intertwined as we have both sought to build our own shining cities on a hill.

We are natural partners because America's values – democracy, the rule of law, individual freedom and opportunity – are Australia's values, too. We have fought together in the Great War, in World War II, in Korea, in Vietnam and, more recently, in Iraq and Afghanistan. Indeed, General Pershing's doughboys first went into battle with the Australians at Le Hamel on 4th July 1918 under the command of General Sir John Monash.

Our destinies are intertwined today, particularly as we meet the scourge of ISIL, or Daesh, which threatens the freedom and the safety of all peoples. At West Point last year, President Obama said that America could not be the world's policeman on its own.

Australia, like America, seeks to defend our interests, our citizens, our values and our friends. America will have more important friends. Occasionally, America will have more useful friends. But America will never have a more dependable friend than Australia.

My message, on this anniversary of the Declaration of Independence, is that America is not alone. America has been able to exercise world leadership because it is the only country in the world that has been prepared to take risks for its values as well as for its interests. America was, is, and will be the indispensable nation – the one reliable bulwark against a world where might is right.

You have been, in President Kennedy's words, "ready to pay any price, bear any burden, meet any hardship, support any friend, oppose any foe in order to assure the survival and the success of liberty."

Our own Prime Minister, John Gorton, said about 40 years ago, "I wonder if anybody ever thought what the situation for the comparatively small nations in the world would be if there were not in existence the United States, if there were not this giant country prepared to make so many sacrifices for others."

So, as we approach this 239th anniversary of the Declaration of Independence, as we honour the light that was lit then and which burns bright around the world today, as it always has, American leadership is as necessary as ever. And in providing it, you won't just have Australia's gratitude, you will have our support as well.

So, Ambassador, thanks to you and to Curtis for your hospitality and, on this day, may I repeat with you: May God bless America. May God bless Australia. May God keep our countries and our world safe and free.

'This has been a great year for PNG'
Port Moresby, Papua New Guinea,
10 September 2015

On the 40th anniversary of Papua New Guinea's independence from Australia, Prime Minister Abbott says the relationship with Australia continues to grow.

I've just finished two years as Australian Prime Minister and this is my third visit to PNG. It's an indication of the importance that the Australian government places on this relationship. It's an indication of the value that Australians place on the relationship with our nearest neighbour.

I'm very conscious of the fact that this is an important time for PNG as you move towards celebrating the 40th anniversary of independence. On the 16th of September 1975 our countries accomplished something remarkable. The night before, the Australian flag had been lowered for the last time at Hubert Murray Stadium here in Port Moresby, and in the words of PNG's first Governor-General, Sir John Guise, "the Australian flag was lowered rather than torn down." With fireworks, not gunfire, a new nation was born.

Just two months after PNG's independence, when Australia went through some political turmoil of its own with the dismissal of the Whitlam Government, Sir Michael Somare remarked that it had not taken long for Australia to be in crisis after PNG had let it go!

Many prophesied that the relationship between Australia and PNG would deteriorate after Independence, but happily, those prophets and gloom and doom have turned out to be wrong. This is a strong relationship – a strong relationship, a good relationship – and it's getting better and stronger all the time.

This year doesn't just mark the 40th anniversary of PNG's independence; it's also the 70th anniversary of victory in the Pacific. For many countries the memories of those wartime days are painful, but certainly, between Australia and PNG, those memories stir bonds of affection because in those days we stood together, inseparable.

I should say, here in Port Moresby, that Australia will always honour the soldiers of the Papuan Infantry Battalion; the men dubbed "the green shadows" by the Japanese. They were legends of the Pacific War.

Likewise, we will always honour the men who came to the aid of wounded Australians, men like the Papuan orderly, Raphael Oimbari, who famously guided the blinded George Whittington down a track near Buna. That of course is an image engraved on Australian hearts. As well, we honour the stretcher bearers who walked the slippery, heart breaking tracks of Kokoda carrying other wounded Australians to safety.

It's been my experience to have walked the Kokoda Track twice and I have nothing but admiration for the PNG nationals who carried their burdens with such care and compassion all those years ago. They are part of our national story just as we are part of their national story.

So, today Australia and PNG meet as partners, strengthened by history, but with both our nations' best days ahead of us. The world's economic and geopolitical centre of gravity is decisively shifting towards our region and naturally enough the Pacific is the subject of growing international interest.

It's fitting that this year PNG is the host of the Pacific Islands Forum which is of course the preeminent body here in the Pacific. I'm thrilled to be hosted by my friend, Peter O'Neill, because of the strong and growing role that PNG plays in our region.

Both Australia and PNG should play a bigger role in the Pacific in the future. But as for Australia and PNG, our economic links are strong. Bilateral trade is around $7 billion a year and businesses like Trukai Rice, a local partnership with Australia's Sun Rice, are bringing good jobs to PNG and good food to household tables. Westpac helps finance the businesses of PNG and through programmes such as its Outstanding Women Awards, it helps to recognise all of the people – the women as well as the men – who are building this great country. All up, Australian investment in PNG is worth almost $20 billion. Our Export Finance and Insurance Corporation provided a $450 million loan to ExxonMobil's PNG LNG Project which was delivered on budget and ahead of schedule last year. This is an extraordinary achievement that the world should know about.

The world should know about all the great business prospects here in PNG because when you prosper, Australia prospers and our region prospers. My distinguished predecessor – John Howard – often said that national competitiveness is like a race with an ever-receding finishing line. It is a race that must go on, always, here in PNG and in

Australia because our competitors aren't stopping or slowing down and neither can we. It's a race that you must run – you business people must run – with government's help because it's business that creates wealth, not government.

The government's job is to take the weights off you so that you can compete here and in the wider world. Both Australia and PNG face an uncertain world economy, so it's critical that both of us remove the barriers to growth because stronger economic growth is the key to addressing almost every national problem. That's why Australia is reorienting our PNG aid programme towards supporting the private sector and encouraging economic growth. We are working with businesses to help where we can to boost the availability of qualified, local workers.

This has been a great year for PNG, with the success of both the Pacific Games and now the Pacific Islands Forum – and Australia certainly looks forward to Papua New Guinea hosting APEC in Port Moresby in 2018.

We were pleased to participate in the Pacific Games because Australians and PNG people share a passion for sport, especially rugby league. I'm delighted that the Prime Minister's XIII – my Prime Minister's XIII – will be playing the Kumuls in just over two weeks, and I want to say that I'm confident that Australia should win but it will be a very tough game because every single fan at the Sir John Guise Stadium will be against us! I won't even begin talking about the Brisbane Broncos and the North Queensland Cowboys.

On that first Independence Day, Australian Prime Minister Gough Whitlam said "our two nations cannot ignore and escape our historical links, our geographic proximity, the past we share, the future we share." And that's the thing, it's the future we share.

I thank the members of the Australia-PNG Business Council for your commitment to deepening the relationship between PNG and Australia and I pledge to work with you to make our shared future as golden as it possibly can be. And yes, I have had fruitful discussion with Prime Minister O'Neill this morning. There are some hardy perennials in the relationship and we're working on them all the time.

We do want to ensure easier movement of people between Australia and PNG. We don't quite have visa on arrival, but nevertheless in Cairns and Brisbane we've got fast entry queues for people from PNG and I know the PNG government is always working with us to try to ensure that it's as smooth as it possibly can be.

It's great that so many people from Australia are happy to make a life or a part of their life here in PNG. While developing themselves professionally, they are maximising their contribution to the welfare and progress of PNG.

I'm disappointed that our 73 police have not been more operational. You won't be surprised to learn that one of the principal subjects that Prime Minister O'Neill and I discussed earlier this morning was making them as operational as possible because PNG has many opportunities and all of those opportunities will be better maximised if we can have as harmonious and as tranquil a society as possible. Obviously a very, very effective Royal PNG Constabulary is an important part of that.

So, everyone, thank you so much for being here. I really am thrilled to see so many people here with such enthusiasm. It's an absolute honour for me to be here on my third visit to PNG as Prime Minister in just two years.

5

INDIGENOUS AFFAIRS

'A stain on our soul'

House of Representatives, Canberra,
12 February 2014

Reporting on progress in "closing the gap", an objective set by the previous Government six years earlier, Prime Minister Abbott notes that indigenous rates of child mortality and education participation have improved but that life-expectancy, employment, literacy and numeracy are still inadequate.

When Prime Minister Keating made his famous Redfern speech in 1992, I was an opposition staffer. My job was to disagree with everything he said. While I could quibble with aspects of that speech, I couldn't disagree with its central point: that our failures towards Australia's first people were a stain on our soul. That was a watershed moment for me, as for others.

Many of us have been on a long journey. I can't say that I have always been where I am now. The further this journey has gone, the more, for me, Aboriginal policy has become personal rather than just political. It has become a personal mission to help my fellow Australians to open their hearts, as much as to change their minds, on Aboriginal policy. We are a great country – I firmly believe the best on Earth. But we will never be all that we should be until we do better in this.

There is no country on Earth where people are made more welcome. There is no country on Earth whose people have more innate generosity to others. Yet for two centuries – with fragrant exceptions, of course – Australians had collectively failed to show to Aboriginal people the personal generosity and warmth of welcome that we have habitually extended to the stranger in our midst.

Even as things began to change, a generation or two back, our tendency was to work "for" Aboriginal people rather than "with" them. We objectified Aboriginal issues rather than personalised them. We saw problems to be solved rather than people to be engaged with. If that hardness of heart was ever really to melt, I thought, that change had to include me. Because you can't expect of others what you won't demand of yourself. So as a backbencher, I spent a few days every year in central Australia and always included a dinner with Charlie Perkins. As a minister, I tried to spend a few days every year in remote Aboriginal communities – especially in Cape York and later in the APY lands for which my portfolios had particular responsibilities. Yet after 14 years in the parliament, I found that I had visited dozens of Aboriginal and Torres Strait Islander places and not spent more than 12 hours in any one of them.

As shadow minister for Aboriginal Affairs, I asked Noel Pearson if he would help me to spend some serious time in individual communities where I could be useful – rather than just another seagull, as Aboriginal people so often called officious visitors. So I spent three weeks in 2008 as a teacher's aide in Coen; 10 days in 2009 as a truancy helper in Aurukun; four days in 2011 doing bush carpentry near Hopevale; and another four days in 2012 helping to renovate the Aurukun school library. Later this year, as Prime Minister, I will spend a week in East Arnhem Land along with enough officials to make it, if only for a few days, the focus of our national government. After 226 years of intermittent interest at most, why shouldn't Aboriginal people finally have the Prime Minister's undivided attention for seven days!

None of this makes me more worthy or less fallible than any of my predecessors – but it does demonstrate that this Government is serious about Aboriginal policy. No less serious than it is about stopping the boats, fixing the budget, and building the roads of the 21st century.

I pay tribute to former prime minister John Howard for first proposing to recognise indigenous people in the constitution. I pay tribute to former prime minister Kevin Rudd for the national apology. I commend former prime minister Julia Gillard for continuing these annual Closing the Gap statements to focus the parliament's attention on problems that might otherwise be neglected or glossed over. I thank Kirstie Parker and Mick Gooda and members of the Closing the Gap steering committee. I welcome the presence today of Warren Mundine and other members of the Prime Minister's advisory council. I welcome the presence of Andrew Forrest and others working on indigenous employment. I especially welcome Fred Chaney, a former minister for Aboriginal affairs and mentor to me, whom I have often described as a distinguished elder – and who is now officially recognised as Senior Australian of the Year. And I acknowledge the Australian of the Year, Adam Goodes, who has personally demonstrated, when bitter offence could have been taken, the "better angels of our natures". I welcome the first indigenous Member of the House of Representatives, Ken Wyatt, and the first indigenous woman member of this parliament, Senator Nova Peris – and I look forward to the day when the parliamentary representation gap is finally closed. Most of all I welcome everyone the length and breadth of this great land who wants tomorrow to be better than today.

I can report that our country is on track to achieve some of the Closing the Gap targets. The target to halve the gap in child mortality within a decade is on track to be met.

We are already close to meeting the target to have 95 per cent of remote children enrolled for pre-school – and should soon know what percentage are actually attending as well as just enrolled. And the target to halve the gap in Year 12 attainment by 2020 is also on track to be met. That's the good news.

The bad news is that there's almost no progress in closing the life expectancy gap between Aboriginal and other Australians – which is still about a decade. There's been very little improvement towards halving the gap in reading, writing and numeracy. And indigenous employment has, if anything, slipped backwards over the past few years. We are not on track to achieve the more important and meaningful targets. Because it's hard to be literate and numerate without attending school; it's hard to find work without a basic education; and it's hard to live well without a job.

We are all passionate to Close the Gap. We may be doomed to fail – I fear – until we achieve the most basic target of all: the expectation that every child will attend school every day. Generally speaking, the more remote the school, the more excuses are made for poor attendance. Last year, in metropolitan areas, only 81 per cent of indigenous Year 9 students met the National Minimum Standards for reading. In very remote areas, just 31 per cent of indigenous students reached the same minimum standard. Yet it's being demonstrated in places like Aurukun that a strong education in traditional culture is actually helped by a good education in English.

Right around our country, it should be possible to be proudly Aboriginal and a full participant in modern Australia. That doesn't just mean *access* to a good education in cities, towns and remote settlements – it means actually going to school.

So I propose to add a new target to our existing Closing the Gap targets: namely to end the gap between indigenous and non-indigenous school attendance within five years. I hope I am here long enough to be judged on its achievement.

We will know that this gap has been all-but-closed when schools achieve 90 per cent plus attendance regardless of their percentage of Aboriginal students. This was the strong consensus of my indigenous advisory council's first meeting: that no one ever received a good education by not going to school. Every day, in every school, the roll is taken. Every school knows its attendance rates. Every education department knows the attendance rate for every school. The lower the attendance rate, the more likely it is that a school has problems. The lower the attendance rate, the more likely it is that a school is failing its students. It's the duty of every teacher and every education department to try to ensure that every child attends school unless there's a very good reason.

One of the worst forms of neglect is failing to give children the education they need for a decent life. That's why every state and territory has anti-truancy laws. That's why the former government, to its credit, tried to quarantine welfare payments for families whose children weren't at school. That's why, at my first COAG meeting, every state and territory agreed with the Commonwealth on the need to publish attendance data from every school. And that's why, at 40 remote schools, the Commonwealth is already funding new anti-truancy measures that, on day one of the 2014 school year, in some communities, seem to have boosted attendance from under 60 per cent to over 90 per cent.

Our job is to break the tyranny of low expectations. That's why indigenous school attendance data will be part of the next Closing the Gap report and all subsequent reports under this Government. The parliament will be brought up-to-date on the relative success or failure of Aboriginal education because a good education is fundamental to a good start in life.

Future Closing the Gap reports should also include data on work programme participation and data on communities without a police presence. These reports, after all, should be less about what government is doing and more about how people are living. We will know that Aboriginal people are living better when children go to school, adults go to work and the ordinary law of the land is respected and enforced.

The first Aboriginal member of this parliament, Senator Neville

Bonner, once warned his colleagues that history would judge us all. We shouldn't have to wait for the judgment of history and, thanks to these Closing the Gap statements, we don't have to.

A fair go for Aboriginal people is far too important to be put off to the judgment of history. We have to provide it now – or as soon as we reasonably can. I am confident of this: amidst all the mistakes, disappointment and uncertain starts, the one failure that has mostly been avoided is lack of goodwill. Australians are now as proud of our indigenous heritage as we are of all our other traditions. The challenge is to turn good intentions into better outcomes.

I am confident that, these days at least, for every one step backwards we are also taking two steps forward. To give just one example: on every ministerial visit to the APY lands, I used to complain that there were just eight police for 3000 people spread over an area the size of Scotland – and that none of them lived in any of the places where they were needed. Six years later, these are hardly model communities, but every substantial settlement has a permanent police presence – thanks to the good work of the South Australian Labor government – because this was an objective beyond politics.

As Fred Chaney has just said, reflecting on a lifetime of work with Aboriginal people: there is so much left to do but – in this area – these really are the very best of times.

There is probably no aspect of public policy on which there is more unity of purpose and readiness to give others the benefit of the doubt. On this subject, at least, our parliament is at its best. Our duty is to make the most of this precious moment.

Indigenous contribution to our national ethos
Old Parliament House, Canberra, 12 February 2014

Prime Minister Abbott tells the annual Reconciliation Australia dinner, sponsored by Rio Tinto, the largest private employer of indigenous Australians, that formal recognition in the Constitution would be his "crowning achievement".

Today, in the parliament, I spoke about the specific things that we could do to close the gap; in health, in education, in employment and in life expectancy. It was about concrete actions to produce concrete change. What I would like to speak about briefly this evening is about the symbolic change that our country needs too.

I am too young to have served in this building. There are very few members in the current parliament who actually served in this building when it was operating as a parliament, but I did come here back in 1999 for the constitutional convention which some of you would remember.

One of the most powerful speeches at that constitutional convention was the speech given by a friend, former senator Neville Bonner, who I had come to know as a member of Australians for Constitutional Monarchy on whose foundation council he served. He gave an extraordinary speech about how his people had suffered the indignity of dispossession, and had endured the life that had been given to them by more powerful newcomers. Part of that was the Crown. He said they came to accept it – perhaps reluctantly – but nevertheless they had come to accept it, and now another generation of white fellas were saying, "Well, we got it wrong we want to rip it off you" and he wasn't happy. He wasn't happy.

It was a very, very powerful speech. In it he quoted an Indigenous poet, a Korean War veteran, Cec Fisher. It was a pretty black poem that Neville Bonner quoted. Talking about "for all the talk of reconciliation, time will not diminish the black deeds of history. We will carry forever the memories of the pain." That was what Cec Fisher said and that is what Neville Bonner quoted.

Interestingly, some years later Cec Fisher wrote another poem which he called *Reconciliation* – a very different poem. He said, "We sit here to unite, we sit here black and white, we sit here in celebration, we sit here in education, we sit here no more hate and sorrow, we sit here planning our tomorrow, reconciliation is what it is all about, reconciliation we're talking about it."

Now, maybe it's not the greatest poem. Maybe this is not Kenneth Slessor, it's not Shakespeare or anything like that. But this is a decent, honest, Aboriginal Australian talking about the journey that he has been on and the patience, the decency and the forgiveness which is evident in that poem characterises the indigenous people who it has been my privilege and honour to meet over the last 20 years or so of my public life.

There is a great spirit in Indigenous people. I often think that we Australians underestimate the contribution that Indigenous people have made to our national ethos; the stoicism, the laconic humour, and the endurance that has come to characterise us as a nation. I doubt it came ashore in 1788 because, frankly, it doesn't characterise the English, the Irish or the Scots but it came to characterise Australians. I suspect that the interaction on our frontier between the white fella and the black fella has produced in the Australian character that stoicism and that humour which is now very much a part of our ethos, indeed a part of our soul.

Now, when we came together as a nation, as a Commonwealth in 1901 we had a British heritage which was embodied in our constitution. We also had indigenous heritage which was very much part of us, but which was not in any way recognised or acknowledged in that constitution and it is high time that we rectify this defect.

I have nothing but admiration for our constitutional founders. I have nothing but pride in the history of Australia. That doesn't mean that everything was perfect. That doesn't mean that everything they did was right in every respect. It is overdue to do what we can to complete our constitution by finally acknowledging the indigenous people in it - significantly acknowledging indigenous people in that constitution.

But I don't think anyone should underestimate the difficulty of that task. There is an abundance of goodwill. As Fred Chaney has said and as I have quoted a couple of times today these aren't necessarily perfect times, they are not even necessarily great times but they are the best of times and there is no better time than now to push along with this.

As those of you who have followed the constitutional debates earlier in our history would know, it is easy to say no. Back in 1977 both major parties ordered a referendum supposedly to recognise local government in our constitution. As I recall, it was defeated basically because of a couple obscure Queensland Senators – habitual naysayers – ran a campaign which ultimately succeeded in obtaining a majority.

So, if we are going to succeed in this vital task, it is so important that all of us approach it in the spirit of that poet Cec Fisher, in his poem *Reconciliation*. To sit down in education, celebration, and in planning. It might take quite a long time. I know some of us are thinking let's try to get it done in six months or 12 months or 18 months. If we could do it that quickly that would be magnificent but let us not underestimate how easy it is for people to become nervous and anxious about these things. We can't be too ambitious and we can't be too hasty because the worst thing that could happen for our country and for reconciliation would be for something to be put up that failed.

As far as I am concerned, if we can get this through in my time as prime minister I would regard it as a crowning achievement. But I have to say to you nothing worthwhile is easy. This is extremely worthwhile but we do have a big task ahead of us.

As far as I am concerned it is as worthwhile a task as anything we undertake but we have to be careful not to force people to take sides, because, if we do, some will take sides and it won't be the right one. What we have to do is invite people to see things from the best perspective. We have to invite people to be their very best selves. In the same way that Cec Fisher was transformed; we have to invite all Australians to be transformed.

Recognition a 'victory for all of us'
Neville Bonner Oration
Sydney, 28 November 2014

The Prime Minister tells an audience of monarchists, who
are reluctant to change the Constitution, that recognition
of indigenous people would complete the nation's founding document.

It's an honour to give this lecture in memory of Neville Bonner, the
first Aboriginal Member of the Australian Parliament, a member of the
Foundation Council of Australians for Constitutional Monarchy, and
a delegate to the 1998 Constitutional Convention to consider whether
Australia should become a republic.

There were many fine speeches at that convention but Neville Bonner's was the one that gripped people's soul. This is what he said:

> We have come to accept your laws. We have come to accept
> your Constitution. We have come to accept the present system.
> We believed you when you said that a democracy must have
> checks and balances. We believed you when you said that not
> all positions in society should be put out for election. We be-
> lieved you when you said that judges should be appointed, not
> elected. We believed you when you said that the Westminster
> system ensures that the government is accountable to the peo-
> ple. We believed you when you taught us that integral to the
> Westminster system is a head of state who is above politics.
> We believed you when you said that, as with the judiciary,
> Government House must also be a political-free zone.

This magnificent old man, went on to say:

> How dare you! You told my people that your system was
> best. We have come to accept that. We have come to believe
> that. The dispossessed, despised adapted to your system.
> Now you say that you were wrong and that we were wrong
> to believe you. Suddenly you are saying that what brought
> the country together, made it independent, ensured its de-
> fence, saw it through peace and war, and saw it through
> depression and prosperity, must all go.

It was by far the most powerful speech of that intense period in our nation's life. As he sat down the supporters of the 'no' case all rose in their seats – and the republicans remained frozen in theirs. And then the most unlikely figure rose in his seat – it's Neville Wran, standing to honour the dignity, conviction and wisdom of a great man. And the rest then rose as one. It was the only standing ovation at that convention.

Despite the many indignities that might have soured his outlook, Neville Bonner had a great love for our country, its institutions and its people. He grasped that modern Australia has an indigenous heritage, a British foundation and a multicultural character.

His final speech brings to mind another image from Old Parliament House. On the day of its opening back in 1927 along with the Duke of York and numerous dignitaries there was just one indigenous man present. He was not an official guest. He had no place of honour. Yet his presence was as much a symbol of unity as that of our future King.

Although unacknowledged, uncounted in any census and not dressed in the finery of others, Jimmy Clements – for that was his name – carried with him an Australian flag. It was his demonstration that he loved our country as much as anyone – despite not sharing in all its benefits.

As a constitutional conservative, like Neville Bonner, my instinct is to keep the constitution; to conserve the constitution exactly as is. "Don't fix what isn't broken" was the rally cry of the 'no' campaign at the Constitutional Convention and at the subsequent referendum. Like John Howard, my distinguished predecessor as leader of the Liberal Party and of the Liberal National Coalition, I don't normally seek to change the constitution.

I don't seek to remove the Crown. I don't seek to change the separation of powers. I don't seek to change our representative system of government. These days, I don't even seek to change the states' constitutional role because I appreciate that we should not lightly change that which has stood the test of time. I understand that change is often far more trouble than it is worth. I do, however, seek constitutional recognition of Aboriginal people in a form that would complete our constitution rather than change it.

Today, I invite the friends of our constitution to suspend scepticism. As a constitutional conservative, I would never seek change unless I was convinced that it would be change for the better. That, after all, is what the founders of our constitution envisaged when they provided a mechanism for changing it.

Changing the constitution was meant to be hard: it requires an act of Parliament, a vote of the people and a majority of four of six states. It is rightly much harder than changing a law but it is not meant to be impossible because our constitution's founders never imagined that the constitution should never change. Sometimes, after all, change is necessary for survival and sometimes change is desirable for improvement.

The opening of our constitution states that the Australian people "humbly relying on the blessings of Almighty God have agreed to unite in one indissoluble federal Commonwealth under the Crown". It is an acknowledgement of our British and our Christian heritage that has not in any way hindered the development of a free, multicultural nation which gives people a fair go and encourages them to a have a go.

It is precisely because we have done so well under the constitution we have that we should be so cautious about changing it. Our whole history, though, is one of change for the better – change that builds on what we have rather than throw it away to start again. The challenge is to find a way to acknowledge Aboriginal people in the Constitution without otherwise changing it. That's the task now engaging the Government and our Parliament.

I do not underestimate its difficulty but I don't underestimate its importance either if we are to achieve all we can as a nation. You are rightly cautious about any change to our constitution. So was Neville Bonner. And so is anyone who appreciates the scale of the Australian achievement over the past century. Still, it would be an odd constitutional conservative who cherished every single clause in our constitution except the clause allowing it to be changed. The establishment of this lecture, in his honour, was Australians for Constitutional Monarchy's tribute to Neville Bonner.

Today, I am asking you to consider a change that, if done well, I am sure he would have asked you to support. If done well, acknowledging indigenous Australians in the constitution would strengthen our country, not weaken it. Constitutional recognition can't substitute for real action to improve the lives of Indigenous Australians – but it can complement it. Every day, this Government is working with Aboriginal people: to get children to school, adults to work and to make communities safe – as we should, because by far the most troubling feature of our national story is the dispossession and marginalisation of Aboriginal people.

It's not that our constitutional founders made a mistake – they simply failed to give Aboriginal people more than a passing thought. So, in addressing this subject, our job is not to correct their work but to complete it.

Like John Howard, I have come to support the recognition of Aboriginal and Torres Strait Islanders in the constitution because it already recognises our British heritage and, if we are to acknowledge part of our history, we should acknowledge all of it.

My hope is that any future referendum to recognise Aboriginal people will echo the successful 1967 changes, not the unsuccessful 1999 ones, which, as you will remember, were to insert a recognition preamble as well as to become a republic.

1967 was a small change to our constitution but a big change for our country. It was Australians' first acknowledgement that Aboriginal people mattered. It was the first sign that they should not be treated as second class citizens in their own country. Like 1967 – but unlike 1999 – any future referendum campaign should be an act of affirmation rather than a political argument. If there is to be a victory, it has to be one for all of us – as 1967 was.

Consideration of a proposal should be a conversation as much as a debate: careful, considered and civilised – because if it is to build national unity it can't be a 'winner takes all' contest.

Both sides of politics, and all Members of Parliament, are now working together on a good way forward and the best possible wording to be put to the Australian people. The bipartisan committee chaired by the House of Representatives' first Indigenous MP, Ken Wyatt, will soon make final recommendations about the precise changes that could be made.

We should be prepared to consider and refine any proposal for some time because it is so much better to get this right than to rush it. The worst of all outcomes would be dividing our country in an effort to unite it. A successful referendum would be another demonstration that Australia can in every way be a beacon of hope and an exemplar of unity and decency.

As the constitution's fiercest defenders, our temptation is to dismiss all change as constitutional vandalism – but today I invite you to consider this change more as renewal and refurbishment; as a grace note in this most serviceable of foundation documents. Indigenous culture, after all, is part of our common heritage as Australians; as much as our language, our Parliament, our system of law and our Crown.

If all Australians are to walk forward together, the least we can do is acknowledge the first of us in our foundation document.

'I recognise your impatience'
Recognise Inaugural Dinner
Sydney, 11 December 2014

Recognise, a branch of Reconciliation Australia, holds its inaugural dinner in Redfern, Sydney, with Prime Minister Abbott as guest of honour. He says the 50th anniversary of the 1967 referendum would be a "richly symbolic time to complete our Constitution".

About two years ago, I was discussing with Noel Pearson the merits of the expert panel's recommendations. And I have to admit, I was expressing concern about the expert panel's support for an anti-discrimination clause in the Constitution on the grounds that it could turn out to be a one line bill of rights.

"You know what your problem is?" said Noel. "You have never personally experienced the reality of racial discrimination!"

And that's true. Anglo Australian males from middle-class families tend to have had a magic carpet ride through life. Still, this hasn't stopped the "whispering in my heart" that our most serious failure as a nation has been our difficulty in acknowledging the people we displaced.

It started to nag at me about the time I first entered federal Parliament. How could I hope to help guide the destiny of our nation and not do whatever I could to reconcile the first Australians with the rest of us?

So, almost every year as a Member of Parliament, starting with trips to Alice Springs in the mid-1990s that invariably included dinner with Charlie Perkins, I have tried to spend as much time as I could with Indigenous Australians in Indigenous communities.

I do not claim to be better hearted or more insightful than any of my predecessors, all of whom, at least in recent times, have acted with abundant goodwill for this cause. But to the best of my knowledge, I'm the first Prime Minister who's sought to run the country from a remote location over the best part of a week talking with Galarrwuy Yunupingu and the other elders of East Arnhem Land.

Our country has many challenges. Our people face many problems. But there is almost nothing that this generation of Australians could do that would more impress posterity than enabling black and white Australians to walk forward together, forever, as one united people.

I am a supporter of constitutional recognition because I want our country to transcend the "them and us" mindset to embrace "all of us" in the spirit of generous inclusion that has always marked Australians at our best. Not "them" and "us" anymore – just us.

Like John Howard before me – and like Kevin Rudd and Julia Gillard, and at least 60 per cent of the population – I am a strong supporter of constitutional recognition. But 60 per cent support for a principle does not guarantee success at a referendum. I know that because I helped to defeat the republican cause that was overwhelmingly supported by the Labor Party, significantly supported by the Liberal Party, and backed by every big media outlet in this country.

So, the question, at a dinner like this, that we have to ask ourselves, is not whether we support constitutional recognition – of course we do – but whether we want it passed. Because to be passed, constitutional change has to satisfy a majority of the people in a majority of the states. In practice, it has to gain the support of both major political parties and all state governments and avoid the opposition of any group of substance.

A fortnight ago, I delivered the Neville Bonner Oration to my former colleagues at Australians for Constitutional Monarchy. I invited them to suspend their scepticism. And I told them that it was impossible to cherish every single clause of a constitution, except the provision to change it.

Tonight, I say to my friends here at RECOGNISE, we have to temper our ambitions, because nothing would set back the cause of our country and the rightful place of Aboriginal people at its heart, than a referendum that failed.

Now, I recognise your yearning for that rightful place and I recognise your impatience to get on with it.

I am pleased that my friend and colleague, Ken Wyatt, the first Indigenous Member of the House of Representatives, along with Senator Nova Peris, the first Indigenous woman in the national Parliament, and the other members of the Joint Select Committee, have put forward three options for change. I thank Ken, Nova and the Committee for their tireless, painstaking, and conscientious work. Their first two options, I fear, would run into the same problem as the expert panel's recommendation. It would subject too much legislation to judicial review of its merits. The third option, I fear, doesn't do enough to recognise Indigenous people – indeed, it hardly does so at all.

I appreciate the work that Marcia Langton, Megan Davis, Noel Pearson and others have done to reach out to constitutional conservatives because – make no mistake – we will be a diminished nation if we cannot find a way to acknowledge the first Australians in our nation's foundation document. But we must not underestimate the "lions in the path" of this vital project.

I am prepared to sweat blood on this. This is at least as important as any of the other causes that this Government has been prepared to take on. I want this to happen. I want this to happen as quickly as it can. I hope that it might happen on the 50th anniversary of the 1967 referendum, the 27th of May 2017. That would be a richly symbolic time to complete our constitution. But I do not want it to fail because every Australian would be the loser. It is more important to get this right than to try to rush it through.

We will get constitutional recognition – and when it comes, I suspect, that it will take the form of a pact – a heartfelt pact – between Indigenous people and conservative Australia. Indigenous people have to accept that any proposal put forward is worth doing because it does sufficiently acknowledge them as the first Australians. And conservative Australia has to accept that any proposal put forward really is completing our constitution rather than changing it.

So this, it seems to me, is the way forward. The Wyatt Committee will deliver its final report in the first quarter of next year. Then, all the significant proposals need to be socialised among the people of our country.

To this end, I announce that the Government will provide a further $5 million to Recognise. People from all walks of life and all shades of opinion, from the city to country and the outback, black and white, will need every opportunity to talk through their hopes and fears for our country's future. These consultations will accelerate and intensify in the new year.

The referendum should be held as soon as possible once we are comfortable that we have the proposal with the best chance of success. Not a 'guarantee of success' because any proposal guaranteed to succeed might hardly be worth doing. Nevertheless, a proposal that is, on a realistic assessment of any forces that might be against it, likely to succeed.

More than 100 years ago, Australians decided to unite in one indissoluble Federal Commonwealth under the Crown. This country we created, as a matter of undisputed fact, has an Aboriginal heritage, a British foundation and a multicultural character and it is high time that this reality was recognised in our Constitution. Constitutional recognition will be a victory for Aboriginal people and will be the culmination of a long, long, long fight for justice.

To succeed, though, it will also have to be a victory for all Australians: a vindication of our magnanimity as a nation whose Constitution will finally belong to all of us. To this solemn and sacred task, I pledge myself.

6

ARTS, SPORT & CULTURE

'This is a night of triumph and celebration'
Address to *Quadrant*'s 500ᵗʰ Edition Dinner
Fort Denison, Sydney, 16 October 2013

The Prime Minister marvels at the achievements visible all around from this gala dinner in Sydney Harbour and applauds *Quadrant*'s optimism for Western civilisation and its pursuit of moral truth.

This is a night of triumph. It's a night of celebration. But I must say that I also feel, as I talk to the people here and look at the faces around me, a sense of humility amidst the excitement and the exhilaration because I am in the presence of my betters and my mentors.

We are here to celebrate something which is bigger than any of us – that is to say, the civilisation and the culture which has nurtured us and which *Quadrant* magazine celebrates in every one of its issues.

I am conscious of the fact that many of the people in this room have been an important part of my life, in some cases for many, many years; in some cases for just a few years, but nevertheless an important part of my life and can take considerable credit in what has recently happened.

I see Trevor Sykes, my first editor. I see Nick Cater and Rebecca Weisser, my subsequent editors. I see Peter Coleman, along with B.A Santamaria, my earliest significant political mentor. And of course, John Winston Howard, my greatest political mentor – the man in whose shoes it is my honour to follow.

So we are here tonight to celebrate *Quadrant,* but we are here to do more than that. We are here to celebrate and to honour everything that *Quadrant* represents, everything that *Quadrant* argues for and fights for – a civilisation based on the great Christian insight that every human being is a person of equal worth and dignity created in the image and likeness of God, and a justice based on the biblical injunction to do unto others as you would have them do unto you.

So I hope you will allow me to begin with a sentence from Genesis: "On the seventh day of creation, God saw everything that he had made, and indeed it was very good."

Now, here on Sydney Harbour, from this vantage point, we can look out on what we think is the most beautiful city, in the most marvellous country. We can see the bushy headlands protected from development. We can see the pristine waters, cleaned up over the past generation or so. We can see the Opera House, one of the built wonders of the modern world. We can see the Naval base, from which our ships deploy to protect our interests and uphold our values. We can see the glittering towers where business is transacted. We can see the merchant ships that carry our commerce. We can see the factories and the warehouses that supply our needs. We can see the yachts that manifest our sense of adventure. We can see the garden suburbs and the gleaming units where our people live.

Of course Sydney and its environs is not the totality of the Australian story but it is an iconic part. We are not gods, these days, hardly Christians, sadly. Still, we can see everything that we have made, and indeed, it is very good.

As a people we can love what we have made and we can love what has made us. Not without qualification, perhaps, but wholeheartedly. Or we can feel ambivalent about these things and be forever torn.

I'm pleased to say that what characterises this gathering, this *Quadrant* dinner, is respect for what this country, this culture and this civilisation has achieved. We are not resentful at what was, we are not embarrassed at what is and we are not fearful at what will be. We are grateful to our families, to our communities, to our country and to our culture for what we have been given. We honour the institutions that have shaped our society and the values that have underpinned our country – a country as free, as fair and as prosperous as any on earth.

Of course we can be better. We will be better. We must be better. But we will build on our strengths, not tear it all down and start again from scratch.

So my friends, just as every faith requires a sacred text, and every culture requires a canon, every way of thinking requires a publication to sustain it. There are plenty of journals for those who dwell on Australia's failures and are convinced that things will only get worse, especially under a conservative government, but if I may say so, *Quadrant* is intellectual nourishment for everyone who thinks that this country and this civilisation has largely got it right and is optimistic about our capacity to do even better.

Quadrant is Australia's best antidote to intellectual pessimism and cultural despair. Certainly if *The Australian* newspaper is a liberal conservative's daily consumption, and if the *Spectator Magazine* is our weekly tonic, *Quadrant* nourishes the insights, the arguments and the historical depth needed to be truly confident about our country and its future.

As James McCauley, along with Les Murray our greatest poet and *Quadrant*'s first editor said in *Quadrant*'s first issue, "In spite of all that can be said against our age, what a moment it is to be alive in". From that time on, for more than half a century, *Quadrant* has consistently displayed a scepticism of new paradigms and panaceas, a willingness to put forward a rational counterpoint to the breathless enthusiasm of the next big thing, an empirical philosophy that judges ideas not by their source or popularity, but by the strength of the evidence and argument and above all else a deep regard for the lessons of the past and the institutions and the traditions and the intuitions that build and protect our society.

This, says Keith Windschuttle, our current editor, is the source of *Quadrant*'s predisposition to get things right. So yes indeed, we have seen everything that *Quadrant* has wrought and it is very good. Very good indeed.

'The true spirit of Australia'
Sydney, 15 July 2014

At a party to celebrate the 50th anniversary of *The Australian*, the Prime Minister, himself a former journalist, applauds the newspaper's ability to reflect the nation's ambitions and character.

The essential thing about *The Australian* is that it's a paper for a nation. Every other newspaper serves a city. The Australian alone is dedicated to our country. It has a national perspective, not a parochial one. This alone should make it uniquely influential in our nation's life.

On any particular day, though, *The Australian* is not necessarily the most influential publication in our country. Arguably, *The Australian*'s News Corp siblings, with their vast circulations and gift for story-telling both in pictures and in words, can more powerfully shape our popular culture. And if it breaks a big enough story, any paper can shape the news.

But at least since Les Hollings' time as editor, no newspaper has more profoundly or more consistently shaped the intellectual life of our country. No think-tank, no institution, no university, has so consistently and so successfully captured and refined the way we think about ourselves.

As Paul Kelly put it on the weekend, through all the twists and turns of time, three themes recur in *The Australian*'s writing: Australia as a big country, not just physically but spiritually, wanting always to be bigger, bolder, smarter and more successful than we currently are; Australia as a globally engaged and regionally oriented power, seeking closer ties with our neighbours and with our allies; and Australia as a successful economy where everyone is equipped and encouraged to have a go.

In my judgment, no paper more closely corresponds with the true spirit of Australia. *The Australian*'s tone may sometimes be light but its purpose is always serious: how can our country be better, today, tomorrow, next week, next month and always.

While the paper has long had a consistent perspective, it's barracked for causes rather than party; it's promoted issues rather than individuals; and the editorial "line" has never precluded well-argued dissent.

Anyone seeking arguments against – as well as for – a price on carbon; support for the monarchy as well as criticism of it; evidence against government spending as well as in favour of it; and the case for smaller rather than bigger government would have found these in The Australian and, often enough, only in *The Australian*. Its main competitor, the *Australian Financial Review*, is a much improved paper – but mostly since it poached an editor from News Corp!

I pay tribute to all the editors of *The Australian* with whom I have worked and who have been substantial influences on my life: Frank Devine, who recruited me, whose daily admonition to his editorial writing team: "What do we feel strongly about today and how will it make a difference to people's lives?" has turned out to be an excellent template for politics; Paul Kelly, a fine editor and Australia's best contemporary historian of politics and government, who went way out of his way to impress upon a very green political staffer the importance of well-developed and thoroughly-articulated ideas in shaping our nation; and David Armstrong, who first recruited me to mainstream journalism after I'd been (ever-so-politely) sacked from the *Catholic Weekly* because the Cardinal didn't like being lectured to by a seminarian in his own newspaper!

Papers normally only shape events over time rather than dictate them on a day-by-day basis. In my judgment, though, it was *The Australian*, late in 1995, that cleared the way for John Howard to return to the leadership of the Coalition and then become our most successful recent prime minister by putting on the front page his change of mind on Asian immigration.

To its credit, when *The Australian* is campaigning, it makes no bones about it and while its preferences are clear, its mind is almost never closed. It campaigned for Gough Whitlam in 1972 and against him in 1975; it campaigned for Howard in 1996 and against him in 2007; it supported Labor when Bob Hawke and Paul Keating were economic reformers and would gladly do so again, I'm sure, if evidence of reform were ever found.

As prime minister, there's nothing of substance written about Australia that I don't want to read – which means that I often spend more-time-than-I-have-to-spare reading *The Australian*. On our country's media, I am not a detached observer; still, under editor-in-chief Chris Mitchell, it seems that *The Australian* has become one of the world's very best newspapers.

As a former leader writer, there's one urban myth that I believe I can and should kill: the claim that News Corp papers are ciphers for Rupert Murdoch. It's out of character for *The Australian* to support a strike but support a strike we did: the pilots' strike of the late 1980s even though it was directed against an airline that Rupert Murdoch part-owned.

Another cheap shot is that wealthy business-people are only interested in making money. *The Australian* has been supported despite oceans of red ink; it's been Rupert Murdoch's investment, not in his future but in his country's.

It's been a poor financial return for him but a priceless return for us. He may have become an American by necessity but he's always been an Australian by conviction. *The Australian* has borne his ideals but not his fingerprints; it has been his gift to our nation. As he memo-ed staff back in 1965: "Please note that we are not a left-wing Labor paper nor are we tied to any particular party or philosophy. We are simply in the business of reporting, interpreting and sometimes commenting on the facts – in that order".

The paper has had its critics, often in its own pages. In its very first week it published a letter, from Balmain, declaring: "*The Australian* is a real flop and unless several radical changes are made.... (I see it) folding up altogether before very long." Fifty years later, *The Australian* continues to annoy and unsettle all who imagine that they have a monopoly on wisdom or virtue.

Back in 1992, when I was an ex-journalist and somewhat disgruntled political staffer, Paul Kelly told me that I would always have a job at *The Australian*. When I tried to redeem that pledge, shortly after the 1993 election, the paper was having one of its periodic budget crises. I never went back but like to think that, in spirit, I'd never left.

Smaller government, bigger people; lower taxes, greater freedom; pride in our country and its achievements; determination to build on our strengths; support for all that may help us, individually and collectively, to come closer to being our best selves: this is what The Australian stands for.

Long ago, *The Australian* found its authentic voice; that has helped governments and people to find theirs.

'Welcome to the team'
Sydney, 26 January 2014

On his first Australia Day as Prime Minister, Abbott articulates the joys of becoming Australian.

Today, across our country, we celebrate one of the greatest gifts imaginable – to be Australian. While Australia Day formally marks the anniversary of the arrival of the First Fleet, today celebrates something richer and deeper. We celebrate the nation and the people we have become.

We are the grateful inheritors of two rich strands of history: a British heritage and an Aboriginal one. The First Australians - along with the millions from around the world who have made their home here since 1788 – have become one people, sharing one land.

We are fulfilling the aspiration in the opening words of our Constitution: 'that we the people...have agreed to unite in one indissoluble Federal Commonwealth'.

Twenty three million of us have found unity in our diversity, respect in our differences and have built a modern nation on the idea that all of us can get ahead provided we are prepared to "have a go".

This Australia Day, we welcome the thousands of new Australian citizens who have chosen to "join our team". It is a fitting day to celebrate new citizens as it was on 26 January 1788 that Australia's first modern migrants arrived.

Today is a significant milestone as it is the 65th anniversary of the Australian Citizenship Act. Since that time, more than 4.5 million people from all around the globe have chosen our country as their home.

I am proud to say that one of those families was my own. On 7 September 1960, along with my father, mother and sister, I left Tilbury in England for Australia. My parents had great hope in Australia.

My wife had great hope in Australia when she came here from New Zealand in 1983. Australia has not disappointed them. My hope is that it won't disappoint anyone.

My duty, as your Prime Minister, is to ensure that, as far as possible, in this great land of ours, no one is left behind.

To the men and women taking the Citizenship Pledge here today – and to the almost 18,000 taking the Pledge around Australia, I say "welcome to the team". You - our newest citizens - will play your part in building our country and making it your home.

Today we celebrate the history that has made us who we are; the country that we love and the values and institutions that underpin it. May God bless you and may God bless our country on this special day.

Speaking truth to power
Canberra, 10 September 2014

At the 50th anniversary dinner of the National Press Club, the Prime Miniser reflects on the changes to the nation since his predecessor Robert Menzies addressed the club's opening.

As some of you would know, like Alfred Deakin and John Curtin, I was a journalist before eventually becoming a prime minister. I have often said that as a journalist, I was a frustrated politician; and as a politician, I am a frustrated journalist; and while a trainee priest, I was just frustrated!

I once observed that it was my hope to raise the status of both occupations; to which a wag replied: by leaving journalism to become a member of parliament, you did!

There's always an element of tension in the relationship between members of parliament and members of the media. We are both deeply interested in everything that impacts on people's lives. We're both committed, I hope, to advancing the national interest and to helping people to come closer to being their best selves. The National Press Club's roll call of guest speakers – national and international leaders, thinkers and doers who have changed Australia and the world – testifies to that.

Yet the media's job is to sit in judgement on politicians. For our part, we must put up with it but we don't usually like it! In the end, though, our country and our world are stronger thanks to a media that speaks truth to power.

On my very first day as an MP, I walked proudly through the House of Representatives entrance. "Where's your pass?" said the attendant. "I didn't think I needed one anymore," I said. "Come on, show me your pass," insisted the attendant. "Look," I said, "I'm the newly elected Member of Parliament for Warringah." "Sure," said the attendant, "and I'm Paul Keating." Just at that moment who should walk past but the late, great Paul Lyneham, who told the attendant that I was in fact who I claimed to be. It was, I thought, probably the only time in history that the presenter of the *7:30 Report* would ever help a Liberal politician out of trouble!

So, I wholeheartedly acknowledge the media's role in our national life and in our polity. Indeed, the country we are owes much to the quality of our journalism. Yet the media's job is to improve our country as well as to report it.

The best contribution, if I may say so, the media could make right now – is not to be more right wing, or more left wing – but to be more ready to give credit where it's due; and to acknowledge the strengths as well as the weaknesses in our country and its people.

Of course, now as 50 years ago, there is much that could be improved: our country doesn't always seize its opportunities; too many people, as always, feel trapped and helpless in the face of life's challenges; and governments could always be braver, surer, and more compassionate.

Still the fact that Australia is undoubtedly amongst the freest, fairest, and most prosperous countries on earth means that we must be doing something right. It means that all of us are doing something right; and that should be acknowledged and celebrated even as we strive for more and for better.

Fifty years ago, middle class Australian families typically had one car, one bathroom, and one telephone. The last five decades has seen the greatest explosion in material wealth in human history. To be born Australian, as always, is to have won the lottery of life; but while the lives of many of us have gone from comfortable to luxurious, the lives of billions of people across the globe have gone from precarious to comparatively prosperous. In Australia, lifespans have gone from under 70 to over 80; in the rest of the world, they've gone from under 50 to over 60.

This is the best antidote to pessimism about the future, particularly pessimism about future conflict: the fact that everyone, these days, has so much more to lose from war and conflict.

People are often irrational but governments rarely are – thanks to collective decision making, even in countries without a democratic tradition.

Of course, here in Australia, there's more family breakdown and more mental illness and more people dependent on social security than 50 years ago. Yet there's also more freedom for individuals to be whoever they really are, and there's far more sympathy for the social and cultural outsider. There's more diversity – sometimes challenging diversity.

Paradoxically, the assurance that Australia stands ready to give to everyone – that you can be part of our team – means that national unity has probably never been stronger. I think it was Lord Salisbury who said that change is to be resisted to the last possible moment because change is always for the worse. I prefer Disraeli's view that change is to be welcomed; provided it's change that accords with the best customs and the best traditions of our people.

Most of the past 50 years' changes have been to make us freer to be our authentic selves – or at least, that's been their intention if not always their outcome. There are better and worse times; but there is no perfect time, there never has been a perfect time to which we need return.

The past is to guide us and to inspire us, not to shackle us. That, at any rate, is my idea of true conservatism. At least in this country and in our culture – with our strong tradition of freedom – liberalism and conservatism are no more than opposite sides of the same coin.

I will leave others to judge how far, and how well, I might have changed over the 30 years that I have been in the public eye and the 20 years I have been in Parliament.

For my part, I will admit to two significant policy areas where I am now different. I've shifted from being a critic to a supporter of multiculturalism, because it eventually dawned on me that migrants were coming to Australia not to change us but to join us. And I've shifted from being an opponent to an advocate for paid parental leave, because it dawned on me that if modern women were to have children they needed encouragement to be both mothers and workers. In other words, there were good conservative reasons – liberal conservative reasons – for changing a traditional position.

Over the past 30 years, the two greatest political leaders – perhaps the greatest leaders of their Parties ever – were Bob Hawke and John Howard; both, of course, on numerous occasions, speakers at this National Press Club.

Howard and Hawke were both true to the best elements in their Parties' tradition – Hawke wanting to give workers the best chance to get ahead; and Howard wanting to combine economic freedom with social cohesion. Both, of course, adapted these to the realities of modern Australia. Both were strong leaders with strong cabinets. Both were tough minded reformers, prepared to take on vested interests – although, in Hawke's case, he could usually rely on the support of the Opposition. Hawke's achievement was to overcome internal dissent; Howard's was to overcome the initial contempt of almost the entire politically correct establishment.

And so in light of your opening vignettes, I ask, how does Menzies rate against them? There's a marvellous passage in Heather Henderson's book where she quotes her father describing his three and a half weeks of the 1961 election campaign: he's the Prime Minister, he is fighting the election campaign and this is what he does in three-and-a-half weeks. He says there's 13 meetings, six ten minute broadcasts, and several appearances on TV "so I will not be unemployed", says Menzies. You should have organised more for him Tony![1]

The gulf between political life then and now is so vast that comparisons are simply impossible. Menzies was the titan of his time; Hawke and Howard are the giants of ours. Australia's comparative economic strength owes everything to a quarter century of reform under Hawke and Howard and almost nothing to the six wasted years that followed.

The Budget – much criticised for poor politics but not for poor economics – is a sign that the age of reform has merely been interrupted, not ended. This Government's mission is to demonstrate that the six years between 2007 and 2013 – the political instability and the policy retreats – were just an aberration, not the new normal. Our success or failure will determine whether or not Australia is doomed to bad government. It is that important.

Like most politicians, I am often asked about my vision for Australia. The last thing people should want is someone else – even a prime minister – dictating their lives and their dreams for them. My vision for Australia is a country where every person is better able to realise his or her own vision. Yes, my vision is better schools, better hospitals, and more productive businesses – but a government that tries to dictate this will end up wasting billions of dollars. The best way to achieve better schools, better hospitals and more productive businesses (that employ more people and pay higher wages), is to liberate our people and our institutions so that they can do what they know must be done.

My vision is not for bigger governments but stronger people, whether it's in:

- The Work for the Dole scheme – about giving people a chance to show what they can do, not what they can't
- Entrenching the fee for service principle in the health system so that people will respect what they get
- Establishing the Cole Royal Commission when I was the Workplace Minister into the construction industry – so the rule of law cannot be flouted
- Setting up first the Green Corps, and now the Green Army – so that we can give our children a better environment than that we inherited
- Or even supporting the crown in our constitution – because we should never lightly junk what's stood the test of time.

There is, if I may say so, a consistent thread running through this public life. People deserve a fair go – that's the Australian way; and they need to have a go too – because that's also the Australian way. Everyone can be good at something. Our challenge is to empower each person to discover what that is and to make it happen.

Finally, I want to thank you for being here at the National Press Club to celebrate 50 years of discourse on public policy. A better life, in a better country, in a better world is the star that guides us all. And I have to say, tonight, is my vision for the National Press Club – a speech with no questions afterwards. Thanks very much.

'A delight to the mind and a light for the soul'
Melbourne, 8 December 2014

Literature challenges our perceptions and opens us up to new ideas, Abbott tells the Prime Minister's Literary Awards ceremony in Melbourne.

In February 2012, I received what I thought was an innocuous tweet asking whether I was reading anything at that moment that I'd recommend to others. So, I replied: "I've just read Nikki Gemmell's *With My Body*; a captivating successor to *The Bride Stripped Bare*!"

Now it's not often that the Twitterverse comes to a standstill – but for a moment there was, it seems, a pause: perhaps an inaudible but palpable gasp of surprise. Not least from Nikki Gemmell who wrote and "here was I thinking that the spring in his step was because of the machinations on the other side of politics!" This was in 2012, I hasten to add.

There seems to have been a shared assumption that my reading must be a dull reflection or reinforcement of views already held. Likewise, when I respond to questions from young people about what they should read with the answer, the classics, Shakespeare and the Bible, it is seen as proof of a pre-existing world view – rather than an invitation to understand and appreciate the works that have shaped our culture and our world.

If I thought that young people had no need of such counsel – because they were already reading what's sometimes called the Western canon – I would not offer that advice. Our reading, after all, should challenge our thinking, not just confirm it. And literature is at its best when it reveals to us a world not seen, a perspective not understood, or an aspect of life not yet contemplated.

Through literature, we can grasp the fullness of life without necessarily having to have lived that aspect of it ourselves. If music is art for the ear, and art is joy for the eye, then literature is surely a delight to the mind and a light for the soul. And my life, like that of so many in this room, has been defined by a love of words. Like prime ministers Deakin and Curtin before me, I was a journalist before I entered Parliament.

As I've sometimes said: As a journalist, I was a frustrated politician;

as a politician, I am a frustrated journalist – and when I was a trainee priest, for three years in my twenties, I was just frustrated.

It shouldn't surprise anyone that most Australian prime ministers over the past half century have, in fact, written books: Menzies, Whitlam, Fraser, Hawke, Keating, Howard and most recently Julia Gillard. They have done so because they understood the power of the written and the spoken word.

I am reminded of a story by Sir Robert Menzies who during 1941 spent several weekends with Winston Churchill at the British Prime Minister's retreat "Chequers". On one evening, Menzies walked into Churchill's study and found him pacing up and down, dictating a draft for broadcast. Menzies offered to withdraw but Churchill would have none of it; offering the Australian prime minister a cigar and waving him to a chair.

And Menzies later recounted Churchill's method: "He tried every word, every phrase, for weight, for meaning, for sound. He knew, of course, that a broadcast speech must come effectively to the ear and must, if possible, achieve its instant persuasion and inspiration." The result, said Menzies, "as we know to our advantage, was all clarity, and feeling, and inspiration."

Every writer is willing to create meaning, to persuade, to touch and to inspire. That's a writer's gift to an audience. Now, it's not without its risks, of course. When asked about how he wrote best sellers, Bryce Courtenay said that no one ever sets out to write worst sellers! To use the words of Richard Flanagan: "somewhere in that abyss between ambition and failure often lies greatness".

So tonight I salute the contribution of Australia's writers – and that of those who work with you. Because, as an author, I know that behind every successful writer is another writer, the editor.

My first editor was the late Christopher Pearson. I came to rely on him, almost as a medieval potentate might have relied on his food taster, to alert me to infelicities of style, non sequiturs and offences against the canons of political correctness. It wasn't a fool-proof system. Still, he helped to shape my public life and my political character and it is right that we collectively pay tribute to those who make and shape our literature.

So I am proud to continue this tradition of the Prime Minister's Literary Awards. I thank the writers, the editors and publishers of all the nominees for their contribution to a deeper, better, more thoughtful and more inspired national life. Because the point of writing, as Pearson often reminded me, is to draw people closer to being their best selves. I also acknowledge the judges who have read, weighed and debated the books in every category.

I recall one of my teachers, the English master from Riverview College, Joe Castley, admonishing his class far ago in the 1970s not to waste the summer break. You must read, he said, not play, read! "Read", he said, "with voracious appetite". It's a phrase that I've never forgotten after all these years and have mostly tried to live by.

Literature has always made a vital contribution to our nation's cultural and intellectual life. In October, when Richard Flanagan won the Man Booker prize, I wrote, as many of you would have, offering my congratulations. And he sent me a most gracious reply – which I hope he won't mind me sharing. Too often, he said, in Australian politics, the arts are seen as the province of the left, "and arts and artists (are) therefore to be shunned by the right".

He noted that this is not the norm in most political cultures and hoped that "at some time, it might cease to be (so) in ours". Well, that's my hope, too. Because every government should want to encourage all of the voices – all of the voices – in Australian life, but these voices can only be heard if they're listened to.

To that end, I announce tonight that the Government will establish the Book Council of Australia to promote good reading as well as good writing. Tonight's awards acknowledge the importance of our national stories as well as the excellence of our story-tellers. They celebrate our literature, as well as those who are creating it. Once you tell your stories, they become our stories.

So I congratulate everyone associated with all of the nominated works and I look forward to spending quality time with some of them over the coming Christmas break.

Celebrating a 'most unusual man'
Sydney, 30 July 2015

At the launch of Gerard Henderson's biography of B.A. Santamaria, Prime Minister Abbott pays tribute to his earliest political mentor.

We're here to celebrate a great book and we're here to celebrate a great life. B.A Santamaria has been dead 17 years, held no public office and claimed to have failed in all his principle endeavours, yet he has spawned a more extensive literature than most prime ministers.

Gerard Henderson's life is the first full biography but Santamaria was the main subject of four earlier books including Gerard's own *Mr Santamaria and the Bishops* on his pivotal role inside the Australian Catholic Church.

Why is this long dead 'failure' still fascinating? Why has one of our country's foremost public intellectuals devoted years to his study? Why, indeed, did the likes of Greg Sheridan and I drive to Melbourne several times in the late 1970s to attend Bob's conferences? Why did our nation's leaders regularly seek his counsel and why was his last visitor the then Prime Minister himself?

B.A Santamaria was, of course, a spellbinding speaker who often held audiences rapt for an hour without a note. It's hard now to know why the fact that 1976 was the 1500th anniversary of Fall of Rome was so fascinating, but listening to Bob, it was. He was a powerful and usually consistent polemicist in print with a widely read, and even more widely denounced, news magazine that continues to this day and a column in *The Australian* that ran for almost 30 years.

Perhaps his legendary modesty, as our author suggests, was a little affected. Still, he wasn't too proud to spend many hours individually mentoring teenagers with promise and would always take a call from any friend of the Movement.

He might have lost the fight for the soul of the Labor Party in the 1950s. He might have despaired of the direction of the Church, despite admiring Pope John Paul II and Cardinal Pell among many other prelates. He might have privately despised many of Australia's public figures, including some who had helped him. Yet if his life was the failure he often protested it was, it was a magnificent failure that changed and improved our country and hundreds if not thousands of its leading citizens.

Of course, he was profoundly right on the big struggle which changed our times. "When the bullets of the communists hit the statue of Jesus outside the Cathedral of Valladolid, for some it was just lead striking brass," he famously told the great Melbourne University Spanish Civil War debate, "but for me they were piercing the heart of Christ the King".

Santamaria and the Movement he helped to inspire and lead, working with Labor's industrial groups, did defeat communism inside the Australia's trade unions. Arguably, this saved Australia from long-term industrial anarchy. Certainly, it saved the Labor Party as a middle-of-the-road social democratic party that could sometimes be trusted with government.

After Doc Evatt's paranoid denunciation, like Moses, Santamaria led his followers out of the Labor Party and, like Moses, he failed to find the Promised Land. Nevertheless, thanks to Bob Hawke, some eventually went back to Labor and helped to make that government the best Labor government ever. Thanks to John Howard, some found their way into the Coalition and helped to make that government the best conservative government, at least since Menzies'.

Santamaria became the extra parliamentary conservative conscience of both parties; upbraiding Labor for its socialism and the Coalition for its alleged heartlessness – and why not, as political parties, no less than individuals, are often improved when someone they respect calls them to account.

In the first edition of his memoirs, contemplating the defeat of all his causes, Santamaria observed: in all this, we were but minnows swimming in giant and stormy seas; yet even the minnow must do what he can. Santamaria was a pessimist who never gave up. His life exemplifies the difference you can make even when you don't succeed. It demonstrates that a good cause is worth failing for.

Will there be a revival of support for the traditional family? Will there ever be a restoration of authority and self-confidence within the Christian churches? It's hard to imagine, but much that's ridiculed today seemed self-evident a generation ago, and what the zeitgeist now condemns, it may one day again endorse. If that day comes, Santamaria will seem more like a prophet than a failure – the Edmund Burke per-haps of Australian conservatism.

It is impossible to grasp Australian politics over the past 70 years without some appreciation of B.A Santamaria. Gerard Henderson has done signal service in producing this comprehensive and judicious life; and like so many of the best authors, he hasn't just studied the struggles he's written about, he's actually lived them and that's what makes his account riveting, as well as interesting.

For me, launching this book is an act of piety towards my tribe; it's an act of piety towards someone who was for some years almost a father to me. He helped to shape me, he helped to shape us. He was, indeed, a most unusual man. He had to be to do what he did.

'More than a piece of old parchment'
Parliament House, Canberra, 24 June 2015

The Magna Carta, the first document to outline the demo-cratic rights of citizens, was born of practical experience rather than abstract theory, the Prime Minister says at an 800th anniversary celebration in the Great Hall organised by the British High Commission.

Often it is in retrospect that particular events assume their greatest im-portance. When the English barons gathered at Runnymede to parley with King John, they weren't thinking of history; they were thinking of themselves. They weren't conscious of universal rights; they were conscious of their own grievances.

For the most part, the Magna Carta reads like a log of claims against the king. Merely to make such claims, though, reveals a clear under-standing that the king can't do what he likes, and that a subject has rights even against a sovereign.

Even in the 13th century, this was not a novel concept. Even then, the king's coronation oath typically included a promise to govern ac-cording to law. It wasn't long, though, before the Magna Carta came to be seen as a constitutional watershed binding all future kings.

So tonight we remember the events 800 years ago that have so shaped the way we think about government. And we celebrate the rule of law without which freedom cannot exist and without which might is the only right.

It is paradoxical that this event, so associated with the rule of law, was the product of a barons' mutiny. As Winston Churchill once ob-served, the English-speaking world "owes more to the vices of King John" than it does to the labours of many virtuous sovereigns. This birth certificate of democracy owed almost nothing to abstract analysis and everything to a practical bargain between discontented nobles and their grasping king. It became a landmark in our constitutional evolution be-cause it formulated that growing sense that the exercise of power and the imposition of taxes should not be arbitrary.

That first Magna Carta lasted just ten weeks, but another was issued in 1216, and another in 1217. Henry the Third re-issued it again in 1225 after more contention with the barons over tax. In 1258, the Provisions of Oxford further developed the notion that the king governed by consent. Edward the First inspected and confirmed Henry the Third's version in 1297 and directed judges to administer it as part of the common law of England.

It would take centuries of further argument to put beyond doubt the principles of Westminster democracy: that taxing and spending requires the consent of parliament; that the monarch governs through ministers; that the executive is subject to the parliament; and that the parliament should be elected through universal suffrage.

Even so, at key moments in our constitutional history, people have looked to the Magna Carta for inspiration and guidance: in the struggle between the king and parliament leading to the Civil War; at the time of the Glorious Revolution and the English bill of rights; and in the build-up to the American War of Independence which the colonists saw as an assertion of the traditional rights of Englishmen against a distant despot.

It's not so much what Magna Carta said or did as much as what it has come to represent: people's freedom to live the life they choose; and political authority chosen by the people and constrained by law.

Thus, Magna Carta has come to be seen, in the words of the famed British jurist Lord Denning, as "the greatest constitutional document of all time, the foundation of the freedom of the individual against the arbitrary authority of the despot".

Our longest serving prime minister, Sir Robert Menzies, appreciated the historical significance to Australia of the Magna Carta. When an impoverished school in the English West Country put up for sale one of just four surviving originals of the 1297 Magna Carta, Sir Robert decided that it should come here. So while the British Museum refused to budge from its bid of £2000, Australia offered the full £12,500 asking price. Of course, in 1951, £12,500 was thought an exorbitant amount for a "piece of old parchment"; you could say it was Bob Menzies' Blue Poles moment. But he has been well and truly vindicated and this priceless manuscript now resides in this building – the focus of our democracy.

In 1948, when the United Nations General Assembly adopted the Universal Declaration of Human Rights, Eleanor Roosevelt declared that it would become 'the international Magna Carta for all men everywhere'.

In pluralist democracies such as ours, it's tempting to think that democracy and the rule of law represent the universal aspirations of mankind. Given the option of selecting your rulers, or having them imposed; of submitting to law, or to arbitrary diktat, people's preferences would indeed seem self-evident. But things are rarely so clear-cut in the real world.

If Nazi Germany had won World War Two, or if Soviet Russia had dominated the subsequent peace, would the United Nations even exist, let alone the Universal Declaration of Human Rights? The Nazis and the Soviets paid lip service to legality but in practice Nazi law and Soviet law was whatever the government wanted it to be. The only check on power was power.

How should a democracy deal with those who would destroy it; how should the rule of law handle those convinced that might is right; and what rights should be accorded to those who don't themselves respect rights? It seems that in every generation, liberal democracies must find contemporary answers to these perennial questions.

Freedom can't be sacrificed in order to be preserved; yet plainly a man with a gun preparing to shoot can hardly be dealt with by a court order. The citizens of liberal democracies must never be as ruthless or as unprincipled with terrorists as terrorists would be with them. Still, we have every right to defend ourselves effectively against those who would do us harm.

The rule of law serves just as much to protect us from criminals as it does to protect us from tyrants. At least in the English-speaking tradition, the executive government has far more often been a protector of people than a persecutor. The law of the land should be as concerned to protect people from violent criminals as it is to protect them from the excesses of government especially if it's government "of the people, by the people, for the people".

Democratic governments can be incompetent and heavy-handed but they are rarely vengeful or ill-intentioned in the way that individuals sometimes can be, even in an easy-going country like Australia.

In New York on September 11 2001, in Bali in 2002 and again in 2005, in London and in Jakarta, Australians were the victims of al Qaeda-inspired terrorism. This was not political violence over a local grievance. This was terrorism with global ambitions.

Islamist terrorism boasts that it is coming for everyone. Especially since the spin-off of Daesh from al Qaeda and the declaration of a caliphate, Islamist terrorism confronts the world with a chilling choice: submit or die.

The only difference between medieval barbarism and Daesh rule is that the beheadings, crucifixions, mass executions and sexual slavery are now recorded for social media.

Daesh currently dominates an area about the size of Italy with eight million people.

Its affiliates are active in large parts of Libya and Nigeria and it is seeking to establish a "far province" in Southeast Asia.

At least 120 Australians are now fighting with terrorist armies in Syria and Iraq among about 20,000 foreign fighters, including nearly 4000 westerners. At least 160 Australians here are actively supporting them with financing and recruitment. ASIO is currently pursuing more than 400 high-priority counter-terrorist investigations.

There have already been two Daesh-inspired terrorist incidents here in Australia: the attack on two policemen in Melbourne last September and the Martin Place siege in Sydney before Christmas. Police and security agencies have disrupted six imminent terrorist attacks. Daesh social media routinely urges sympathisers to mount attacks in Australia, sometimes observing that all you need is a knife, a flag, a camera-phone and a victim.

Australians should never abandon our freedoms in order to defend them; but defend them we must. Arguably, the greatest freedom of all is the freedom to live without fear and dread; particularly the fear, and the morbid fascination with evil, that's at the heart of this darkness.

Along with our allies, Australia is mounting air strikes against Daesh forces in Iraq and training and assisting the Iraqi army to retake their own country. Working with local community leaders, and with families, we're trying to ensure that impressionable young people do not succumb to the lure of this death cult. We're trying to prevent people from leaving our country to become terrorists; we're trying to prevent hardened terrorists from coming back; and we're striving to lock up any that we can't keep out.

We have a clear message to young people thinking of joining terrorist armies overseas: don't leave because you're likely to be killed;

but if you do leave, don't come back, because Australians won't have terrorists loose on our streets.

We now have counter-terrorist units at all international airports, have questioned hundreds of travellers to the Middle East, and we've cancelled at least a 120 hundred passports. Still, as things stand, putting Australian foreign fighters in gaol is easier said than done, despite new laws making it an offence merely to be present in designated terrorist-controlled areas. We can't readily put informers on the witness stand or always make available intelligence without risk to sources and it wouldn't usually be possible (nor desirable) in such cases to bring witnesses from the Middle East to testify.

On the standard rules of evidence, without a confession, securing a conviction is hardly straight-forward, let alone for crimes committed offshore in ungoverned space. Bringing foreign fighters back to face trial in Australia risks leaving them free on our streets rather than in our gaols. That's why the government has introduced legislation to strip citizenship from terrorists who are dual nationals.

Since 1948, section 35 of the Citizenship Act has provided that dual nationals who serve in the army of a country at war with Australia automatically lose their citizenship. This section provides for renunciation by conduct. An Australian who fights against Australia has automatically forfeited the right to be one of us – provided forfeiture doesn't make someone stateless.

The government is modernising this section by providing that a person participating in terrorism against Australia, likewise, automatically forfeits citizenship. Stripping citizenship from terrorists who are dual nationals could mean that up to fifty per cent of those who have gone to the Middle East to fight can't come back.

I stress that this legislation is directed at terrorists, not dual nationals. Most dual nationals, in fact, are migrants who have become first-class Australian citizens. Migrants, after all, have voted with their feet for Australia; hence their massive enthusiasm for our country.

To help demonstrate that this is a national security measure (rather than a dual citizenship issue), as part of the citizenship consultation now taking place, the government will consider further measures to stop Australian foreign fighters with no other citizenship from readily returning here.

Fighting for a terrorist group at war with Australia is the modern form of treason – and those who have left our country to fight against us may require a modern form of banishment. Foreign fighters and home-grown terrorists present the biggest security challenge we have faced for many years. They must be dealt with in accordance with the principles of a just and decent society; but they must be dealt with.

The first duty of government is the protection of the community; or as Cicero put it 1200 years before Magna Carta: 'Salus populi suprema lex', the safety of the people is the supreme law. The administration of justice according to law is only possible in a peaceful and orderly society. So if you leave Australia to fight for terrorist armies in the Middle East, we don't want you back – and if you're a dual citizen, we certainly won't let you back.

On the 800th anniversary of Magna Carta, we shouldn't just celebrate the rule of law; we must defend it. This means ensuring that people trying to kill us, for who we are and for what we believe, should not be at liberty to do us harm.

The Daesh death cult has abundantly demonstrated that the first people it's coming for are the vast numbers of Muslims who don't agree with it. Here in Australia, the right to speak your mind is taken for granted. "Death to the infidel" has never had any currency here in Australia. We have become appalled at the very idea of killing in the name of God.

An Australian, for instance, could freely echo President al Sisi of Egypt's warning that Islam needs a religious revolution, without fear of official persecution or need of police protection. In Australia, and other western countries, along with everyone else, Muslims are entirely free to proseletise for their beliefs.

In parts of the Muslim world, however, the wrong proselytism is punishable by death. If Islam is to further develop an appreciation of pluralism, it may need Muslims protected by the rule of law and the other principles of liberal democracy that Magna Carta so potently represents. Australians could help to encourage the easy-going versions of Islam that the world so hopes for.

Security under the law is what our tradition has given people; it's what the Magna Carta represents. It's hard to imagine any human progress without it.

7

THE ANZACS

Keeper of the ANZAC flame

Australian War Memorial, Canberra, 15 April 2014

At a dinner honouring military historian C.E.W. Bean, Prime Minister Abbott outlines plans for forthcoming WWI centenary celebrations, and explains the nartion's debt to Bean's "enthusiasm for what Australia could be".

Every nation has a story and every nation has its storytellers. What actually happened matters but so, too, does how it is perceived. A nation, after all, is shaped by its historians as well as by its history.

World War I was the crucible in which the Australian identity was first forged and CEW Bean is the person who first and best told us what it meant. In 1901, six British colonies had formed the Commonwealth of Australia. We had a parliament and a flag but no real sense of nationhood because our story, up till then, was that of New South Wales, of Victoria, of the other colonies and of the wider British Empire. In Bean's words, when our soldiers sailed for war, they left "a nation that did not yet know itself".

For those who lived through it, the Great War blotted out everything that had come before. From an Australian population of just under five million, 417,000 enlisted; 332,000 served overseas; 152,000 were wounded; and 61,000 never came home. Of men aged 18 to 42, almost one in two enlisted and, and of those who served overseas, almost one in five were killed in action. Of the 270,000 who returned, more than half were wounded. We cannot imagine how many were psychologically scarred.

Other countries suffered no less grievously which is why the Great War still casts a long shadow. But this was our "baptism of fire". For us, it's akin to what the War of Independence was to America. It's when we were first put to the test and not found wanting.

Charles Bean went ashore at Gallipoli on April the 25th 1915. He had complete freedom of the front, reported the war continuously through all four years and carried a Turkish bullet in his thigh for the rest of his life. He then dedicated the next 30 years to writing and editing the monumental Official History and to establishing the Australian War Memorial dedicated to the memory, and commemorating the character of all who'd served to build up the nation for which they'd given their lives.

The War Memorial is more than a shrine and more than a museum. It is also a priceless archive of letters, diaries and photographs that has enabled later generations of writers and historians to add their insights to those of Bean and his contemporaries.

Bean deeply grasped the heavy responsibility on those providing the "first draft of history". His rival correspondent, Keith Murdoch, said of him that "no accounts of actions could be more accurate than his – no description of the men's suffering and gallantry could be more sympathetic. He is always in the place where he can see and help most, however dangerous it may be."

This is not to suggest that Bean was without fault. He intrigued against General Monash and tried to stymie his appointment as commander of the Australian army corps – but was man enough, subsequently, to revise his judgments.

Over time, Bean became much more than a reporter. Every Anzac Day, it's his voice that echoes around the dawn services and it's his lessons that make the Remembrance Day silence so eloquent.

Over four years of war, recording scenes from darkest nightmares, witnessing death upon death upon death, Bean knew the toll taken on his young country. He became the "keeper of the ANZAC flame", to use Les Carlyon's words. Carlyon, of course, is the modern Bean. His magisterial works, *Gallipoli* and *The Great War*, are worthy successors to Bean's *Official History* in their sympathy and in their scholarship and have helped to renew our nation's foundation stories.

Carlyon has ensured that we are a country of memory as well as of memorials. As we move towards the Centenary of Anzac, and through all the anniversaries of the next four years, Bean and Carlyon should be our teachers. We honour this sacrifice by learning from it.

For us, commemorations will begin in September to mark Australia's first action: the capture of German New Guinea. Then, there's the centenary of the sailing of the first ANZAC convoy from Albany in Western Australia, guarded by a Japanese cruiser as well as by the Emden-bound HMAS Sydney and ships of the Royal Navy.

Obviously, April 25th next year will be a pivotal moment but there will be other Gallipoli anniversaries: such as Lone Pine, the Nek, and the only unambiguously successful part of the whole campaign, the evacuation.

Over the next four years, some major war memorials will be upgraded and restored with help from the Anzac Centenary Public Fund that's being marshalled by Angus Houston and Lindsay Fox. This includes the shrines in Melbourne and Sydney and the travelling exhibition being overseen by the War Memorial to visit towns across Australia.

There will, of course, be local commemorations funded by the $125,000 that the Commonwealth government is providing to each federal electorate. It's my hope that more schoolchildren will research war veterans from their area so that the example of those young Australians might work on the imagination of today's young Australians: not to glorify war but to promote the ideals of duty and service.

All these commemorations should unflinchingly acknowledge the terrible sacrifice. Over the next four years, we should acknowledge "the good and the bad, the greatness and the smallness" of the entire Anzac story.

For most of the past century, Gallipoli has shaped Australians' thinking about the Great War. But when all is said and done, Gallipoli was a defeat; a magnificent loss perhaps, but a loss nonetheless. Then came the carnage of the Western Front, especially the horror of Fromelles, with more than 5,000 Australian casualties in a single night.

Under Sir John Monash, undoubtedly one of the very best allied generals, Australians eventually mastered the organisation of infantry and armoured attack behind a creeping artillery barrage in ways that changed the war. Between March and November 1918, the five divisions of the AIF, operating together for the first time under Monash, bested no fewer than 39 enemy divisions. They took 29,000 prisoners, captured 338 guns, and advanced over more than 40 miles of contested ground. They comprised less than 10 per cent of total British Empire forces but made almost a quarter of all the gains in the war's decisive final months.

Gallipoli was a magnificent defeat. The Western Front was a terrible victory. There may be more lessons in defeat than in victory. Still, we should remember our victories at least as much as our defeats.

Perhaps more than any other time, this was the moment when Australians have most shaped history. In the words of Professor Robin Prior, it's the only time when our forces have engaged the main enemy on the main battlefront and made an appreciable difference to the outcome.

We should remember the Western Front; and tell that story, as well as the Gallipoli one. That's why our commemoration of Anzac won't just climax on the 25th of April next year.

The government is considering the establishment of an interpretative centre alongside the Australian National Memorial at Villers-Bretonneux. This would be a lasting tribute to General Monash and his men, and its opening would be a fitting conclusion to Australia's commemoration of the war that shaped us.

As Bean put it, it's "in disaster that human character is most clearly exhibited and, though she had known fire, drought and flood, Australia had never seen the one trial that, despite civilised progress, all humanity still recognises – the test of a great war…"

"And then" says Bean, "during four years in which nearly the whole world was so tested, the people of Australia looked on…They saw their own men – those who had dwelt in the same street or been daily travellers in the same trains – flash across the world's consciousness like a shooting star. In the first straight rush up the Anzac hills in the dark; in the easy figures first seen on the ridges in the dawn sky; in the working parties stacking stores on the shelled beach without the turning of a head; in the stretcher bearers walking, pipes in mouths, down a bullet-swept slope to a comrade's call, unconsciously setting a tradition that may work for centuries; in things seen daily from that first morning until the struggle ended, onlookers had recognised in these men qualities always vital to the human race. Australians watched the name of their country rise high in the esteem of the world's oldest and greatest nations. Every Australian bears that name proudly abroad today and by these daily doings, great and small…the Australian nation came to know itself".

In no way should the Centenary of Anzac glorify war but it should commemorate what's best in our human character and acknowledge that the worst of times can bring out the best in us.

As Bean observed, to an unusual extent among British forces, Australian troops "had the habit of reasoning why and not merely of doing and dying". Among officers and men alike, the Australian soldier's "unspoken, unbreakable creed was the miner's and the bushman's: stand by your mate".

Soldiers do indeed sometimes have to do terrible things but they should always remain decent people. This, I believe, has been the characteristic of Australian Forces from that day to this: in East Timor, Iraq and Afghanistan as much as in the Great War. Our times deserve a Charles Bean to tell this story too.

At the end of the war, Bean took two weeks' leave and, characteristically, spent it writing about the future of our country. He called the tract "In your Hands, Australians". "We have to make up our minds", he said "right here and now…whether we are going to work…for ourselves or for Australia … We have done with the war, God knows – we are only trying to make full and real use of the peace for which our finest Australians fought…and died; and that is a struggle in which we all can join, even those who honestly opposed the war."

That he could look so clearly to the future, after four years witness to carnage on a daily basis, gives us the measure of the man.

With his optimism and his enthusiasm for what Australia could be; with his desire to learn from the past but not be shackled by it; and with his quest to be helpful, not difficult, he had the true measure of our country.

'An unquenchable patriotism'

Australian War Memorial, Canberra, 25 June 2014

General Sir John Monash (1865-1931) was one of the greatest Allied generals of World War I. At the launch of the digital version of Monash's 10,000 papers, letters, maps and other records by the Australian War Memorial, Prime Minister Abbott says, "the more you read Monash, the more you admire him".

It is a real honour for me to be here because Sir John Monash was a true Australian hero and I applaud the Australian War Memorial on this Anzac Connections project.

Fortunately for us John Monash was as meticulous in recording his thoughts as he was in planning his military operations. His papers, his letters, his diaries all give us so much insight into the man – a man who changed the course of history. He was a citizen soldier. Who along with so many other Australians answered the call of King and country in the 1914-18 war.

He was one of the best generals of that war – arguably the most successful allied general of the war. In the words of prime minister Lloyd George the "most resourceful general in the whole of the British Army".

At the centenary of his birth in 1965, Prime Minister Sir Robert Menzies said of Monash: "He has an assured place in military history, a place founded not only on his brilliant understanding of the art and science of war, but also on his unsurpassed capacity for communicating his ideas; in other words, his advocacy in the greatest sense".

The more you read Monash, the more you admire him and this is why it's so important that his papers be widely available.

Two days before the landing at Gallipoli, Monash wrote prophetically: "... long before this letter can possibly reach you, great events, which will stir the whole world, and will go down in history, will have happened – to the eternal glory of Australia and all who have participated." Monash's writings show a dedication to his comrades, a love of family, and an unquenchable patriotism.

And then of course he went from Gallipoli to the Western Front. He was an engineer, and engineers are problem solvers. He put his mind, his creativity, and his initiative to solving the fundamental problem of the Western Front. How can you attack defensive positions guarded by barbed wire, machine guns under the most awful artillery barrages? And he perfected battle plans which materially contributed to the victorious conclusion of the war.

The role the Australian Corps played in defeating the German offensives of March and April 1918, and in the subsequent victories, ensures that our country's name is written in the annals of military history.

Gallipoli – magnificent though it was – was ultimately a defeat. The Western Front – terrible though it was – was ultimately a victory. And so much of that victory was due to Monash, his thinking, his planning and his execution.

My hope is that the commemoration of the Centenary of Anzac gives us here in Australia a better appreciation of our role in that war and an understanding that while defeat has its lessons, victory is worth celebrating and remembering too.

It's extraordinary that the deeds of the Australian Army on the Western Front are much better remembered in France than they are here in Australia – that should change. That's why one of the main outcomes of the Anzac Centenary will be the establishment of an interpretive centre to honour the contribution and the sacrifice of the Australians who served on the Western Front.

It is fitting that this centre will be named after General Monash, and established alongside the Australian National Memorial at Villers-Bretonneux, the principal site that Monash and his fellow soldiers chose to dedicate to their comrades' service and sacrifice.

We should be as familiar with the story of the Western Front as we are with the story of Gallipoli. Australians should be as least as familiar with the achievements of John Monash as we are with the heroism of John Simpson Kirkpatrick.

Monash, the man who turned the tide of history, remained humble and gracious in the face of prejudice. He believed that the effort, sacrifice and the suffering of war and that the ANZAC tradition of loyalty to a common cause of courage, comradeship and mutual cooperation could build a better Australia.

He was a great military leader, a military leader of rare genius who went on to become a great civilian leader in the post war world. An industrial pioneer and also a champion of education of which he said: *"You must not imagine that your education is given to you only for your individual benefit. It is not; but is given [to] you to fit you for national service, and for the discharge of your higher duties of citizenship."*

It's no wonder that on his death, 250,000 Australians turned out for his funeral – including tens of thousands of the men who had served under him. Monash changed the course of history. He lived to the eternal glory of our country and all Australians for all time, should know his name. I thank the Australian War Memorial for giving us General Monash's words and thoughts so that more Australians will know his name – and will never forget his achievements.

'Two foes who have become friends'
Istanbul, Turkey, 23 April 2015

On the eve of the centenary of Anzac Day, Prime Minister Abbott addresses a peace summit in Istanbul attended by leaders from Australia, New Zealand and Turkey, saying that when the wounds of battle have healed, adversaries often see the virtue in each other.

In November last year, Prime Minister Davutoglu addressed Griffith University in Queensland, on the eve of the G20 summit. He explained that his great-uncle had fought the Australians at Gallipoli 100 years ago.

In some parts of the world, to enter the homeland of a former enemy, even two generations on, would be to invite hostility and suspicion; but Prime Minister Davutoglu was welcomed as a friend in Australia.

Likewise, I have not only been welcomed here as a friend but invited to address this Peace Summit, notwithstanding Australia's role in the 1915 attack on Turkey.

As Prime Minister Davutoglu said, it is "very rare...in history" that two nations which fought so fiercely should become such friends.

Indeed, our friendship proves that when the battle is over, when the wounds have healed and when the ground has cooled, warriors can see their enemies' virtue.

The Gallipoli campaign (or Canakkale Savasi as you call it here in Turkey) was a dreadful baptism of fire for the young Commonwealth of Australia.

Some 60,000 Australians fought here; nearly 9,000 died, over 20,000 were wounded and thousands more carried the unseen scars for the rest of their lives.

An Australian historian wrote of the trauma of the Great War: "dreams abandoned, lives without purpose, women without husbands, families without family life, one long national funeral for a generation and more after 1918". It would have been like that for Turkey too. That's why, this week, Australia salutes the magnanimity of Turkey towards us as well as the courage and self-sacrifice of our own countrymen.

To those who despair of reconciliation in the midst of conflict, I say: look to Turkey and Australia – two foes who have become friends.

In a place of honour, next to the Australian War Memorial in Canberra, there is a memorial to Mustafa Kemal Ataturk – a worthy and resourceful leader, who embraced his fallen enemies as sons of Turkey.

Ataturk's famous words of consolation to the grieving mothers of Australia, that their sons were lying in the soil of a friendly country, will echo around the Anzac services held in our country this week – as they stand in stone on the sacred soil of the Gallipoli Peninsula.

One of the Australians impressed by Ataturk's statesmanship was our 8th Prime Minister, Stanley Bruce, a Gallipoli veteran who'd been wounded at Suvla Bay. But in 1936 he chaired an international conference in the Swiss town of Montreux which restored Turkey to full control over the Dardanelles. The man who, in 1915, had fought to seize control of the Dardanelles for the Allies, in 1936 worked hard to return them to Turkey.

In Bruce's closing remarks at the Conference, he declared that Turkey had provided a "magnificent example" to the world in trying to reach a solution to international problems through legal methods. It was a practical manifestation of Ataturk's dream of "peace at home and peace in the world"; a dream that's shared by Australians.

Ataturk had been generous to us as a people – and grace begat grace.

For the last century, under successive governments, Australia's determination has been to advance our interests, protect our citizens and uphold our values.

We have never believed that we can save the world single-handedly; nor have we shrunk from shouldering our responsibilities. We seek to act towards others as we'd have them act towards us. After all, keeping commitments, valuing human life, protecting property and extending freedom are universal aspirations, not just Australian ones.

Since 1947, Australia has provided more than 65,000 personnel to more than 50 multilateral peace and security operations.

We are not accustomed to turning back, once we've put our hand to the plough. In Afghanistan we worked with Turkey in the NATO-led force. On our side of the world, when leadership is needed, we step up, as we did in Bougainville, the Solomons and in Timor-Leste. I acknowledge Turkey's contribution of police to UN missions in Timor-Leste, a wonderful gesture of friendship to a new country and mark of good international citizenship.

Today, Turkey and Australia are working to defeat terrorism in all its forms. Australia condemns the occupation of Turkey's consulate in Mosul by Daesh terrorists.

A terrorist movement calling itself "Islamic State" insults religion and mocks the duties of a legitimate state towards its citizens. In declaring a caliphate, this death cult has declared war on the world. Regrettably, some Australians have joined this madness.

We've changed our laws to ensure that foreign fighters returning home can be arrested, prosecuted and gaoled for a very long time indeed. And we're working to prevent more people joining this conflict.

Our planes and soldiers are part of the international coalition to disrupt, degrade and ultimately destroy the Daesh death cult at the request of the Iraqi government. We are doing so because the threat it poses respects no national boundaries.

Any group proclaiming "submit or die" is a threat to our lives and values – and to the lives and values of all decent people. Australia is a free, fair and, above all, a pluralist society. It's our pluralism that shows that freedom and fairness is real. Some 70,000 Australian citizens have Turkish descent. This year is the Year of Turkey in Australia. And it is the Year of Australia in Turkey.

Important cultural exchanges will complement our increasing economic ties. This morning I invested Dr Haluk Oral with an award in the Order of Australia. He has been honoured for his service to our shared history and to the commemoration of the Centenary of the Gallipoli Campaign.

A subject of Dr Oral's research was Dr Charles Snodgrass Ryan, an Australian who'd served as a military surgeon at the siege of Plevna, where he repeatedly ran to the aid of wounded Turkish soldiers under fire. He returned to Turkey in 1915 with the Australian Imperial Force.

On 24 May 1915, when a truce was called to bury the dead, Turkish officers thought that Dr Ryan's medals might have been stolen. In rusty Turkish, Dr Ryan responded "They were pinned upon my chest because I fought at the siege of Plevna with Gazi Osman Pasha".

Sir Charles Ryan was a brave man; a healer and a saver of lives. His story belongs to Australia and it belongs to Turkey too.

As we honour our soldiers and remember their sacrifice, we also honour those who lifted their hands in peace and were a bridge between our peoples. I honour them all today, Australian and Turkish alike; I honour all who work for a just and lasting peace based on the universal decencies of mankind.

'Ordinary men did extraordinary things'
Gallipoli, Turkey, 25 April 2015

At the dawn service commemorating the centenary of the Gallipoli landing, Prime Minister Abbott tells the 10,000 Australians and New Zealanders who had travelled to Anzac Cove that, just as the Anzacs had been as good as they could be in their time, the challenge for us is "to be as good as we can be in ours".

It's one hundred years since Australians and New Zealanders splashed out of the sea, right here. So now we gather in the cold and dark before dawn; wondering what to say and how to honour those whose bones rest in the hills and the valleys above us, and whose spirit has moved our people for a century.

Year after year, we journey to what's now a peaceful coast to remember things that, normally, we might try to forget. Year after year, from all over our country, from every walk of life, from every background, young and old make this pilgrimage.

We aren't here to mourn a defeat or to honour a success, although there was much to mourn and much to honour in this campaign. We aren't here to acknowledge a legacy in this country, although Gallipoli shaped modern Turkey as much as it forged modern Australia and New Zealand.

Few of us can recall the detail, but we have imbibed what matters most: that a generation of young Australians rallied to serve our country, when our country called, and they were faithful, even unto death.

Beginning here, on this spot and at this hour, 100 years ago, they fought; and all-too-often they died: for their mates, for our country, for their King and – ultimately – for the ideal that people and nations should be free.

The first Anzacs were tradesmen, clerks, labourers, farmers and professionals; they were from every conceivable occupation, from every rung in the ladder of society, and from every point under the Southern Cross. Instead of landing here, they would have longed for the homes they'd left behind, the times they might have shared with their families, the backyard sport they could have played with their mates. But ordinary men did extraordinary things.

"They lived with death and dined with disease" because that was where their duty lay. In volunteering to serve, they became more than soldiers; they became the founding heroes of modern Australia.

If they had not been emblematic of the nation we thought we were, Anzac Day would not have been commemorated from that time until this – in every part of our country, in every place where Australians gather, and in every military base where Australians serve.

If they were not still emblematic of the nation we think we are, none of us would be here.

But like every generation since, we are here on Gallipoli, because we believe that the Anzacs represented Australians at our best. It's the perseverance of those who scaled the cliffs under a rain of fire. It's the compassion of the nurses who attended to the thousands of wounded.

It's the conquest of fear, often through a larrikin sense of humour. And it's the greatest love anyone can have: the readiness to lay down your life for your friend.

It's this that's ennobled those Anzacs to all who have come after them: they faced the hardest possible test and they did not flinch. The Gallipoli campaign was a failure, of course; the only really successful part was the evacuation. But the survivors of Gallipoli and their reinforcements went on to become some of the world's finest soldiers. The Australian and New Zealand mounted infantry spearheaded the British army that captured Jerusalem and Damascus. In March 1918, it was the Australian army corps that held the last great German attack that had split the British from the French armies. And it was Monash, the engineering genius and citizen soldier, the commander who'd struggled at Gallipoli but succeeded in France, who pioneered the all-arms warfare that led to victory, by breaking the bloody stalemate on the Western Front.

Over the past century, the Anzacs' descendants have honoured that tradition: in the Second World War, Korea, Malaya, Borneo, Vietnam, Iraq and – our longest war – Afghanistan.

Those serving on peacekeeping and relief missions have likewise kept faith with the original Anzacs.

Even now, our armed forces are serving in the Middle East and elsewhere, defending the values that we hold dear.

Today, all of us who have not been tested in war salute all of those who have. Most of us have never worn our country's uniform. We have not climbed the steep cliffs of Gallipoli. We have not trudged through the snow of Bullecourt. We have not struggled through the mud of Passchendaele. We have not experienced the horrors of Hellfire Pass, or fought through the jungles of Kokoda or Vietnam, or shaken the Uruzgun sand from our clothes. We have not risked being shot out of the skies over Germany or torpedoed in the Med or in the Pacific. But we are the better for those who have.

Because they rose to their challenges, we believe that it's a little easier for us to rise to ours.

Their example, we believe, helps us to be better than we would otherwise be. That's why we're here: to acknowledge what they have done for us – and what they still do for us.

The official historian, Charles Bean, said of the original Anzacs: "their story rises as it will always rise, above the mists of ages, a monument to great hearted men; and, for their nation a possession forever". Yes, they are us; and when we strive enough for the right things, we can be more like them.

So much has changed in one hundred years but not the things that really matter. Duty, selflessness, moral courage: always these remain the mark of a decent human being.

They did their duty; now, let us do ours. They gave us an example; now, let us be worthy of it. They were as good as they could be in their time; now, let us be as good as we can be in ours.

'We wonder at their selflessness'
Lone Pine, Gallipoli, 25 April 2015

At the Lone Pine Australian memorial in Gallipoli, the Prime Minister channels liberal philosopher Edmund Burke, saying Australia, like all societies, is a compact between the "dead, the living and the yet-to-be-born".

The men whose names are carved into this memorial, were the hope of their day; just as you young people, who are gathered here right now, are the hope of ours. To us, they are Anzacs; but in their day, they were fathers, sons, parents, children, cousins and mates – just as you are now. You walk among their headstones, you read the inscriptions, you hear the epitaphs and you hear their families speak. In these inscriptions, in these epitaphs, we hear the echoes of our country, a century ago. We feel that spirit beckoning us, to bigger, more honest and less selfish lives. From this place, from those who are buried here, we draw sustenance and inspiration. We don't come here merely to lament. We come here to show respect – because their stories have become our stories.

Our nation is not just a place on a map, or a mass of people who happen to live somewhere. Our nation is shaped by our collective memory; by the compact, between the dead, the living and the yet-to-be-born. And this is the mystery, and the wonder of Lone Pine: this home that is so far away from our home; this place of peace that was once a battlefield. The Gallipoli of August 1915 reeked of death. It was a place of disease and lice, of dysentery and flies, of headaches and fevers from dehydration, of frayed nerves from living under months of gunfire. Lone Pine was a battle of bayonets, hand held bombs and knives; and when there was nothing left to fight with, fists, knuckles, boots and teeth. Of all the bastards of places, this is the greatest bastard in the world, wrote a soldier who had lived the horror. Woe is to be found everywhere, wrote another.

The Lone Pine attack was meant to be a distraction, while a larger operation took place elsewhere on this peninsula. Of itself, it had little strategic purpose. But that didn't stop both sides fighting with an intensity that shocks us and moves us, even a century on.

In just four days in August 1915, some 800 Australians lost their lives; and 1500 were wounded in and around the trenches that run across this cemetery. The Turkish casualties were almost three times ours.

It's hard to fathom so much loss for what seems so little. Yet it was not for nothing. It was for country, empire, king, and the ideal that people and countries should be free. It was for duty, loyalty, honour and mates: the virtues that outshine any cause.

So here, at Lone Pine, we remember those men called upon to do things in their country's name that took them to the very edge of their physical and emotional limits, and beyond. We remember them and how they somehow found strength in each other. We wonder at their selflessness. We wonder at their capacity to face death, and not to falter. We wonder at what possessed them to charge into machinegun fire, or to push friends out of the way of unexploded bombs. And we remember everyone who served on this peninsula: Australians, New Zealanders, Britons, French, Indians, Canadians – and Turks too. We remember the brave, the scared, and the confused. We remember the good and the bad; the greatness and the smallness of it all.

For when the battle is over, when the wounds have healed, and when the ground has cooled, great warriors can see their enemies' virtue. The care taken of this place reflects the foe that is now a friend. So today, I salute a noble adversary and I thank the Republic of Turkey for accepting our sons with theirs.

On the headstones here, on the graves with no name, are etched the words: their glory shall not be blotted out. It is taken from the Scripture: Their seed shall remain forever. Their glory shall not be blotted out.

A century on, we re-affirm this truth. Our nation has grown from their seed. Australia thrives and prospers, nourished by their example. Here at Lone Pine, the pact between the past and the present is renewed for the future; for all who seek to understand what it means to be Australian.

8

DEFENCE & VETERANS

'We remember our work here with pride'
Tarin Kot, Afghanistan, 28 October 2013

At a special ceremony at Tarin Kot, the Australian-run base in the Uruzgan province of Afghanistan, Prime Minister Abbott announces Australia's "bittersweet" withdrawal from a long conflict.

Australia's longest war is ending, not with victory, not with defeat, but with hope for an Afghanistan that's better for our presence here. For a year in 2001, and again since 2005, Australian soldiers have been in Afghanistan. Since 2005 a special operations task group, and subsequently a reconstruction taskforce have been deployed here in Uruzgan in support of the Provincial Reconstruction Team.

Some 20,000 Australian men and women of our armed forces have served here in Afghanistan. Forty have died, 260 have been wounded, many more carry mental scars that may never heal. We salute their service. We mourn their losses and we honour their achievement. All Australians do, as this the first ever bipartisan visit to Afghanistan shows, and I thank the Australian Leader of the Opposition for his presence here today.

Thanks to Australia's presence here and that of our American, Dutch, Singaporean and Slovakian allies, there are now 26 girls' schools out of 200 schools in Uruzgan – that's a twentyfold increase since 2001. Up to 80 per cent of expectant mothers receive at least some prenatal care, care that was almost non-existent a decade ago and 200 kilometres of roads and bridges have been upgraded. This is still a poor and a difficult province – even by Afghan standards – but it is richer and better governed than it was thanks to Australia and thanks to our allies. Afghanistan is a better place for our presence here.

Australia is better too. The threat of global terrorism is reduced. Our reliability as an ally is confirmed and our commitment to the universal decencies of humanity that we fought for here is made obvious.

Australians have re-found a martial tradition that might have faded away with our parents and grandparents. We have discovered new heroes in Mark Donaldson, Ben Roberts-Smith, Dan Keighran and others whose names will emerge in time, more than worthy to stand with the original Anzacs and we have learnt that all the fierce and indomitable people of this beautiful but forbidding land, are worthy of respect.

Australians don't fight wars of conquest. We fight wars of freedom. We fight for peoples' right to live their own lives and to worship in their own way and for their duty to respect others' right to do likewise. That fight goes on, even though our fight here in Uruzgan is ending.

Elsewhere in Afghanistan, Australians will continue to train the Afghan Army. We will continue to fund Afghan development and we hope that the education of women and the growth of a freer society will go on, not because we're pushing it, but because Afghans have concluded that it's what's best for them, that it's an element of their best selves.

Still, this is a bittersweet moment for Australia; sweet because hundreds of soldiers will be home by Christmas; bitter because not all Australian families have had their sons, fathers and partners returned; sweet because our soldiers have given a magnificent account of themselves; bitter because Afghanistan remains a dangerous place despite all that has been done.

Our armed forces and our officials have done their duty. That duty never ends, although our duty here has. Now, the future of Uruzgan is in the hands of its own people. We hope they will remember us with pride as we remember our work here with pride.

Lest we forget.

'A task this Government will never shirk'
Canberra, 25 June 2015

Addressing a conference of the Australian Strategic Policy Institute, Prime Minister Abbott says Australia is a peace-loving international citizen, but it still must have an adequate defence force "to defend its citizens, advance its interests and uphold its values around the world".

"Expect the unexpected" has to be the first law of defence planning.

Prior to the event, who would have thought that Australia would send 5,000 troops to East Timor in 1999? In early 2001, who would have thought that Australia would participate in military operations in Afghanistan later that year; let alone the invasion of Iraq two years afterwards? Who would have imagined that our subsequent military rotations in Afghanistan, lasting over a decade, would ultimately involve almost 35,000 Australian troops? Who would have imagined, at the beginning of last year, that Australian personnel would be retrieving our dead from Ukrainian fields under the noses of the Russian army; or that a decade after the execution of Saddam Hussein, another Australian contingent would be in Iraq with no early end in sight to this deployment?

As the world's 12th largest economy and as a major trading nation; as one of the United States' principal allies; and as a treaty partner to many of our important neighbours, Australia has global interests and needs some global reach. The job of Australia's armed forces is to defend our territory, contribute to a more secure region, and help build a safer world.

First and foremost, our armed forces should be capable of successfully repelling any regional adversary and inflicting very severe damage on any attacker. But because Australia does have global interests, our armed forces should be capable of contributing proportionately to our allies' military operations around the globe. And because the stability of our region is essential for the safety and security of our own country, our armed forces should be capable of mounting independent combat operations anywhere close to home.

Thanks to the decisions made in the 2000 Defence White Paper and subsequently, Australia's armed forces are now more capable than ever before. Last year, without assistance, Australia was able to deploy 200 police to Ukraine and 250 soldiers to the Netherlands within just a few days of the MH-17 atrocity.

Just three days after refugees became trapped on Mt Sinjar in Iraq, an Australian Hercules – loaded by Australians with Australian supplies at an Australian facility in the Middle East – was undertaking humanitarian air drops.

Refuelled by an Australian plane, six Australian strike fighters flew virtually non- stop to the Middle East where they now regularly hit targets in Iraq from a base as far away as Sydney is from Alice Springs.

When the HMAS Adelaide amphibious ship joins HMAS Canberra and HMAS Choules and the new air warfare destroyers are operational, Australia will be able to conduct significant amphibious and humanitarian operations throughout our region.

Right now, our armed forces are active around the globe. Australia has about 500 soldiers training and assisting the Iraqi armed forces to retake their own country. We have about 350 personnel involved in air strikes against Daesh targets in Iraq and supporting the air campaign over Iraq and Syria as well. We have about 400 personnel engaged in logistical and transport operations in the UAE and a ship constantly deployed on anti-piracy operations near the Horn of Africa. We still have some 400 personnel deployed to Afghanistan on a training and logistics mission; and there are still military and police personnel in the Solomon Islands.

Australia seeks no dominion. We threaten no one. We seek only to be a good neighbour, a reliable ally, and a steadfast friend. But a serious country needs capable armed forces: to defend its citizens, to advance its interests and to uphold its values around the world.

As a peaceful, pluralist democracy, Australia never picks fights. Our instinct is to settle differences, not to inflame them. Still, we've never shirked our share of responsibility: to help people in trouble, to keep the peace and to deter and defeat aggression. That's our record as a good international citizen.

In an uncertain world, we have a responsibility to be prepared. More than in most other fields, defence preparedness requires continuous effort – not just over weeks and months – but continuous effort over years and decades.

Our 1999 expedition to East Timor did expose very serious gaps in our capability. The men and women of our armed forces were enthusiastic, determined and professional, but faced serious risks because of the range of operations they simply weren't equipped for.

The Howard Government swiftly commissioned a new Defence White Paper to reassess our long term defence capability on the basis of these new insights into the challenges we faced.

That White Paper was delivered a year before our perceptions of the world were to change on September 11, 2001 – but it has served us well for over a decade. The 2000 white paper affirmed that we should pay for the defence we needed; rather than suffer the defence we'd actually paid for. It faced up to the historical reality that successive Australian governments have tended to put off investing in defence because threats were perceived to be vague or distant. This short-sightedness has often lulled governments into making short-term cuts or deferring investment to another day.

During the last parliament, for instance, defence funding fell to its lowest level, as a percentage of GDP, since 1938. As you all know, 1938 was the eve of the greatest ever military threat to our country and our world – yet a nation in denial had allowed its defences to become pitifully inadequate. While domestic and international circumstances are vastly better now than then, defence decisions are neglected or deferred at our peril.

Our armed forces constantly need new capabilities as they adapt to current and future challenges.

Of course this Government understands that economic security and national security are interdependent. That's one of the reasons why the Government is working to repair the Budget. A stronger budget does mean more capacity to invest in our long-term national security capabilities.

Already, in last year's Budget, this Government committed $1 billion more to defence – and, in this year's Budget, has committed an extra $1.2 billion for national security. That includes $450 million to strengthen our intelligence capabilities, to support metadata retention and to counter terrorist propaganda and violent extremism. This year's Budget also includes more than $750 million for defence operations in the Middle East, Afghanistan and Iraq.

At a time when the armed forces of like-minded nations are facing cuts, Australia is boosting defence spending to almost $32 billion next year and $132 billion over the forward estimates. That is an increase of almost $10 billion compared with the four-year estimates announced in last year's Budget.

The Defence White Paper to be released in the next few months won't be an unfunded wish list; it will be a costed, sustainable, long-term plan. It is now being rigorously tested because it will provide the foundation for our country's defences over the next two decades.

We've listened to the experts from defence, from our intelligence services, from industry, academia, think tanks and broader government. All the big projects and programmes in the portfolio have been assessed by industry analysts. For the first time, there has been an externally validated assessment of defence costs so that we can be more confident that defence spending is finally value for money. Most defence capability projects won't come to fruition for 10 to 20 years but good planning demands that the money is there when the bills arrive.

A future force structure is at the heart of the coming White Paper. The Government has reassessed what our armed forces should be able to do. We understand that our adversaries will hide in cities and caves; that they will exploit the vulnerabilities of modern communications; and that they will take advantage of our diversity and our tolerance to attack our values and weaken our society.

We must expect our opponents and our competitors to use every means to challenge us. This could include potential use of weapons of mass destruction and offensive cyber capabilities. So, the White Paper will specify a force structure that enables our military to be even more effective in securing our nation and to make an even more active contribution to regional and global security.

As history has repeatedly shown, the defence of Australia begins far from our shores, sometimes on the other side of the world, so our armed forces must be capable of conducting independent operations in our region and contributing meaningfully to military operations around the globe.

Obviously such a potent, balanced, versatile and sustainable future force does need a range of capabilities – but rather than just list them on a service-by-service basis, there is a joint plan that aligns capabilities with Australia's strategic needs.

We need an army that can take and hold ground against a very wide range of opponents; a navy that can deter aggressors, protect our sea lanes, and put our army ashore where needed in the region; and an air force that can strike far afield and support our troops around the globe.

We will invest in the key enablers to make this possible:

- Comprehensive intelligence, surveillance and reconnaissance to ensure that our armed forces know what is happening around them
- Enhanced cyber and electronic warfare capabilities
- Upgraded communications systems and integrated command and control systems so information can instantly be shared
- Strong and sustainable partnerships with industry.

We need a strong defence industry to support and sustain our armed forces. The White Paper will re-set this critical relationship. It is certainly not necessary or practical that all our defence equipment be made here in Australia but it is necessary that it be sustainable in Australia. That said, our preference will always be for local build where world class equipment can be obtained at a reasonable price in a way that doesn't limit interoperability with our allies.

A competitive evaluation process is now underway to choose the next Australian submarine, building on a French, German or Japanese design. Obviously, we want to maximise Australian involvement in its build, including work on combat systems integration, and this will result in the creation of at least 500 new highly skilled jobs. And, because there will be more submarines, there will more sustainment work in Adelaide too.

Notwithstanding cost blowouts and delays – very significant cost blowouts and very significant delays – in the air warfare destroyer programme, the ANZAC frigate programme and Austal's work around the world including for the US Navy, demonstrates that Australia can successfully build surface warships under the right conditions.

It is the government's intention to develop a continuous build of major surface warships here in Australia to avoid the unproductive on-again, off-again cycle that has done this industry so much damage.

There will be further announcements about naval shipbuilding within the next few weeks.

The White Paper, a Defence Investment Plan, covering major equipment and its sustainment, the Defence Industry Policy Statement, a Naval Shipbuilding Plan and our commitment to increase funding — in combination — will provide the clarity and certainty that the defence of Australia needs.

Today, I reaffirm our commitment to increasing the defence budget to two per cent of GDP by 2024. In a difficult and uncertain world, and in a region where other countries are spending more on defence, this is the least we can responsibly spend.

In Iraq, Afghanistan and elsewhere we ask our uniformed personnel to put themselves in harm's way for our country so we do have a heavy responsibility to equip them properly for the task.

Every decision we take today, every investment we make, must be geared to that goal. It is not a case of asking defence to do more with less, it is a case of ensuring defence can do even more with more.

For Army, the focus will be on continuing to develop and implement Plan Beersheba, producing a stronger force better prepared for every contingency. The key to this will be replacing Army's armoured combat vehicles; preparing for future amphibious operations from the Canberra Class ships; and integrating new intelligence, surveillance and communications technology with other joint capabilities.

The future submarine and frigate programmes, along with the Canberra Class amphibious ships and Hobart Class air warfare destroyers, will be the heart of the future navy.

The air force will move to the F-35 Joint Strike Fighter, Growler electronic warfare planes and more unmanned aircraft, and will have significantly stronger command, logistics, transport, and surveillance capabilities.

But succeeding in the future will depend on more than high-end capabilities. It's the integration and the sharing of information between platforms and systems that will make our armed forces truly interoperable and allow us to maintain an edge in our region. Properly knitted together, these capabilities will be more than the sum of their parts and will ensure a more mobile, agile, adaptable, and potent Australian Defence Force.

To make our country safer over the long term, the Government has already identified significant reforms with the Department of Defence itself.

The First Principles Review of Defence confirmed that our armed forces have high international standing and a fine record of delivering on military operations, and in humanitarian and emergency support. But, and this will surprise none of you, it also identified the empire-building and feather-bedding that tends to build up in large, traditional institutions.

There will be simpler management lines to provide clear direction, transparency and accountability; and we will remove the red tape that causes higher costs and delayed decision making. This transformational change will be overseen by the Secretary of the Department and the Chief of the Defence Force, there will also be an external oversight board, including all of the members of the review team.

All of this is about making our armed forces better prepared to meet the challenges of the present and the future. To do so, we must give our serving men and women the resources, equipment and support they need to do the difficult jobs we of ask them.

More than anything else, the most important capability Defence has is its people. This Government will do the right thing by defence force personnel – with the best equipment, good pay and conditions, and support long after their service has ended. And we'll support ADF families – because it's their resilience and solidarity that makes possible the service of our fighting men and women.

There is a compact between the Australian people and those who wear our uniform. It is a compact first settled at Anzac Cove 100 years ago in the baptism of fire that shaped our nation. Back in 1915 the troops who landed at Gallipoli were from every walk of life. They were labourers, farmers, office-workers and artisans who volunteered to serve for their mates, for our country, for their King and – ultimately – for the ideal that people and nations should be free.

It's a very different armed force today, but with the same values at its core. Today's personnel are highly trained, highly skilled professionals. Many are seasoned veterans with extensive operational experience – gained defending the freedoms and the values that we hold dear.

We owe it to those in uniform, we owe it to our country and to our citizens, we owe it to the wider world in which we are a force for good to ensure that our armed forces are becoming more potent and more capable all the time.

This is a task that this Government will never shirk.

'Worthy successors to the Anzacs'

House of Representatives, Canberra, 25 May 2015

Prime Minister Abbott formally offers to repatriate the remains of 25 soldiers killed in Vietnam who never made it home.

On the 100th anniversary of the landing at ANZAC Cove, thousands of Australians made the journey to Gallipoli. The descendants of the fallen, as well as strangers, walked among the graves, read the epitaphs and touched the walls of granite where the names of the missing are inscribed. In both world wars and in Korea, our dead lie close to where they fell. As every visitor to our war cemeteries knows, the Commonwealth War Graves Commission reverently maintains the shrines where they rest.

Madam Speaker, shortly after the commencement of our involvement in Vietnam, Australian policy changed. We decided to bring home the bodies of the fallen. We can never restore those who have died in the service of our country. But we can and we should offer solace and support to the families left behind.

Fifty years ago this week, the first contingent of the 1st Battalion, Royal Australian Regiment departed for South Vietnam. Eventually, almost 60,000 Australians, including Army, Air Force and Navy personnel, served in Vietnam.

Some 521 of them are listed on the Roll of Honour at the Australian War Memorial. Of the 521, all but 25 were brought home. Of the 25 not brought home, 24 of them lie at Terendak Cemetery in Malaysia.

Terendak Cemetery is situated on a peaceful slope, surrounded by trees. The graves are tended with respect – and I thank the Government of Malaysia for the care it has shown for almost half a century. However, the cemetery is located within a large, operational Malaysian military base, and security restrictions understandably limit the access of families to the graves of their loved ones.

Among those buried in Terendak Cemetery, is Private Ronald Field of the First Battalion, Royal Australian Regiment. Private Field, a forward scout, was killed in action on the 9th of October, 1965. Also lying there is Warrant Officer Max Hanley of the Australian Army Training Team

Vietnam. He earned the Military Medal in the Malayan Emergency and was also awarded the US Bronze Star for exceptional heroism while serving as a platoon leader in Vietnam. Warrant Officer Hanley was killed in action in South Vietnam on the 20th of February 1967. Also interred at Terendak, alongside our Vietnam veterans, is Lieutenant David Brian of the 3rd Battalion, Royal Australian Regiment. Lieutenant Brian was killed during operations on the Thai-Malaya border on the 5th of March 1964.

Mrs Dianne Field, the widow of Private Ronald Field; Mrs Marie Hanley, widow of Warrant Officer Max Hanley; and Mrs Sara Ferguson, the widow of Lieutenant David Brian are with us in the gallery today. You are our honoured guests. Today we remember the sacrifice of your husbands made in the service of our country – as well as the burdens that you and your families have carried.

The natural instinct of governments is to resolve problems to the satisfaction of their citizens. We don't want soldiers killed in the same war treated differently. Hence, the Government will offer to repatriate the remains of all the Australians interred at Terendak Cemetery.

This offer will also be extended to the family of Warrant Officer Kevin Conway, who died in the Vietnam War, and is buried in Kranji War Cemetery in Singapore. Because of the unique circumstances of Terendak Military Cemetery, with its limited access for families, this offer will be extended to all the families of those interred there, including those of service dependants.

In making this decision, the Government has consulted with the RSL, the Vietnam Veterans' Association and the Vietnam Veterans' Federation, as well as with families. I want to acknowledge the fine work of the Minister for Veterans' Affairs, Senator Ronaldson in this matter and also the advocacy of the Member for Solomon.

The decision to take up this offer of repatriation rests, as it should, with the soldiers' widows, children or immediate family. They can start to bring their loved ones home or they may choose to let them rest where they lie. Either way, their decision will be respected.

I can assure those who choose repatriation, that we will bring our soldiers home with full military honours. They will be reburied in Australia at a cemetery of the family's choosing. The Commonwealth will bear the full cost of repatriation and burial.

The former Chief of Army, General David Morrison, once observed that the Australians who served in Vietnam laid the foundations for the modern, professional Australian Army. They fought well in a difficult and a controversial war. They are worthy successors to the ANZACs we remembered a month ago. Today's decision will ensure that all the Australians who died in the Vietnam War receive equal treatment. It is a policy worthy of a country that honours all who wear our uniform and who serve in our name.

We do remember all who served in the Vietnam War. We especially remember those who were faithful, even unto death. They did their duty. They remain an example. Their selfless sacrifice will never be forgotten by the country they served.

'You have set a standard of strength and decency'

Torrens Parade Ground, Adelaide, 15 August 2015

At the 70th anniversary of Victory in the Pacific, Prime Minister Abbott notes the high price Australia paid in the conflict and the long period of peace and prosperity that has followed it.

As I begin – could I ask all of our Second World War veterans either to stand or to raise your hand so that we may salute you. On behalf of the Commonwealth of Australia, I thank you for defending liberty, for opposing tyranny and above all for building a lasting peace.

For all our problems in these days and for all the perils that we face now, these are the best times in human history and that's largely thanks to you.

For every one of us who is not of the wartime generation, it is an honour to be with every one of you who is. You fought, you suffered, you won, you made history, and you shaped our world.

On this day, seventy years ago, our nation and our allies celebrated the greatest victory the world has ever seen. Our country had emerged from six atrocious years with our alliances secure, our values upheld and our freedoms safe.

As Prime Minister, Ben Chifley declared on this day 70 years ago: "The war is over. Let us offer thanks to God…and remember those whose lives were given that we may enjoy this glorious moment and may look forward to a peace which they have won for us." So, on this anniversary, we remember the exhilaration of victory and we remember the grim struggle by which victory was won. Australians had fought in the air and on the sea; in the jungle and in the desert. Australians had suffered in prison camps. Australians had kept families together while spouses, parents and siblings served far away. Everyone who lived through those times was caught up in the struggle to defend our country and to preserve our freedom. Almost a million Australians, men and women, served in the Second World War. Almost 40,000 died.

To all of them, to all of you, we owe a debt of gratitude that can never fully be repaid.

So, today, tonight, we honour the volunteers of the Second Australian Imperial Force who pushed the Italians out of North Africa and the French out of Syria. We honour the veterans of the Greek and Crete campaigns, including those who spent long years in captivity. We honour the Ninth Division at El Alamein – one of the decisive units in the decisive battle where the tide of war turned. We honour the men of the Royal Australian Navy for their part in the British victories in the Mediterranean and the US victories in the Pacific. We honour the Australians flying in our own squadrons and in the Royal Air Force who helped to win the Battle of Britain and who took the war to Germany.

On this anniversary of Victory in the Pacific, we honour the Australians who harried the Japanese down the Malayan peninsula, who defended Singapore, and who dealt the Japanese their first defeat on land at Milne Bay. We look back in awe at the men who fought through the mud and blood of New Guinea and the other islands and we remember with pity those who starved and died on the Burma railway. Here in Brisbane, we remember those aboard the Australian Hospital Ship Centaur, torpedoed off Stradbroke Island and we thank our American comrades in arms, to whom we turned in our dark hour. We acknowledge all who served, all who suffered, all who died in the service of our country; and all those they left behind. We thank them, we thank you, for the democratic and free Australia that is your true legacy, and we resolve always to strive to be worthy of this sacrifice.

On this day 70 years ago, addressing the people of the British Commonwealth and Empire, King George – the Queen's father – had this to say: "Great is our responsibility to make sure…that the peace gained amid measureless trials and suffering shall not be cast away…For great as are the deeds that you have done, there must be no falling off from this high endeavour. We have spent freely of all that we had. Now, we shall have to work hard to restore what has been lost and to establish peace on the unshakeable foundations, not alone of material strength but also of moral authority…If you carry on in the years to come as you have done so splendidly in the war, you and your children can look forward to the future, not with fear, but with high hopes of a surer happiness for all." The King concluded, "It is to this great task that I call you now and I know that I shall not call in vain."

So let us for a moment consider what has been achieved in the postwar world: 70 years of peace in western Europe; 70 years of peace between China and Japan; a rules-based international order, guaranteed by the United States, that has fostered the greatest expansion of safety, of prosperity and of democracy that the world has ever seen; with many hundreds of millions of people, especially in Asia, moving from the Third World to the Middle Class in just two generations. Let us savour that. Let us ponder the epic nature of this achievement no less than the achievement of victory 70 years ago.

Now, of course, there is always more to do; there is always injustice to be overcome; there is always the evil, alas, that lurks deep in the human heart and can never quite be banished; yet the world that the heroes of World War II created has been golden beyond the imagining of any previous generation.

The wartime generation built a lasting peace because you never let the grim necessities of war harden your hearts or misshape your characters. You rose to the challenge of war and you rose again to the challenge of peace and all of us are your beneficiaries. Perhaps you were the first generation in human history to be as resolved to build a peace as you were to win a war. Perhaps you took to heart Churchill's dedication of his war memoirs: "in defeat defiance, and in war resolution; but in victory magnanimity, and in peace, goodwill." You certainly rose to the challenge King George posed and the faith he so beautifully expressed.

Men like Gunner Russell Savage of the Second/Tenth Field Artillery Regiment, in a prison camp in Northern Japan, when the war ended; asked by a liberating comrade: "Which of these bastards do you want shot?" he shrugged off the question. "We were beyond caring about past atrocities," he said, "and simply wanted to be away home."

Men like my former constituent, Captain Norman White, a Japanese POW for more than three years, who eventually ran a friendship circle for Japanese business people in Sydney.

Whether it was your grace, or your humanity, or just your exhaustion, there was a substantial lack of the reprisals, the retribution and even the reparations that had marked every previous war won. There was little "victors' justice" but a rare and fragrant abundance of victor's goodwill and magnanimity. It's this that allowed Germany and Japan to rise again in peace and freedom so swiftly; to become exemplary international citizens.

It was the grace of Russell Savage, the generosity of Norman White, the goodness of "Weary" Dunlop, and the decency of countless others of the wartime generation that paved the way for initiatives like the

Colombo Plan and the Japanese trade treaty and all the other measures that, in the post war world, have turned strangers into friends and enemies into partners.

This is your world. I hope that you are proud of it; for we could not be more proud of you.

You have set a standard of strength and decency – a gold standard to which every future generation should aspire.

I thank you.

'I stand in humble awe of all who served'
Canberra, 18 August 2015

At a Vietnam Veterans Day Remembrance Service, Prime Minister Abbott acknowledges the magnanimity of the Vietnam who have befriended their former foes and credits this for Australia's present friendship with Vietnam.

As someone who has never served in our armed forces, I stand in humble awe of all who have – particularly, the decorated veterans I see before me.

We gather today to remember those who served in the Vietnam War. From the arrival of the Australian Army Training Team in 1962 to the final withdrawal of the Embassy guard 11 years later, over 60,000 Australians, including army, air force and navy personnel, served in Vietnam – 521 of them died. Over 3,000 were wounded. Many suffered unseen scars that never healed.

This year marks a half century since the first contingent of the 1st Battalion Royal Australian Regiment departed and today marks the 49th anniversary of the Battle of Long Tan. It was at Long Tan that 108 Australian and New Zealand soldiers prevailed in the pouring rain against an estimated 2,000 North Vietnamese and Viet Cong troops. As their commander Lieutenant Colonel Harry Smith said, "although nowhere near the same scale, Long Tan will be remembered alongside Kapyong, Tobruk and Gallipoli."

As always, victory came at a high price. Long Tan was the most costly action single action by Australian soldiers in Vietnam, with 18 dead and 24 wounded. Courage, determination, resourcefulness and unflinching loyalty to mates marked that battle and, indeed, the entire Australian experience in Vietnam.

At Long Tan, at Fire Support Base Coral, at Fire Support Base Balmoral, at Binh Ba and in countless contacts and fire fights throughout that war, Australian soldiers proved themselves worthy successors to the Anzacs, as did our naval and air personnel who provided vital logistic support.

I regret to say that back home we did not always appreciate that at the time. People were entitled to question the war, but they should never have doubted our soldiers. Eventually we would see what was always true: that in you, was and is, the best of Australia. Eventually we saw the duty, the courage, the integrity and the examples of men and women at their best. That is what you were, and are. Australia is proud of you and we honour you for your service to our country.

The former Chief of Army David Morrison observed that the soldiers who served in Vietnam laid the foundations for the modern professional Australian Army. The friendship that now exists between Australia and Vietnam owes much to veterans determined to befriend their former foes as the Anzacs did two generations earlier.

Today, we remember all who served in the Vietnam War. We remember those who died. We remember those who were scarred physically and mentally. We remember their families, and their loved ones, that suffered with them.

You did your duty. You remain an example. Your sacrifice should never be forgotten by the country you served.

9

NATIONAL SECURITY, COUNTER-TERRORISM & AIR SAFETY

'It is not a state, it is a death cult'
Parliament House, Canberra, 1 September 2014

As Islamic State fighters threaten a massacre in a key Shiite town in Iraq, Prime Minister Abbott tells parliament that Australia, like the United States, cannot idly stand by in the face of preventable genocide, and that prevention of terrorism at home also needed more funding.

Many Australians are understandably apprehensive about the risk of becoming involved in another long and costly conflict in the Middle East. The situation in the Middle East is indeed a witches' brew of complexity and potential danger. Doing anything involves serious risks and weighty consequences. But doing nothing involves risks and consequences too.

As things stand, doing nothing means leaving millions of people exposed to death, forced conversion and ethnic cleansing. So far this year, more than a million Iraqis have been driven from their homes. We have all seen on our screens the beheadings, the crucifixions and the mass executions. Peoples and cultures that have existed for millennia are faced with extermination. Thousands of women have been forced into sexual slavery. President Obama has labelled what is happening at the hands of the ISIL movement as a potential genocide.

I refuse to call this hideous movement "Islamic State" because it's not a state; it is a death cult.

In good conscience, Australia cannot leave the Iraqi people to face this horror, this pure evil, alone or ask others to do, in the name of human decency, what we won't do ourselves. It is right to do what we prudently and proportionately can to alleviate this suffering, to prevent its spread and to deal with its perpetrators. So far, Australian aircraft have participated in humanitarian airdrops to people trapped on Mount Sinjar and, just yesterday, to the besieged inhabitants of the town of Amerli.

Yesterday's airdrop was mounted in conjunction with American, British and French aircraft.

In coming days, Australian aircraft will join an airlift of supplies, including military equipment, to the Kurdish regional government in

Erbil. American, British, French, Canadian and Italian aircraft will also be involved. This involvement has been at the request of the Obama administration and with the support of the Iraqi government.

So far, we have met requests for humanitarian relief and for logistical support. So far, there has been no request for military action itself.

Should such a request come from the Obama administration and supported by the government of Iraq, it would be considered against these criteria: Is there a clear and achievable overall objective? Is there a clear and proportionate role for Australian forces? Have all the risks been properly assessed? And is there an overall humanitarian objective in accordance with Australia's national interests?

Like President Obama, Australia has no intention to commit combat troops on the ground. But we're not inclined to stand by in the face of preventable genocide either. Australia is not a country that goes looking for trouble but we have always been prepared to do what we can to help in the wider world.

Madam Speaker, many Australians, understandably, will shrink from reaching out to this conflict on the other side of the world but this conflict is reaching out to us.

At least 60 Australians are fighting with terrorist groups across Iraq and Syria. They are supported by about 100 more. And we know – or at least should prudently assume – that many of them will seek to return to Australia. They will return accustomed to kill.

Around two thirds of Australians who returned from fighting with terrorist groups in Afghanistan a decade or so back subsequently became involved in terrorist activities here. A number are still serving long jail sentences.

The Australians and their supporters who have joined terrorist groups in the Middle East are a serious and growing threat to our security. That's why the Government is boosting counter-terrorism funding by $630 million and updating our laws so they keep pace with evolving technologies and the developing threat.

At the same time we have stepped up engagement with community groups here in Australia.

I want to stress now as I always do, that the threat is extremism, not any particular community. The target is terrorism – not religion.

We need to understand that people who kill without compunction in other countries are hardly likely to be law abiding citizens should they return to Australia. They have come to hate us no less than they hate their victims in Iraq and Syria. The don't hate us for what we do; but for who we are and for how we live. They hate us because we let people live and worship in whatever way they choose and I thank God that we do.

I am grateful that the Government's actions so far have been fully supported by the Opposition Leader. This is as it should be when our nation faces threats to its national security.

Obviously, Madam Speaker, the Parliament will have a chance to speak to this statement and that of the Opposition Leader in coming days. That, too, is as it should be in a free and fair democracy such as ours.

'Against terrorism, not religion'

House of Representatives, Canberra, 22 September 2014

After major raids on suspected terrorists in Sydney and Brisbane, Prime Minister Abbott tells Parliament: "I can't promise that hideous events will never take place on Australian soil, but I can promise that we will never stoop to the level of those who hate us."

Because protecting our people is the first duty of government, it's right that I should update the House on developing challenges to our national security.

I acknowledge the commitment of all MPs to keeping our people safe and I especially acknowledge the support that the Leader of the Opposition has given to the Government on this subject. On questions of national security, it's always best if government and opposition can stand together, shoulder to shoulder. It lets our enemies know that they will never shake our resolve. It's a sign that hope is stronger than fear and that decency can prevail over brute force.

From me and from all ministers in this government, there will be three key messages: First, the government will do whatever is possible to keep people safe. Second, our security measures at home and abroad are directed against terrorism, not religion. And third, Australians should always live normally because terrorists' goal is to scare us out of being ourselves.

As we all know, there have been major anti-terrorist raids across Sydney and Brisbane. Our police and security agencies will always strive to stay at least one step ahead of those who would do us harm; and, so far, thank god, they have succeeded. I can't promise that hideous events will never take place on Australian soil; but I can promise that we will never stoop to the level of those who hate us and fight evil with evil.

Regrettably, for some time to come, Australians will have to endure more security than we're used to, and more inconvenience than we'd like. Regrettably, for some time to come, the delicate balance between freedom and security may have to shift. There may be more restrictions on some so that there can be more protections for others.

After all, the most basic freedom of all is the freedom to walk the streets unharmed and to sleep safe in our beds at night. So, creating new offences that are harder to beat on technicality may be a small price to pay for saving lives and for maintaining the social fabric of an open, free and multicultural nation.

For more than two years, the civil war in Syria, followed by the conquest of much of northern Iraq, has been sucking in misguided and alienated Australians. There are at least 60 Australians that we know of currently fighting with terrorist groups in Syria and Iraq, and at least 100 Australians who are supporting them. More than 20 of these foreign fighters have already returned to Australia.

As a peaceful and pluralist democracy, we naturally shrink from getting involved in conflicts on the other side of the world. Sometimes, though, these conflicts reach out to us – regardless of anything that we might do now or might have done in the past.

I refuse to call a terrorist movement "Islamic state" because to do so demeans Islam and mocks the duties that a legitimate state bears to its citizens. It can hardly be Islamic to kill without compunction Shia, Yazidi, Turkmen, Kurds, Christians and Sunni who don't share this death cult's view of the world.

Nothing can justify the beheadings, crucifixions, mass executions, ethnic cleansing, rape and sexual slavery that have taken place in every captured town and city. To do such evil – and to revel in doing such evil – is simply unprecedented. To demand the allegiance of Muslims everywhere, and the conversion or subordination of everyone else, is an ultimatum to the entire world.

As we all know, the Middle East is a difficult part of the world where violence is all-too-common. Indeed it's a witches' brew of complexity and danger.

Nevertheless, it is in the interests of Australia and the world that we here stand ready to join a coalition to help the new Iraqi government to disrupt and to degrade the ISIL movement and to regain control over its own country.

The claim that ISIL's atrocities and threats are a response to something else is an excuse, not a reason. Nothing remotely justifies the mass slaughter of innocents – overwhelmingly Muslims – that the ISIL movement routinely practices. Nothing remotely justifies ISIL's brazen pretension.

It's important to remember that the September 11 attack predated America's involvement in Iraq, just as the first Bali bombing predated Australia's. Groups such as ISIL will cite our involvement but they would attack us anyway for who we are and for how we live, not for anything that we have done.

It's our acceptance that people can live and worship in the way they choose that bothers them, not our foreign policy. ISIL kills because it glories in death and because no one has yet been strong enough to stop it. It's ISIL's success on the battlefield, at least as much as its absolutism, that explains its perverse appeal. Stopping and reversing its advance will help the people of Iraq; it should also reduce its magnetism for people from around the globe who are looking to join a fight.

Last week, together, the Leader of the Opposition and I helped to farewell the Australian force that's ready to join the international coalition against ISIL.

Later this week, I'll be in New York for discussions at the United Nations which President Obama will chair. Subsequently, the Cabinet will again consider the use of our forces to mount air strikes and to provide military advice in support of the Iraqi government.

Last week, the Opposition Leader and I separately thanked our police and security agencies for their work to disrupt an ISIL plot to conduct demonstration executions here in this country.

For some months, operatives in Syria have been urging their Australian networks to prepare attacks against targets here. An urgent review of the safety of Parliament House has recommended that the Australian Federal Police take control of internal as well as external security. In this building, there will be more armed police, fewer points of access, and more scrutiny of parliamentary passes. I thank the presiding officers, particularly you, Madam Speaker, for supporting and for beginning to implement these recommendations. They will mean slightly more inconvenience but considerably more protection for everyone involved in our national government.

Last week, an Australian ISIL operative instructed his followers to pluck people from the street to demonstrate that they could, in his words, "kill kaffirs". All that would be needed to conduct such an attack is a knife, a camera-phone and a victim. Consequently, within 36 hours more than 800 police and security agents were deployed in Sydney and in Brisbane to execute 30 search warrants. One person has been charged with serious terrorist offences and a large amount of evidence has been amassed that will now carefully be sifted so that further charges might be laid.

It was important to respond with great strength to disrupt this imminent terrorist act. It demonstrates that our determination equals that of those who would do us harm. We will more than match the resolve of our adversaries in all things except malice; because our military, police and security personnel have goodwill towards everyone except those who are plotting to hurt us. So today, I pledge that our security agencies will have all the resources and authority that they reasonably need.

In August, the government committed an additional $630 million to the Australian Federal Police, Customs and Border Protection, the Australian Security and Intelligence Organisation, the Australian Secret Intelligence Service and the Office of National Assessments.

Additional ASIO and ASIS officers are being recruited and deployed; biometric screening will start to be introduced at international airports within 12 months; and more Border Force personnel are now being deployed to international airports.

Before Christmas, the government will respond to the review of the national security apparatus that's now underway. Legislation on agency powers is now before the parliament.

Legislation to create new terrorist offences and to extend existing powers to monitor or to detain terror suspects will be introduced this week.

We can't prevent from returning home Australians-born-and-bred who've been foreign fighters, however incompatible with our values their conduct has been. Unfortunately, terrorists don't reform just because they've returned home, as the experience with Australians returning from fighting with the Taliban shows.

My unambiguous message to all Australians who fight with terrorist groups is that you will be arrested, prosecuted and gaoled for a very long time indeed and that our laws are being changed to make it easier to keep potential terrorists off our streets. For one thing, it will be an offence to be in a designated area, for example Raqqa in Syria, without a good reason.

The only safe place for those who have been brutalised and militarised by fighting with terrorists is inside a maximum security prison.

As well, legislation requiring telecommunications providers to keep the metadata they already create and to continue to make it available to police and security agencies will be introduced soon.

If the police and security agencies can make a case for more resources and for more powers, the government's strong disposition is to provide them because it's rightly expected of us in this place that we will do whatever we possibly can to keep people safe. Of course, any such powers would be exercised responsibly, under the watch of the Inspector-General for Intelligence and Security, the Ombudsman, and the joint standing committees of this parliament.

These are troubling times for everyone accustomed to think that terrorism happens in places other than Australia or that history has largely overtaken the use of military force.

Our Australian instinct to assume the best of everyone and our tendency to imagine that we live in the best of all possible worlds is being challenged as rarely before. Still, even in what seem darkening times, I'm sure that we won't lose our perspective and will continue to keep things in proportion.

'A moral victory far surpassing any military success'
New York, 24 September 2014

Prime Minister Abbott tells the United Nations Security Council that Islamic State's terrorism is an insult to the ideals of both Islam and liberal democracy.

I'm happy to be here at your urging, Mr President. It is the weightiest of matters that brings us together today.

Right now, thousands of misguided people from around the world are joining terrorist groups in Syria and Iraq because they claim Islam is under threat and because they are excited by the prospect of battle. But whatever they think or say, these terrorists aren't fighting for God or for religious faith.

At the heart of every terrorist group is an infatuation with death. What else can explain the beheadings, crucifixions, mass executions, rapes and sexual slavery in every town and city that's fallen to the terrorist movement now entrenched in eastern Syria and northern Iraq?

A terrorist movement calling itself "Islamic State" insults Islam and mocks the duties of a legitimate state towards its citizens. And to use this term is to dignify a death cult; a death cult that, in declaring itself a caliphate, has declared war on the world.

So, countries do need to work together to defeat it because about 80 nations have citizens fighting with ISIL and every country is a potential target.

Last week, an Australian operative in Syria instructed his local network to conduct demonstration killings – and this week, an Australian terror suspect savagely attacked two policemen. Now, it's hard to imagine that citizens of a pluralist democracy could have succumbed to such delusions – yet clearly they have.

The Australian Government will be utterly unflinching towards anything that threatens our future as a free, fair and multicultural society; a beacon of hope and exemplar of unity-in-diversity.

Already, more than 60 Australians are fighting with ISIL and al-Nusra. More than 60 Australians have had their passports suspended to prevent them from joining terrorist groups in the Middle East. Our laws are changing to ensure that foreign fighters returning home can be arrested, prosecuted and gaoled for a very long time indeed.

We aren't just dealing with potential terrorists at home; we're tackling their inspiration abroad. Our combat aircraft and special forces are now in the Middle East preparing to join the international coalition to disrupt and degrade ISIL at the request of the Iraqi government.

I congratulate you, Mr President, for the leadership you've shown in assembling a broad coalition. The participation of Middle Eastern countries in this week's strike on ISIL in Syria is the clearest possible demonstration that the West can't solve this problem alone – and won't have to.

Our goal is not to change people, but to protect them; it's not to change governments, but to combat terrorism. Governments that don't commit genocide against their own people, nor permit terrorism against ours – that's all we seek.

But even in what seem to be darkening times, there are grounds for hope: the ISIL horror has generated all-but-universal revulsion. Muslim leaders from Prime Minister Najib of Malaysia, and President Yudhoyono of Indonesia, to the Grand Mufti of Australia, have declared that the ISIL movement is against God, against Islam and against our common humanity. Perhaps the realisation is now dawning for all peoples, all cultures and all faiths that it can never be right to kill in the name of God.

That would be a moral victory far surpassing any military success.

'My Government will never underestimate the threat'
AFP Headquarters, Canberra, 23 February 2015

Reminding our domestic security services – including the Australian Federal Police, ASIO and other agencies – that they are at the front line of the war against terrorism.

Today, I want to speak to you about keeping our country safe. I want to speak to you about the threat that we face; the work done already to keep you as safe as we humanly can; and the things still needed to prevent further terrorist attacks.

Today, my colleagues and I are joined by representatives of the Australian Federal Police, the Australian Defence Force, ASIO and agencies like Crimtrac – which helps police and other law enforcement bodies share information. The men and women in this room are on the frontline of Australia's fight against terror.

There is no greater responsibility – on me, on the government – than keeping you safe. This is the responsibility that's discharged by the men and women in this room.

We know that these are testing times for everyone here – and for everyone sworn to protect democratic freedoms. The terrorist threat is rising at home and abroad – and it's becoming harder to combat.

We have seen on our TV screens and in our newspapers the evidence of the new dark age that has settled over much of Syria and Iraq. We have seen the beheadings, the mass executions, the crucifixions and the sexual slavery in the name of religion. There is no grievance here that can be addressed; there is no cause here that can be satisfied; it is the demand to submit - or die.

We have seen our fellow Australians – people born and bred to live and let live – succumb to the lure of this death cult. We have heard the exhortations of their so-called caliphate to kill all or any of the unbelievers and we know that this message of the most primitive savagery is being spread through the most sophisticated technology.

By any measure, the threat to Australia is worsening. The number of foreign fighters is up. The number of known sympathisers and supporters of extremism is up. The number of potential home grown terrorists is rising. The number of serious investigations continues to increase.

During 2014, the Government consulted with our experts – many of whom are in this room today; we talked with our allies; and we worked with the Opposition, to improve Australia's preparedness for any eventuality.

Last September, the National Terrorist Threat level was lifted to High, which means a terrorist attack is likely. Critics said we were exaggerating. But since then, we have witnessed the frenzied attack on two police officers in Melbourne and the horror of the Martin Place siege.

Twenty people have been arrested and charged as a result of six counter terrorism operations conducted around Australia. That's one third of all the terrorism-related arrests since 2001 – within the space of just six months.

The judgment to lift the Threat Level was correct. In proclaiming a caliphate, the Islam-ist death-cult has declared war on the world. Not only has Australia suffered at the hands of terrorists – but so have Canada, France, Denmark, Iraq, Egypt, Libya, Nigeria, Japan, Jordan, the United Kingdom and the United States.

We have seen the tactics of terrorists evolve. In the decade after 9/11, our agencies disrupted elaborate conspiracies to attack our electricity supplies, the Grand Final at the MCG and the Holsworthy Army Barracks in Sydney. Now, in addition to the larger scale, more complex plots that typified the post 9/11 world, such as the atrocities in Bali and London, sick individuals are acting on the caliphate's instruction to seize people at random and kill them.

Today's terrorism requires little more than a camera-phone, a knife and a victim. These lone actor attacks are not new, but they pose a unique set of problems. All too often, alienated and unhappy people brood quietly. Feeling persecuted and looking for meaning, they self-radicalise online. Then they plan attacks which require little preparation, training or capability. The short lead time from the moment they decide they are going to strike, and then actually undertake the attack, makes it hard to disrupt their activities.

Police do not have the luxury to wait and watch. They apply their best judgement – and they do so, fully aware that armchair critics, will find fault. Still, police act because they have enough facts to make an informed judgement. Some of these raids may not result in prosecution. But frankly, I'd rather lose a case, than lose a life. The protection of life must always rank ahead of the prospects of a successful prosecution.

The arrest of two men in Sydney earlier this month, who'd already recorded a pre-attack message, is just one example of how quickly a threat can develop. I should add that without our Foreign Fighters legislation, it is highly unlikely that these arrests could have been made.

This new terrorist environment is uniquely shaped by the way that extremist ideologies can now spread online. Every single day, the Islam-ist death cult and its supporters churn out up to 100,000 social media messages in a variety of languages. Often, they are slick and well produced. That's the contagion that's infecting people, grooming them for terrorism.

Already at least 110 Australians have travelled overseas to join the death cult in Iraq and Syria. At least 20 of them, so far, are dead. Even if the flow of foreign fighters to Syria and Iraq stopped today, there's an Australian cohort of hardened jihadists who are intent on radicalising and influencing others.

The number of Australians with hands-on terrorist experience is now several times larger than those who trained earlier in Afghanistan and Pakistan. Of that group, two-thirds became involved in terrorist activity back here in Australia.

The signs are ominous. ASIO currently has over 400 high-priority counter-terrorism investigations. That's more than double the number a year ago. We are not alone in facing such challenges. The same phenomenon is evident across Europe, in the United States and in South East Asia.

Many of those involved in anti-Western attacks in Indonesia over the last decade are now being released from prison—some neither reformed nor rehabilitated. Australian and Indonesian agencies will continue to work closely together to tackle extremists – because it is in both our interests to do so.

In Australia and elsewhere, the threat of terrorism has become a terrible fact of life that government must do all in its power to counter. So far, this is what we have done.

Within weeks of taking office, I asked the Attorney-General to develop a government response to foreign fighters.

Last August, the Government invested $630 million in a range of new counter-terrorism measures. This funding gives our security agencies the resources they asked for to combat home-grown terrorism and to help prevent Australians participating in terrorism overseas.

The effect of these new measures has already been felt.

- Counter-Terrorism teams now operate at all eight major international airports
- Sixty-two additional biometric screening gates are being fast tracked for passengers at airports to detect and deal with people leaving on false passports
- Forty-nine extra AFP members are working in Sydney, Melbourne and Canberra on the foreign fighter threat
- Seven new financial analysts have been engaged to help crack down on terrorist financing
- A new "violent jihadist network mapping unit" in ASIO has been created to improve intelligence agencies' understanding of the threat facing Australia
- A Foreign Fighters Task Force has been established in the Australian Crime Commission with access to the commission's coercive powers
- Last Thursday, the Attorney-General announced a series of measures designed to combat terrorist propaganda online
- We have legislated to cancel the welfare payments of individuals assessed to be a threat to security.

This is not window dressing – as of last September, 55 of the 57 Australian extremists then fighting with terrorist groups in Syria and Iraq had been on welfare. We have made it easier to ban terrorist organisations which promote and encourage terrorist acts. We have strengthened the offences of training with, recruiting for and funding terrorist organisations. We have made it easier to prosecute foreign fighters by making it illegal to travel to a declared area overseas. Last December, we proscribed travel to Syria's Al Raqqa province – where the death cult is based – without a legitimate purpose. We are now looking at listing Mosul district in Ninawa Province, in Iraq, which the death cult also controls. And we have given ASIO the further power to request an Australian passport be suspended, pending further security assessment - that's happened eight times so far.

This year, we will consider what further legislation is needed to combat terrorism and keep Australians safe. But we cannot do it alone. The Government is working with local communities to counter violent extremism. I acknowledge the readiness of parents, siblings and community leaders to let the police know about people they think are falling under the death cult's spell. Our law enforcement agencies could not operate without their help. I acknowledge the cooperation the Commonwealth enjoys with all States and Territories on counter-terrorism issues.

That cooperation was highlighted by the Martin Place siege. Yesterday, Premier Mike Baird and I released the Martin Place Siege Joint Commonwealth - New South Wales Review. What we learnt from that Review was that there were no major failings of intelligence or process in the lead up to Martin Place. Everyone did their job as required by law. But now, there's more to do.

It's clear that in too many instances the threshold for action was set too high – and the only beneficiary of that was the Martin Place murderer himself. For too long, we have given those who might be a threat to our country the benefit of the doubt. The perpetrator was given the benefit of the doubt when he applied for a visa. He was given the benefit of the doubt for residency and citizenship. He was given the benefit of the doubt at Centrelink. He was given the benefit of the doubt when he applied for legal aid. And in the courts, there has been bail, when there should have been jail.

This report marks a line in the sand.

There is always a trade-off between the rights of an individual and the safety of the community. We will never sacrifice our freedoms in order to defend them – but we will not let our enemies exploit our decency either. If Immigration and Border Protection faces a choice to let-in or keep out people with security questions over them – we should choose to keep them out. If there is a choice between latitude for suspects or more powers to police and security agencies – more often, we should choose to support our agencies. And if we can stop hate-preachers from grooming gullible young people for terrorism, we should.

We have already made a start on removing the benefit of the doubt for people who are taking advantage of us. We've introduced legislation to refuse a protection visa to people who destroy evidence of their identity.

And the same applies if you present a bogus document. This Bill is currently stalled in the Senate. It's reasonable. It's in our country's interest. And I call on all senators to support it.

The Government's Data Retention Bill – currently being reviewed by the Parliament – is the vital next step in giving our agencies the tools they need to keep Australia safe. Access to metadata is the common element to most successful counter-terrorism investigations. It's essential in fighting most major crimes, including the most abhorrent of all – crimes against children. Again, I call on Parliament to support this important legislation.

We need to give our agencies these powers to protect our community. Today, I am releasing the Counter Terrorism review that the Government commissioned last August. The Review finds that we face a new, long-term era of heightened terrorism threat, with a much more significant 'home grown' element.

While the Review did not recommend major structural changes, it did recommend strengthening our counter-terrorism strategy and improving our cooperation with at-risk communities. The government will carefully consider the findings and act as quickly as possible.

In fact, some recommendations have already been acted upon. We will ensure returning foreign fighters are prosecuted or closely monitored using strengthened control orders. We will appoint a National Counter Terrorism Coordinator.

We want to bring the same drive, focus and results to our counter terrorism efforts that worked so well in Operation Sovereign Borders and Operation Bring Them Home.

Over recent months, I spent many hours listening to Australians from all walks of life. learly, people are anxious about the national security threats we face. Many are angry because all too often the threat comes from someone who has enjoyed the hospitality and generosity of the Australian people. When it comes to someone like the Martin Place murderer, people feel like we have been taken for mugs.

Australian citizenship is an extraordinary privilege that should involve a solemn and lifelong commitment to Australia. People who come to this country are free to live as they choose – provided they don't steal that same freedom from others.

We are one of the most diverse nations on earth – and celebrating that is at the heart of what it means to be Australian. We are a country built on immigration and are much the richer for it. Always, Australia will continue to welcome people who want to make this country their home. We will help them and support them to settle in. But this is not a one-way street. Those who come here must be as open and accepting of their adopted country, as we are of them. Those who live here must be as tolerant of others as we are of them. No one should live in our country while denying our values and rejecting the very idea of a free and open society.

It's worth recalling the citizenship pledge that all of us have been encouraged to recite: *I pledge my commitment to Australia and its people; whose democratic beliefs I share; whose rights and liberties I respect; and whose laws I will uphold and obey.* This has to mean something. Especially now that we face a home-grown threat from people who do reject our values.

Today, I am announcing that the Government will look at new measures to strengthen immigration laws, as well as new options for dealing with Australian citizens who are involved in terrorism. We cannot allow bad people to use our good nature against us. The Government will develop amendments to the Australian Citizenship Act so that we can revoke or suspend Australian citizenship in the case of dual nationals. It has long been the case that people who fight against Australia forfeit their citizenship.

Australians who take up arms with terrorist groups, especially while Australian military personnel are engaged in Afghanistan and Iraq, have sided against their country and should be treated accordingly.

For Australian nationals, we are examining suspending some of the privileges of citizenship for individuals involved in terrorism. Those could include restricting the ability to leave or return to Australia, and access to consular services overseas, as well as access to welfare payments.

We will also clamp down on those organisations that incite religious or racial hatred. No-one should make excuses for Islam-ist fanatics in the Middle East or their imitators here in Australia. For a long time, successive governments have been concerned about organisations that breed hatred, and sometimes incite violence. Organisations and individuals blatantly spreading discord and division – such as Hizb ut-Tahrir – should not do so with impunity.

Today, I can confirm that the Government will be taking action against hate preachers. This includes enforcing our strengthened terrorism advocacy laws. It includes new programmes to challenge terrorist propaganda and to provide alternative online material based on Australian values. And it will include stronger prohibitions on vilifying, intimidating or inciting hatred. These changes should empower community members to directly challenge terrorist propaganda.

I've often heard Western leaders describe Islam as a "religion of peace". I wish more Muslim leaders would say that more often, and mean it. I have often cited Prime Minister Najib of Malaysia, who has described the Islamist death cult as "against God, against Islam and against our common humanity". In January, President al Sisi told the imams at Egypt's al Azhar university that Islam needed a 'religious revolution' to sweep away centuries of false thinking. Everybody, including Muslim community leaders, needs to speak up clearly because, no matter what the grievance, violence against innocents must surely be a blasphemy against all religion.

I can't promise that terrorist atrocities won't ever again take place on Australian soil. But let me give you this assurance: My Government will never underestimate the threat. We will make the difficult decisions that must be taken to keep you and your family safe. We have the best national security agencies and the best police forces in the world. Our agencies are working together. All levels of government are working together. We are doing our duty.

That is what you have a right to expect – and to demand of me and of us.

Australians killed in the downing of MH17
House of Representatives, Canberra, 18 July 2014

On 17 July 2014, a scheduled commercial flight from Amsterdam to Kuala Lumpur, Malaysia Airlines Flight 17 (MH17) is shot down by a Buk ground-to-air missile whilst flying over the eastern region of Ukraine. Prime Minister Abbott informs Parliament, "the perpetrators must be brought to justice".

I claim the indulgence of the Parliament to make a statement about some very significant events that have happened overnight.

This is a grim day for our country and it's a grim day for our world. Malaysia Airlines MH17 has been shot down over the Eastern Ukraine it seems by Russian backed rebels. 298 people have been killed. At least 27 Australians have been killed. Our hearts go out to the families of all the dead. Our thoughts and prayers especially are with the families of the Australian dead. We can't restore them to life but we can and will do everything to support them in this sad and bitter time because that is the Australian way – we help in times of trouble.

A Department of Foreign Affairs team is preparing to leave for Kiev. Next of kin and families will be notified as soon as possible. They'll be offered counselling and assistance and bodies will be repatriated to Australia as quickly as possible.

We owe it as well to the families of the dead to find out exactly what has happened and exactly who is responsible. As things stand, this looks less like an accident than a crime. I want to repeat this: as things stand, this looks less like an accident than a crime. If so, the perpetrators must be brought to justice.

So I can inform the House that as quickly as possible Australia will be working at the United Nations Security Council for a binding resolution calling for a full and impartial investigation with full access to the site, with full access to the debris, with full access to the black box and with full access to all individuals who might be in a position to shed light on this terrible event.

I can also inform the House that the Minister for Foreign Affairs will shortly summons the Russian Ambassador to seek a categoric assurance from the Ambassador that the Russian government will fully cooperate in this investigation.

Madam Speaker, we owe it to the dead and their families, we owe it to the peace and stability of the wider world to establish the facts and we will do all we humanly can to bring that about.

Let me conclude with this: the bullying of small countries by big ones, the trampling of justice and decency in the pursuit of national aggrandisement and reckless indifference to human life should have no place in our world.

'Russia needs to reflect on this'

Opinion piece for News Corporation Publications, 20 July 2014

The Prime Minister offers both emotional and practical support to the grieving families of victims in the MH17 atrocity, and promises justice.

The downing of MH17 is not an accident, it's a crime. There were 298 men, women and children on this aircraft - and their deaths offend our sense of justice.

We grieve for all, but particularly for the 28 Australians who have lost their lives. Many others were travelling to Australia on MH17, including AIDS researchers and health workers who work every day for a better world. Our hearts go out to all their families

We know that Flight MH17 was shot down. It was shot down over Russian-backed rebel territory, likely by Russian-backed rebels, quite possibly with a Russian-supplied weapon. That's why it's so important that Russia now fully cooperate with an immediate investigation to identify precisely what happened.

Australia has been responding on a range of fronts. On Friday, the Department of Foreign Affairs 24 hour Consular Emergency Centre took over 900 calls from people concerned about the fate of family members or loved ones.

A consular officer has been assigned to the family of each Australian victim. These officials will help them through the difficult time ahead. They are being offered counselling and assistance.

The Government has also deployed a team of officials and investigators to the Ukraine. It won't be easy work, as it's not an easy part of the world. We will do our best to ensure that the task of repatriating those who were lost will occur as quickly as possible.

In the meantime, though, along with our partners at the UN Security Council, we have demanded unimpeded access to the crash site so that bodies can be treated with respect and an impartial investigation can begin uninterrupted by hostile force.

Foreign Minister Julie Bishop is on her way to New York as part of our efforts to ensure a binding resolution of the UN Security Council requiring a thorough international investigation. The investigation must have full access to the site, to the debris, to the black box recorder and to any persons who may be able to assist with that investigation.

Australia expects to play a leading role in that investigation. Our 28 dead deserve to be represented. There is ample precedent for this in previous investigations of incidents involving airlines

This is not an accident scene, it's a crime scene. The investigation must not be interfered with. Any interference is designed to hide the truth and protect the guilty. On this, there can be no negotiation.

The victims of the MH17 were from around the world. They include citizens from Malaysia, Indonesia, the United Kingdom, Germany, Belgium, the Philippines and Canada, as well as Australia. Holland has borne the heaviest loss with 154 dead. I have spoken with Dutch Prime Minister Rutte and conveyed our shared sadness.

There is extensive diplomatic work underway. Foreign Minister Julie Bishop and I have been speaking with our counterparts from around the world including US President Obama, UK Prime Minister Cameron, Ukraine President Poroshenko and Malaysian Prime Minister Najib. This has been a terrible year for Malaysia.

The world knows there are problems in Ukraine but we also know who is stirring them up. The argument from Russia that none of this has anything to do with them because it happened in Ukrainian airspace does not withstand serious scrutiny. In any event, MH17 was a civilian plane carrying 298 people who were not part of any dispute and who were innocently going about their lives.

Russia needs to reflect on this lest its whole standing in the world be put at risk. There can be no excuses. No buck-passing. No blame shifting. There has to be absolute full cooperation with an impartial international inquiry.

Our country is united in grief and in its determination to ensure that justice is done. I appreciate the support of the Leader of the Opposition. Flags have been lowered. Today, the Governor-General and I will attend a church service along with Mr Shorten as we stand together as a nation. Later, there will be a National Commemorative Service for those lost and for those they have left behind.

Our grief is matched by a determination to provide support and comfort. The nation's thoughts and prayers are with the families who have lost loved ones. We don't just grieve for them, though. Australia will do all we can to ensure that the perpetrators are identified and brought to justice.

Injecting decency into the vilest of situations
St Patrick's Cathedral, Melbourne, 7 August 2014

In the wake of the MH17 tragedy, Prime Minister Abbott declares a national day of mourning, and tells a memorial service in Melbourne, "may the God of mercy comfort those left behind and may the God of justice answer all our prayers."

It is an honour to be here in this cathedral dedicated to God and to the better angels of our natures, with the religious and civic leaders of our country, in sorrow and in solidarity with the families of the victims of MH17 on this National Day of Mourning.

Three weeks ago tomorrow, the families of 38 Australians woke up to the very worst news imaginable. Their plane had been shot out of the sky and 298 innocent people murdered, including 38 men, women and children who called Australia home.

Children had lost parents, parents had lost children and an aching void had opened in hundreds of lives made worse by the wanton cruelty of shooting down a passenger jet.

There will be a time to judge the guilty, but today we honour the dead and we grieve with the living. We cannot bring them back, but we will bring them home, as far as we humanly can.

We do rededicate ourselves today to supporting the bereaved, to obtaining justice for the dead and for their families and to working for a better world. Today the Australian nation expresses its gratitude for the lives so cruelly cut short and we express our solidarity with those who love them.

The dead of flight MH17 reflect what's best in modern Australia: doctors who work with refugees, teachers who work with indigenous people and children with disabilities, volunteers in our armed forces and with local charities, business innovators and pillars of local communities, young people filled with passion for the life before them.

What could be more typical of modern Australia than a Malaysian married to a Dutchman, raising their children in outer-metropolitan Melbourne? And what predicament could be more heart-rending than that of a family now bereft of the children that are every parents' greatest joy?

When those we love are snatched away, nothing can ease the pain. Somehow we who have not been bereaved must reach out to those who have and show, by our love, that love has not abandoned them. You have not been abandoned and you never will be.

As the news of this atrocity broke right around our country, friends and family began calling and visiting those whose world had been shattered. Within a couple of hours, consular officials were making contact with families to let them know that their country was with them in their darkest moments.

Within 24 hours, hundreds of personnel had been mobilised in Canberra and hundreds more were being mobilised to go abroad to bring home our dead with respect and with dignity.

Hundreds of unarmed Australian police and military have been working around the clock to recover remains and belongings from a war zone.

Because this is what Australians do in times of trouble. We reach out to people and do what we can to help. We try to create order in the midst of chaos and we try to inject decency into the vilest of situations.

We cannot fill the void in people's hearts. We cannot dull the ache of loss. We cannot resolve the mystery of needless suffering and death but we can armour ourselves against despair by responding to evil with good – unconquerable good. As the Maslin family have so beautifully put it – love conquers hate.

So I salute all those who have rallied to their fellow Australians and to all the other victims of MH17 and I especially acknowledge Air Chief Marshal Angus Houston, our envoy in Ukraine.

Mostly though, I pay tribute to all those who have lost loved ones. Some of you I have spoken with. Your decency, resilience and compassion have been both humbling and uplifting. One of you even asked me how I was bearing up because in the depths of your own pain, you were still thinking of others.

Long ago it was written "there is a time to die, a time to weep and a time to mourn", there is also a time to mend, a time to love, a time for peace and a time to keep.

In time, our thoughts will linger not on how the passengers of flight MH17 died, but on how they lived. We will remember them as they were - joyful, open, kind and optimistic. A home-sick poet, Dorothea

Mackellar, once wrote: "wherever I may die, I know to what brown country my homing thoughts will fly".

May those who are lost arrive home to the people and the country they loved. May the God of mercy comfort those left behind and may the God of justice answer all our prayers.

'One of the great mysteries of our time'

House of Representatives, Canberra, 5 March 2015

On 8 March 2014, a Malaysia Airlines flight travelling from Kuala Lumpur to Beijing Capital International Airport in China mysteriously disappears over the South China Sea, never to be seen again. Its 227 passengers, including six Australians, and 12 crew are presumed dead. To mark the first anniversary of the flight's disappearance, the Prime Minister convenes a special sitting of Parliament to which the families of the deceased Australians are invited, and pays tribute to the search and rescue mission, despite its lack of success.

For the world, the loss of Malaysia Airlines flight MH370 is one of the great mysteries of our time.

For the families and the loved ones of those on that flight, it is a harrowing nightmare. Seven who called Australia home were on board flight MH370. Rodney and Mary Burrows, Catherine and Robert Lawton, Yuan Li and Naijun Gu, and Paul Weeks were mums and dads, spouses and partners, brothers and sisters, sons and daughters, mates and best friends; all irreplaceable to their families, friends, workplaces and communities.

Every family has a story of loss. We are honoured today to be joined by the Burrows, Lawton and Weeks families. Thank you for joining us. We know these anniversaries are painful beyond words. The message of this Parliament to all of the families of MH370 is that you remain in our thoughts and prayers.

To you – and to all those with loved ones aboard that flight – my pledge is that we are taking every reasonable step to bring your uncertainty to an end. It has been the biggest search operation of its kind in history and it's been an extraordinary example of international cooperation.

In the first few weeks, 28 search aircraft from Australia, New Zealand, China, Japan, Malaysia, South Korea and the United States completed 345 sorties into the southern Indian Ocean. Ships from Australia, China, Malaysia, the United Kingdom and the United States also joined the search.

As the search from the air and on the surface reached its conclusion, Australia began the largest underwater search ever carried out, in an area that had never been mapped before. To add to the difficulty, the search zone is in the 'Roaring Forties', one of the world's roughest stretches of ocean.

Despite these difficulties, over 26,800 square kilometres of the mapped ocean floor have been searched in detail, which is about 40 per cent of the priority search area.

With sadness, I have to admit to the House that, so far, we have not found any trace of MH370. But I do reassure the families of our hope and expectation that the ongoing search will succeed. I can't promise that the search will go on at this intensity forever, but we will continue our very best efforts to resolve this mystery and provide some answers.

It is right on this anniversary that Australia thanks Malaysia and China for their co-operation and friendship in this sad and difficult task.

I acknowledge the presence in the Gallery today of the High Commissioner for Malaysia and the Ambassador of the People's Republic of China and representatives of the other countries who lost their citizens on MH370. We grieve with you for the loss of your people and we thank you for the compassion you have shown to us on the loss of our people.

All of the men and women who have striven – from the sky and on the ocean – to unravel the fate of MH370 deserve our deepest thanks. The members of the Joint Agency Coordination Centre have supported the families of those aboard MH370. In word and in deed, they have demonstrated the best traditions of public service.

I acknowledge the leadership of Air Chief Marshal Sir Angus Houston, one of our nation's great servants. The Australian Transport Safety Bureau is tirelessly going about its work. We have four vessels working in the search area now. We are using cutting edge technology and world experts in underwater search operations.

Finally, on this anniversary, it is right to say that the loss of MH370 demonstrated a fundamental gap in tracking long haul flights, particularly over the oceans. This is not the first major aircraft to go missing and, tragically, it may not be the last.

In this day and age it seems inexplicable that the technology and systems were not in place to provide us with the exact position of this plane at all times. The grief of the families has been compounded by this failure.

Last weekend, the Deputy Prime Minister announced that Australia, Malaysia and Indonesia will conduct a trial to track more closely aircraft over the oceans. I thank our friends in Malaysia and Indonesia for their commitment to this essential project. While it is not a complete answer, it will deliver immediate improvements in the way we track aircraft while more comprehensive solutions are developed and implemented.

We must ensure that no families will ever again have to endure the suffering of the families of the MH370 passengers.

On this first anniversary, we remain hopeful that we will solve this baffling mystery and bring the peace of knowing to the families and friends of all aboard Malaysia Airlines Flight MH370.

10
FAITH

'We pray for all people striving for rights and respect'

Ecumenical Church Service
Melbourne, 11 December 2014

Ukrainian President Petro Poroshenko spends two days in Australia to discuss the downing of flight MH17, supposedly by Russians, over Ukraine. He attends a prayer vigil at the Ukrainian Greek Eparchy of Saints Peter and Paul, in Melbourne, at which Prime Minister Abbott articulates the solace of faith.

President Petro Poroshenko, my friend, thank you for that splendid address. A little bit of it was translated to me and all I can say in response is that shirtfront must have translated well!

In the summer of 1982, I was walking the streets of Kiev. I heard music coming from a church, not unlike this. I went inside and was utterly spellbound by the singing. It was truly the voice of men and angels and it is such a pleasure to hear it again here today. I thought to myself then that it may be only people who suffer for their faith that truly know what faith is.

Stalin used to boast that religion would die out in the Soviet Union because Russia would one day run out of grannies. Well, Russia never did, no country ever has and each generation in turn has found its faith because faith arouses something deep in the human heart.

I'm reminded of the story of the funeral of the Russian dictator, Leonid Brezhnev. He had devoted his life to an ideology that stamped out all opposition, persecuted those of faith and sought to impose the will of large countries on small ones.

But at his funeral, after the last regiment had marched past and the last state anthem had been sung and as the open coffin was about to be closed, his widow leaned over and made the sign of the cross on her husband's chest.

The survival of faith, the flourishing of faith and the survival and the flourishing of the nations that are sustained by it is a timeless story. Here, in this splendid church, I should acknowledge the part that faith has played in our culture and public life; indeed, in the culture and public life of civilised countries.

Our democracy is inspired by the gospel insight that every human being is born with equal rights and dignity in the eyes of God. Our justice is inspired by the gospel insight that each of us should treat others as we would have them treat us.

Today, we pray for the victims of the MH17 atrocity. We pray for all 298 of them. We particularly pray for the 38 Australians who are amongst them. We pray for their families in their time of grief and loss.

We acknowledge the Ukrainian people who did so much for them in that terrible time and who continue to work with Australians, Dutch and Malaysians to ensure that the perpetrators of that atrocity are brought to justice.

I particularly acknowledge today the President of Ukraine, Petro Poroshenko. Israel aside, there would hardly be a country on earth so subject to existential threat as Ukraine is. If the freedom of one country is diminished, the freedom of all is diminished.

I have come to know Petro Poroshenko quite well over the last few months and I want to say that not just Ukraine, but freedom has a great champion in Ukraine's President.

Today, in this cathedral, we pray for all countries and all peoples striving for peace with freedom. We pray for all people striving for rights and respect. We pray for them all and we ask that the good Lord, the living God, will give them strength and success.

'This is a universal code of conduct'
Wollongong, NSW, 1 March 2015

Before an audience of dignitaries of the Buddhist community, Prime Minister Abbott addresses the official opening of the Nan Tien Institute, which offers courses in the arts, health, mindfulness and wellbeing. Although not a Buddhist himself, Prime Minister Abbott says the institute is based on the universal values of decency, generosity, understanding, integrity and moral rectitude, and has much to offer Australia.

My understanding is that Nan Tien means "paradise of the south" – I have waited a long time to get to paradise and it is a real pleasure to finally arrive.

Many years ago in the 1960s, our then Prime Minister Sir Robert Menzies made a marvellous statement, long before we spoke of multiculturalism, of what it meant to be here in Australia. He said, back then, "what we need in Australia is that every person who comes into the Australian community should retain his quality but should add it to the qualities of all the other people in the community, so that finally we get a community of high ideals, and of clear faith, and of generosity and understanding."

That, if I may say so is what this Nan Tien Institute is all about: a community of high ideals, of generosity, and of understanding. This, today, is a very Australian gathering. It is the quintessence of modern Australia: people coming from the four corners of the earth to form one people whose democratic beliefs we share, whose rights and liberties we respect, and whose laws we uphold and obey.

I am not a Buddhist, but all men and women of goodwill are fellow travellers of one another in this journey here on earth.

On the way down, I was reminding myself of the five precepts of Buddhism: don't kill, don't steal, avoid dishonourable conduct, don't lie, and don't over-indulge. I have sometimes failed in at least some of these respects! But this is a universal code of conduct. These are the universal decencies of mankind, expressed in the Buddhist scriptures.

I went on to read of the eight-fold path which incorporates: right knowledge, right attitude, right speech, right action, right livelihood, right effort, right mindfulness, and right meditation. What noble aspirations these are.

Not a single one of us – regardless of our religion or culture – could not try to move closer to these magnificent ideals.

So, on an occasion such as this it is easy to appreciate the essential oneness of humanity and the journey to being our best selves upon which we are all embarked.

The challenge of faith in a difficult world
Old Parliament House, Canberra, 17 June 2015

The Australian Catholic University hosts its first Parliamentary Interfaith Prayer Breakfast in Canberra, attended by Christians, Jews, Muslims, Hindus, Buddhists, Sikhs and Baha'i. Keynote speaker Stepan Kerkyasharian AO, Prime Minister Tony Abbott and Opposition Leader Bill Shorten deliver speeches. Prime Minister Abbott says faith is the "engine of moral progress".

Never have I entered a gathering to the kind of reverential silence that greeted me as I walked in just a few moments ago. I apologise for coming in while you were concluding your prayers.

We have a tradition in the Parliament of a parliamentary Christian prayer breakfast but this is a new and encouraging development. We are broadening out the traditional Christian prayer breakfast to people of all faiths because faith matters and these days it is important – more important than ever – that we have faith.

This is an interesting day in the parliamentary year. We have the Interfaith Parliamentary Prayer Breakfast this morning and we have the Press Gallery ball this evening. We have breakfast with those who are trying to build us up and we have dinner with those who are trying to drag us down!

I have been both a trainee priest and a journalist – no prizes for guessing which gathering I would rather be in!

There's a story about Cardinal Gilroy. One day he was in the archiepiscopal Bentley being driven around his various duties and, as English cars do, the Bentley broke down. The curate chauffeur was fiddling around under the bonnet, failing to get the car going. Eventually, Cardinal Gilroy piped up from the back seat, "What about saying a Hail Mary?" So, the dutiful curate says a Hail Mary, pokes around at the spark plugs and the carburettor, tries the car and it goes.

"Well I'll be buggered!" says the Cardinal from the back seat.

And this, if I may say so, is the great challenge that we all face – the challenge of faith in a difficult world.

Years ago, when I was at the seminary, there was a popular prayer card called 'Footsteps' and on the front of the card there was a photograph of footprints in the sand across a beach and on the back of the card was a dialogue between God and a penitent. God says to the penitent, "At every step of your journey, I have been with you." And the penitent says, "But Father, I look at the footprints on the sand and at times there is only one set", and God says to the penitent, "That, my child, was when I carried you on my back." The challenge for all of us is to believe this.

Now, in the 18 months or so that I have been your Prime Minister, it's been my privilege and my pain to have to speak to people in some of the most difficult circumstances anyone can imagine – parents who have lost children; children who have lost parents; people dealing with the tragedy of life; people about to go into circumstances where they could lose their live. In the end, all you can say to people in those circumstances is that there is some meaning to all of this. There is some purpose when bad things happen to good people.

Faith is all we have in the most difficult circumstances of life – if not necessarily faith in God, faith in others, faith in values. We need that if we are to survive and even occasionally to flourish in all the vicissitudes of life.

So, I have two tasks this morning. First of all, to thank all of you, leaders of our various faith communities, for what you do to maintain people's faith, even in the most difficult circumstances.

Second, to acknowledge the difference that faith makes to our culture and our civilisation.

Our civilisation, our culture, our country would not be what it is but for the influence of faith.

There is that marvellous phrase in the Gospels, 'To love your neighbour as you love yourself'. This phrase which all of us, regardless of our own faith or lack of faith, can repeat because it's been drilled into us from our nursery times – this concept that exists one way or another in all faiths, is the engine of all moral progress.

Faith doesn't make us good, but by God, it makes us better.

We are so much better than we would otherwise be thanks to the faith that reminds us that there is something more than us, something more than the here and now to which we must aspire; that there is a judge over us who is even greater than those who are sitting in judgement over us today.

I recall, the marvellous passage of Betjeman which I learnt all those years ago in the seminary, and I'll try to remember it now: 'What is faith? Not at all for me the certainty of St Paul; no blinding light; a fitful glow is all the light of faith I know which sometimes goes completely out and leaves me struggling round in doubt until I will myself to go and worship in God's house below, my parish church, and even there I find confusion everywhere.'

I have hundreds of letters in the course of a year from people of faith who are saying to me, 'we are praying for you, we want you to do well'. They often say to me, 'we want you to do better', and yes, I want to do better too. I'm sure all my colleagues on all sides of the Parliament get similar letters.

Thank you for those letters. Thank you for what you do to keep us strong.

'You are the beneficiaries of a mighty effort'
Manly, NSW, 7 August 2015

The Prime Minister tells students at St Paul's Catholic College, a high school in Manly, in his electorate, that Catholic schools are a monument to the faith and enterprise of parents and contribute enormously to the character of Australia's young.

I was reflecting a little on the history of Catholic education on the drive up here today. Way back in the 1870s, the then Premier, Sir Henry Parkes, said that education henceforth should be free, compulsory and secular.

And the Catholic bishops and priests of those days quite understandably thought that they wanted their people to be educated not just in reading, writing and arithmetic and the sciences and the high culture of our civilisation; they wanted our young people – their young people – to be educated in the faith as well.

So from the 1880s, a massive effort – a truly massive effort – a mobilisation of money and manpower on a scale today almost unimaginable was put in place by the Catholic Church here in New South Wales and subsequently right around Australia.

The extraordinary edifice of Catholic Education today with almost 2,000 schools around our country, almost a million students around our country is a result of that mighty effort by our forefathers – an extraordinary mobilisation of manpower and money all designed to ensure that young Catholics – young Christians – did not just get the best possible education but were educated in the light of Christian faith.

You are the beneficiaries of that effort.

Despite government funding - that began under Sir Robert Menzies back in 1963 - to come to a school such as this requires a sacrifice. Your parents have made the sacrifice to send you, the students of St Paul's Catholic College, to this school and I hope you feel particularly valued because while all parents make a sacrifice, your parents have made an additional sacrifice Your parents have gone the extra mile so that you can enjoy not just the best possible education but an education in the faith as well.

In a different school, not too far away from here, I had a similar benefit 40-odd years ago. I am sure each one of you, looking back on your school days in a few years' time, will be able to say, "yes, it was special, yes, I got something from it, yes, it wasn't just an education – it was more than that."

I can certainly remember from my own school days; great teachers, great parents, great students and above all else this sense of mission, this sense of destiny which every school of this type imparts to its students. I have no doubt that you have absolutely outstanding teachers here today. Certainly, I had absolutely outstanding teachers in my day at a school such as this.

I remember one of my teachers saying to me, "pray as if everything depended upon God but then work as if everything depended upon you." When I told another Jesuit of this he said, "no that's not right – it is work as if everything depended upon you but then pray as if everything depended upon God." The Jesuits would argue about what comes first – praying or working. It's important to have both and I am sure that is what you have at this fine school.

So, you have good values, you have good teachers and soon you will have a structure, a building worthy of you and the sacrifices that your parents are making for you.

11

EDUCATION, SCIENCE AND HEALTH

Improving the links between science and business
Parliament House, Canberra, 29 October 2014

At an annual black-tie dinner and awards ceremony in the Great Hall of Parliament House, the Prime Minister's Prizes for Science are announced and awarded. The Prime Minister's Prizes for Science, presented at an annual black-tie event in the Great Hall, are a prestigious recognition for achievements in scientific research, innovation teaching. The Prime Minister tells the attendees that Australia punches above its weight in published scientific research but needs to improve the translation of that into practical outcomes.

It was said of Alexander the Great, when he saw the breadth of his dominion, that he wept for there were no more worlds to conquer. Perhaps this is why Winston Churchill said "the empires of the future are the empires of the mind". Because that deep yearning to explore, to discover and to advance is part of the human condition – and now so much of it one way or another has to be intellectual.

The scientists in this room are the great explorers of our day. From Professor Brian Schmidt unlocking the universe, to the workers at Cochlear providing hearing to the deaf, the scientists of our country are revealing the secrets of our world and doing the great works of our time.

Tonight, we honour Australia's scientists who through grit and determination are continuing to tell us what we previously didn't know and sometimes couldn't even imagine. And we wouldn't have great scientists without teachers to transfer their sense of curiosity and wonder to a new generation. Tonight, I especially honour the science and maths teachers who are with us.

I want to assure you that you have a fine advocate in Ian Macfarlane – the Minister responsible for science. He is the son of a scientist. He is the grandson of a scientist. He is one of the most experienced members of Cabinet and he is the second longest Minister for Industry in the history of our country – over seven years so far. And it's good that you have as your Minister one of the steadiest and the most experienced people in the Cabinet.

Science is at the heart of this Government's Economic Action Strategy because you cannot separate science from the advancement of our country.

It is an essential part of modern economic policy – because the commercialisation of science and the encouragement of innovation is essential for jobs, for growth and for prosperity.

And two weeks ago, Ian Macfarlane and I released what we call our Industry Innovation and Competitiveness Agenda. This maps out a vision for science and its role in the future of our country. The overriding themes are: investment in science, technology, engineering and mathematics; entrepreneurship; and collaboration between business and science.

Now as I'm sure you know, in our first year, we have had to bring the Budget back under control. Living within your means always involves difficult decisions and it's rarely popular, but it is necessary if we want our prosperity to be sustainable. But even in a time of budget cutting, we have still made some important new investments as part of the $9.2 billion ongoing annual investment in science and research.

These new investments include $65 million to operate and maintain the CSIRO's new marine research vessel; and $35 million for the operation and maintenance of ANSTO's Opal nuclear reactor. We're promoting international science collaboration by extending the Australia-China Science and Research Fund and the Australia-India Strategic Research Fund. And we have set out to build one of the largest endowment funds in the world for medical research. This $20 billion Medical Research Future Fund will ensure that Australia continues to be a world champion of research and innovation.

And now that our best scientists and our greatest medical researchers are in this building, I hope you will wear out the carpet putting the case for this fund to my political colleagues in other parties because you can't have a fund without funding.

Now, across government, our focus has been on getting maximum benefit for taxpayer dollars. It's what you do in your life every day – you try to get maximum value from your research grants; you try to get maximum value for the funding that the university has given you.

We are seeking to prioritise national research to the challenges that face our nation. Because our ability to compete in global markets does depend on our ability to produce high-quality, innovative products and services. And these products usually require the ingenuity that's born of strong science.

As the Chief Scientist, Professor Ian Chubb put it: we have to do "all the things that we need to do well." That's what our competitors are doing – and so must we. So as part of the Competitiveness Agenda, the Government is providing $12 million more to foster school students' interest in STEM. There's the "Mathematics by inquiry" — maths-in-schools programs. There's computer coding courses. There's a local trial of the American Pathways in Technology Early College High School or P-TECH. And there's more summer schools for STEM students.

These are just some of the things we're doing and there is more to come – including changes to employee share ownership to encourage more start-up businesses so that good ideas can be commercialised here in Australia.

We are recognised globally for our high quality research. In 2013, with just 0.3 per cent of the world's population, this country of ours was responsible for over three per cent of the world's published research. Now, that only ranks us 9th in the OECD. So, we can do better. Especially, we must do better at translating research into practical outcomes.

We are determined as a Government to boost collaboration between science and business because Australia ranks just 29th out of 30 OECD countries on the proportion of businesses collaborating with higher education and public research institutions. And we rank just 23rd out of 32 countries on the percentage of total research publications that are co-authored by industry and the research sector.

We are determined to work with industry and researchers to get a better return on that $9.2 billion a year research investment. And to this end the new Commonwealth Science Council to advise the Government on ways to improve connections between research organisations, universities and businesses will comprise five scientists and five business representatives – including Professor Brian Schmidt, Professor Ian Frazer, Catherine Livingstone and Michael Chaney.

One of its first tasks will be to consider specific proposals raised by the Chief Scientist – for Government funding of science and research to be better targeted. Of course we value "blue sky" or pure research, we always have and we always will, but we still need to improve the links between science and business and to better commercialise our ideas.

Tonight is probably a good time to add something to the Prime Minister's Prizes for Science.

Ian Macfarlane and I have been considering the findings of a review. The review, led by our Nobel Laureate Brian Schmidt, found that too much was being asked of one prize. From next year, and alongside the Prime Minister's Prize for Science, there will also be a Prime Minister's Prize for the Commercial Application of Science. This prize will be awarded to an Australian or Australian team for "the most significant technological innovation that has led to the betterment of humanity". It will allow a broader range of achievements from industry, defence science, rural science and engineering to be honoured. Equal recognition should be given to those who discover and to those who innovate, because without innovation, scientific discovery may never be more than an interesting experiment.

I thank all of you in this room tonight – teachers, researchers and industry innovators. I thank you for your dedication to a better world and to a better Australia. On behalf of the Australian people, congratulations to all the nominees for this year's prizes.

'This is culture-shifting and life-changing'
Parliament House, Canberra, 27 October 2014

At the annual dinner of the Association of Australian Medical Research Institutes, the Prime Minister talks up the nation's world-beating achievements – such as the bionic ear, a cervical cancer vaccine and the first treatment for influenza – and announces a major new funding initiative, the $20 billion Medical Research Future Fund.

My duty – and it's a very happy duty – is to say congratulations to all of you on behalf of our nation and, if I may be presumptuous, to say on behalf of people everywhere thank you for everything that you do for our country and for our world.

We have less than one per cent of the world's population, but we're responsible for close to five per cent of refereed medical research. Eight of our fifteen Nobel Prize winners have been in the field of medical research. Four of the last ten Australians of the Year have been medical researchers and I'm delighted we've got two of them here tonight – Pat McGorry and Ian Frazer – and of course Simon McKeon is not a medical researcher himself, but he's had a lot to do with encouraging medical research. Howard Florey was probably the man who has saved more lives than any other person in history – an Australian medical researcher. Donald Metcalf, the father of modern haematology, is estimated to have saved some 20 million lives. Australians invented the bionic ear, the cervical cancer vaccine, the first treatment for influenza. So, wherever you look in the field of research, in the field of treatments and cures, Australians are there making a difference. May that always be the case.

I was looking before I came along this evening at some recent work which our medical research institutes have done. The Children's Cancer Institute in New South Wales has doubled the survival rate from 35 per cent to 70 per cent for high-risk acute lymphoblastic leukaemia.

The Victor Chang Cardiac Research Institute has recently developed a world first technique doubling the time a donor heart can exist outside the recipient.

The Hunter Medical Research Institute, has a new clot busting drug therapy for stroke victims which has demonstrated major neurological improvement within 24 hours for two thirds of patients and 72 per cent have experienced excellent or good recovery after three months.

The Baker Institute, a world first breakthrough in the treatment of high blood pressure – a paradigm shift in fact – using catheters. This new procedure has been approved for use in Europe and here in Australia and is now being practiced in more than 10 of our hospitals.

Every day, every week, every month, every year our researchers are making a difference. Thanks in large measure to medical research, someone born today can expect to live 25 years longer than his or her great-grandparents.

That's not just 25 years, that's good years – good, healthy years – that we can expect which our great-grandparents couldn't, largely because of the sustained work of medical researchers over the last hundred years or so.

Our life expectancy has gone from under 60 to over 80 in large measure because of the people in this room and your intellectual forebears over the last several decades.

As some of you might know, when I was the Health Minister some years ago I regarded myself as the Health Minister for medical research and now I'd like to regard myself as the Prime Minister for medical research.

Pre-election we promised that we would make it easier for medical researchers through streamlining and simplifying NHMRC grant applications. My Department tells me that all this has been done. I'm always a little cautious when my Department tells me that all this has been done; I'd like to confirm with you that all this has been done! But, I am told that the application forms are very considerably shorter and I'm told that the percentage of five year grants has gone up from about six per cent to at least 20 per cent. So, that sounds to me like proof positive that at least some of our ambitions to make you researchers rather than form fillers are actually coming true.

Of course, post-election in the Budget we announced a world first; a $20 billion Medical Research Future Fund that will more than double our annual spend on medical research.

This is precisely what the 23,000 or so medical researchers in our country need if they are to continue to do their world leading work.

Governments propose, in some respects parliaments dispose, and you can't have a Medical Research Future Fund without funding.

Yes, the funding mechanism is controversial; we are asking for a modest co-payment from people who are visiting their general practitioner. No one likes to pay more for anything, but it seems to me that if it's fair and reasonable for people to make a modest contribution when they get their PBS drugs – the drugs that so many of you have made such a contribution towards – why isn't it also fair and reasonable for this modest contribution when you visit the doctor, particularly when for quite a few years all of the proceeds are going to be invested in what will be a world changing fund that will help people's lives, not just here, but right around the world? This is history making, this is culture shifting, this is life changing.

So, my request to all of you in this room tonight: please don't leave tomorrow without knocking on the door of a crossbench Senator and saying, "For our country's sake – for our country's sake, have a look at this fund".

'A rock of common sense, trust and professionalism'
Canberra, 24 November 2014

The Prime Minister tells the Pharmacy Guild of Australia, which represents 5,700 businesses, that pharmacies are community health services that provide comfort and confidence to people in need.

I believe that community pharmacy is not just a business, it's a service. But it is not just any old service; it is a service which gives comfort and confidence to our people and to our communities. There's hardly a community worth the name anywhere in Australia that lacks a community pharmacy. And in every community where there is a community pharmacist, that pharmacist – that pharmacy – is a rock of reliability, common sense, dependability, trust and professionalism.

When I was the Health Minister for four years, I had lots of complaints about lots of different subjects, but not once can I ever remember anyone coming to me to complain about their community pharmacy. I had lots of people come up to me when I was the Health Minister and compliment me on the work of community pharmacists, and I was very happy to accept those compliments, I have to say!

I love community pharmacy because the pharmacist is always there, the pharmacist is always helpful and the pharmacist is always professional. You may say, well that's all very well and that's a minister in a government – in this case a Prime Minister of a government – saying that pharmacy is one of the pillars of our community.

Well, what am I going to do for you, you may well ask? I will tell you; I am not going to approach the problems of our country in a way which fails to respect the institutions that have made our country strong. I am not going to run around solving non-problems and I am not going to put theory ahead of practice. When I know that something works I will support it.

I won't support something which is untried and unproven against something which is. I never want to promote theory over practice.

As you know, up until 2007, government – it was Coalition government to be sure – but up until 2007, government was regularly delivering surpluses in the order of $20 billion a year.

We know that since then, governments – a Labor government until quite recently – was regularly delivering deficits in the order of $50 billion a year. So, times are different now to those of just a few years ago.

I cannot stand up and say to you that government will no longer be looking for savings – I can't say that to you in all honesty – but what I can say to you is that we want to work with you so that whatever we do in the end is helpful for pharmacy, is helpful for your customers and your communities, and we want to work with you to ensure that the great community pharmacists of our country are providing more services, not less services to the people of Australia, because you are consummate health professionals.

There are few people who are as much in touch with the people they serve as you are. And with government support, I am very confident that community pharmacy can do more for the people of Australia.

Yes, we want to deliver a good Budget outcome for the people of Australia, but we also want to deliver a good health outcome for the people of Australia and the best way of ensuring that we do both is to work constructively with the Guild.

How do you know that I want to work constructively with the Guild? Because that's what I've always done. How do you know that I'm a friend of community pharmacy? Because that' what I've always been. How do you know that I respect the place of the community pharmacy in our economy and in our society? Because the last time there was a serious push to threaten the place of community pharmacy in our society, I stood up against it.

So, my friends, as we go forward, all of us have to do the right thing by our country.

You do the right thing by our country by doing your job as well as you possibly can, and every day you do your job, the Australian people are better off and healthier.

I do my job, Peter Dutton does his job, by helping you to do your job better.

And yes, because you're small business people, we help you do your job better by getting taxes down, getting regulation down; trying to ensure that as far as is humanly possible we work for business, not against business; trying to ensure that we always have an open door and a ready ear to the problems of business whenever they are brought to us.

We want to ensure that we get the best possible deal for community pharmacy in the months and years ahead, because the best deal for community pharmacy is almost certainly the best deal for the Australian people who we are pledged to serve.

13

ENVIRONMENT, ENERGY & INFRASTRUCTURE

'I salute you as people who love the natural world'
Canberra, 4 March 2014

Respect for the environment does not necessarily need to be at the detriment of industry, the Prime Minister tells a dinner hosted by ForestWorks, a lobby group for businesses involved in producing wood, paper, furniture and other timber products.

Thank you very much indeed for that kind introduction. It's nice to have a list of things recounted to an appreciative audience – it really is nice. But the most important fact, at least insofar I suspect as this audience is concerned, is omitted from the official resume, because I had the great good fortune of having as my maternal grandfather a shipwright. And as many of you would know, a shipwright is a marine carpenter. A shipwright is a marine carpenter, at least that's what a shipwright was back in the 1920s when many of our larger ships were still made of timber.

My carpenter granddad recruited me to help build a workbench for the new family home when I was in year seven. He joined me in building a timber canoe which I paddled around the Lane Cove River National Park in year eight. He got me to help him to build a large timber shed down the back of my mum and dad's place when I was in year 9 and for my sixteenth birthday when I was in year ten he gave me a toolset which, until just a couple of years ago when it was lost in a flash flood at home, was still the tools which I used around the house to do the kinds of things which every half useful husband should be able to do!

I can't say that having a shipwright grandfather made me a craftsman; it didn't. I didn't become a craftsman, but I did learn to appreciate the value of timber and the importance of working with one's hands. I came to appreciate the forest wasn't just a place of beauty, but it was a source of resources; of the ultimate renewable resource, of the ultimate biodegradable resource.

So when I look out at an audience such as this, this evening, when I look out tonight at an audience of people who work with timber, who work in forests, I don't see people who are environmental bandits, I see people who are the ultimate conservationists. That's what I see and I want to salute you. I salute you as people who love the natural world, as people who love what Mother Nature gives us and who want to husband it for the long-term best interests of humanity.

I want to say this: we will never build a strong economy by trashing our environment, but we will never help our environment by trashing the economy either. You understand - what I regret to say not everyone does – that it is possible to combine respect for the environment and respect for nature with healthy private business.

Man and the environment are meant for each other. The last thing we do – the last thing we should want – if we want to genuinely improve our environment is to want to ban men and women from enjoying it, is to ban men and women from making the most of it and that's what you do. You intelligently make the most of the good things that God has given us.

So my friends, when I say that I want Australia to be open for business, I mean open for business for the forestry industry.

When I say that Australia is not only open for business, but it is under new management, I mean that the people in charge in Canberra – here – value what the forestry industry does and it would be quite a long time since you've experienced that in Canberra.

I hope that you will be the beneficiaries of the general economic policies that the Coalition is putting into practice. You will benefit from the abolition of the carbon tax, ultimately from the abolition of the mining tax. Many of you will benefit from the cutting of the company tax rate. Most of you will benefit from the reduction in red and green-tape that we are determined to deliver. And while it's not the job of the national government to build the kind of country roads and logging trails which you're all very familiar with, if we do invest more, as we will and are, in the major infrastructure that our country needs, that obviously means that state and local governments can do more for the kind of infrastructure that you depend upon in your daily life.

I am pleased to say that in the six months since the change of government here in Canberra, Greg Hunt, an Environment Minister who appreciates that the environment is meant for man and not just the other way around, has provided environmental approvals for projects worth some $400 million. I am pleased and proud to have an Environment Minister who wants to see projects go ahead. I am pleased that because of Greg Hunt's good work, we now have assessment bilaterals – a one stop shop in other words – for environmental approvals with New South

Wales and Queensland, and are working on these with the other states and have high hopes of getting there well before the end of the year.

I'm pleased that we've also got a Korean free trade agreement and are working well towards free trade agreements with Japan and with China.

But you're not just any other industry. You are an industry which has been officially frowned upon for too long.

This is a Liberal/National Coalition that values what you do and wants you to be able to make the most of your life. We don't support, as a Government and as a Coalition, further lockouts of our forests. We just don't support it. We have quite enough National Parks, we have quite enough locked up forests already. In fact, in an important respect, we have too much locked up forest.

One of the first acts of the incoming Government was to begin the process to try to get out of world heritage listing for 74,000 hectares of country in Tasmania, because that 74,000 hectares is not pristine forest. It's forest which has been logged, it's forest which has been degraded, in some cases, it's plantation timber that was actually planted to be logged. Now I'm all in favour of protecting pristine wilderness in proportion – but why should we lock up, as some kind of world heritage sanctuary, country which has been logged, degraded or planted for timber? Why should we do that? Frankly, when this Government comes across examples of actions which are contrary to common sense, we do our best to reverse them. That's what we do – we try to ensure that government does not do that which is contrary to common sense.

You know, getting that 74,000 hectares out of the world heritage listing is still going to leave half of Tasmania protected forever, but that will be an important sign to you, to Tasmanians and to the world that we respect the timber industry and we want the timber industry to have a vigorous and dynamic future, not just a past. We want the timber industry to be a vital part of Australia's economic future, not just something that was a relic of our history. That's what this Government wants.

I don't buy the Green ideology which has done so much damage to our country over the last couple of decades and I'm pleased to see that there are some sensible Labor Party people who don't buy it either. I know they're a minority inside their own Party, but I applaud those who don't buy the Green ideology.

The Green ideology has done so much damage to Tasmania. We all know that Tasmania has the lowest wages in our country. It's got the lowest GPD per head in our country. It's got the lowest life expectancy in our country. It's got the lowest education attainments in our country and it's got the highest unemployment in our country and funnily enough, for the last eight years it's had a government, in large measure, dominated by the Greens. For the last four years it's had a government which was Green dominated, even though prior to that election, the leader of the government said that it would never happen – well, sadly it did happen. The deal with the devil that was never going to happen did happen and I say, the only way to ensure that this Green ideology which has done so much damage to Tasmania and more recently done so much damage to our country, is expunged, is not just to change the government in Canberra but to change the government in Hobart as well.

I am so pleased that for the first time in many years, you can come into this building and not feel that you are in hostile territory. I want to assure you that this is friendly country. This is friendly country and I want to see many more buildings in the years to come built in this country that are as beautifully fitted-out with marvelous timber products as this building is here.

The forestry industry of this country has done great things for this building and may it do great things for so many more buildings in our country and around the world in the years and the decades to come.

Finally I want to say that we don't claim, in this Government, to be experts on everything; we don't claim to know everything about this industry. Yes, we have an abundance of goodwill towards your industry. Yes, we want your industry to flourish, but we know that we will do better by your industry if we are as well informed as possible and that's why I announce tonight that there will be a Forestry Industry Advisory Council, shortly to be finalised by the Government, but I can announce tonight that the co-chairman of that will be Rob de Fegely who is well known to your industry.

I'm sure you'll keep us on the straight and narrow so to speak insofar as far as your industry is concerned and I'm sure that he will ensure that we make the kind of decisions that ensure that my colleagues and I are welcome at next year's dinner.

'You've kept proving the pundits wrong'
Parliament House, Canberra, 3 June 2015

At the annual Minerals Council of Australia gala dinner, Prime Minister Abbott thanks the industry for its contribution to Australia's economy and overseas trade, especially with China, Japan and South Korea, and promises more free trade and further reductions in red tape.

It is good to have so many of Australia's most productive people here in Parliament House.

We have at least as much to learn from you as you do from us as the presence of so many of my colleagues here tonight testifies.

My first task tonight is to pay tribute to an industry that has done so much for our country and, indeed, for the wider world. Our country would not be what it is today without the resources industry. You are just two per cent of our workforce, but you are almost 10 per cent of our GDP and you are almost 60 per cent of our exports. Over the past decade, you have paid $104 billion in company tax. That's $104 billion towards paying for the social security and the services upon which Australians depend.

The wider world would not be what it is today without the Australian resources industry.

The economic miracles of Japan, Korea and, above all, of China have relied on Australian coal, Australian iron ore and Australian natural gas. Over the years, we have exported enough iron ore to lay all the railway tracks in Japan 300 times or to build the Tokyo Tower 400,000 times. Over the past four decades, our trade with China has increased thirteen-hundredfold – not twofold, or fivefold, or tenfold, but thirteen-hundredfold – and your sector is responsible for over 80 per cent of our exports to China. Last year, your exports to China totalled almost $80 billion. Thanks to you, Australia is the world's largest exporter of iron ore, close to being the world's largest exporters of metallurgical coal and soon will be the world's largest exporter of LNG.

As well, you have built so much of Australia's industrial muscle. Regions like Gladstone, the Pilbara, the Hunter, the Illawarra and the La Trobe Valley are unimaginable without the resources industry.

While the resources investment boom is winding down, world supply has increased and prices have fallen, your industry remains critical to Australia's future. Indeed, just today, our national accounts show that mining remains our fastest growing industry with exports up over six per cent, helping to drive the fastest overall export growth in Australia since September 2000. So please, no gloom. Do not under any circumstances underestimate yourselves.

My second task tonight is to explain how the Government is helping the resources industry as part of our plan for a strong and prosperous economy for a safe and secure Australia.

This Government does have a clear vision for mining. This Government wants our country to have the most competitive and advanced mining industry of any developed democracy.

Under this Government, the carbon tax has gone. The mining tax has gone. One trillion dollars' worth of new projects – many in your industry – have been given the green light.

Red tape is being cut – over $2 billion in costs and over 50,000 pages in regulation so far.

Free trade agreements have been concluded with China, Japan and Korea. Our free trade agreement with China, for instance, will end tariffs on alumina, zinc, nickel, copper, and coking coal. The tariff on thermal coal will be phased out over two years. So, we have made it easier to do business, but it doesn't stop there.

Australia needs more investment, more exports and more jobs and there are a series of measures now in the Senate that will deliver exactly that. They are part of the plan that we took to the people at the last election.

The Senate has legislation to re-establish the Australian Building and Construction Commission, an effective cop on the beat that stamped out thuggery and boosted productivity. Thanks to the ABCC, industry productivity rose by 16 per cent with an economic benefit to the country of about $7.5 billion a year. The ABCC drove construction industry disputes to record lows.

To attract more investment, we want to extend the Commission's powers to offshore work, including the multi-billion dollar resources projects on which our future prosperity depends.

And we are determined to restore the right of entry laws that the former government promised to retain during the 2007 campaign before unions were given the green light to sit in any lunch room. For instance, the Pluto LNG project received over 200 right of entry visits in only four months. BHP's Worsley Alumina plant faced 676 right of entry visits in a single year – they must have done a very good lunch there!

Our changes before the Senate will mean unions can no longer deny workers access to an individual flexibility agreement. Our changes before the Senate will remove the union veto on greenfield projects by allowing the Fair Work Commission to approve an enterprise agreement after three months of negotiation. Our changes mean that productivity will be genuinely considered when employees and employers are making Enterprise Bargaining Agreements. As well, our changes will end the 'strike first, talk later' approach to bargaining. None of these are new policies. They're not new plans. They are precisely what we took to the people. They are the changes that we have a mandate for.

John Howard often said that our national competitiveness was like a race with an ever-receding finishing line. Our goal is to make our resources industry the most competitive in the world.Our reforms across government are about making our country more productive with more jobs and more prosperity for everyone.

To take an example, as an island nation, we depend on an efficient shipping industry because 99 per cent of our trade by volume goes by ship. Between 2007 and 2013, however, the number of Australian ships on the coastal trade halved. Bell Bay Aluminium has said that the freight costs for shipping from Tasmania to Queensland rose by 63 per cent, from $18 a tonne in 2011 – before the former government introduced the Coastal Trading Act – to $29 in 2012.

Because of this Act, it's cheaper to ship sugar from Thailand to Australia than around our own coast. It's also cheaper to ship goods from Melbourne to Singapore than from Melbourne to Brisbane.

Australian jobs in Australian industries depend upon cost-effective shipping. We will untangle this mess because coastal shipping, in all its forms, is vital to our national productivity and competitiveness.

This Government understands in the marrow of its bones that the foundation of a strong economy is strong, productive and competitive business. Since the days of the gold rushes, your industry has been part of our national character as well as our national economy.

You have been strong, innovative and resilient and you've kept proving the pundits wrong. In the 1950s, it was said that bauxite was rare in Australia, that payable oil would never be found here and that our tropical north could not be prospected. But with ingenuity, investment and vision, you have opened deposits once thought unviable and discovered new deposits, even in areas once thought thoroughly explored.

Today, new mines are being developed and high-grade deposits are being reported.

New tungsten mines will once again make Australia one of the top 10 producers of this essential metal. In Dubbo we have one of the world's largest in-ground resources of rare metals and heavy earths and Australia now has the largest and richest deposits of scandium.

So for the innovators in mining, for the intrepid men and women who discover the deposits that will deliver our future prosperity, this Government has introduced an Exploration Development Incentive – a flow through share scheme to support investment in small mineral exploration companies involved in greenfields exploration.

Finally, let me say a few words about the coming climate change negotiations. Australia is a country that keeps its commitments. We more than achieved our first Kyoto target and we will achieve a 13 per cent reduction by 2020 on 2005 emissions levels. But we will do so without a carbon tax and without harming our economy.

Our Direct Action Plan is working. The Emissions Reduction Fund has so far achieved 47 million tonnes of reduction at a cost of just $14 a tonne. We will continue to deliver reduced emissions in ways that don't damage our economy. We will continue to be a good environmental global citizen without taxing investment and jobs.

I look forward to working with you to build a strong economy and a clean environment.

You are citizens as well as business people. You want a better world for your children as well as a better return for your shareholders.

Together, we will build the best possible Australia on the shared understanding that a strong economy makes possible the high environmental standards that we all seek.

So, thank you so much. It's terrific to have you all here in Canberra and it's good to see you in buoyant spirits and may the iron ore price continue to be $63 a tonne or higher.

Building the infrastructure of the 21st century
Parliament House, Canberra, 30 October 2014

In this statement to the House of Representatives, Prime Minister Abbott says infrastructure is often neglected by Australia. It is not simply about building more roads, bridges and dams but about improving the quality of life for Australians with faster commutes, more time spent with family and greater efficiencies for business. He promises new infrastructure projects in every Australian state and territory.

At the last election, the Coalition promised to scrap the carbon tax, to stop the boats, to get the Budget under control and to build the roads of the 21st century. We are honouring all of these commitments – but my task today is to report on one of them, our infrastructure agenda.

I said that I hoped to be the Infrastructure Prime Minister – and that part of that was delivering an annual infrastructure statement to the House of Representatives. So today, I am pleased to report progress in building the modern infrastructure that our country needs.

Infrastructure does matter. It helps determine our quality of life as well as our country's competitiveness, productivity and living standards.

Australia needs an Infrastructure Prime Minister because for too long, infrastructure improvements have not kept pace with population growth for the needs of our people. Too many of us have painful, first-hand knowledge of the problems with our national infrastructure, particularly in our big cities.

People leave for work earlier now than they did a decade ago because the traffic jams just keep getting worse and worse. Parents rack up late fines at child care centres when freeways slow to a crawl. Businesses see their costs rise when trucks idle in traffic. Air travel between our cities is actually slower today than it was a generation ago – because of clogged airports and surrounding road networks. And exports can be held up at bottlenecks in key freight networks, particularly again in congested cities.

That's why building the infrastructure of the 21st century is an essential part of the Government's Economic Strategy to build a strong and prosperous economy for a safe and secure Australia. This Budget committed $50 billion to infrastructure. It's the largest infrastructure investment in our history – and it's forecast to generate a record $125 billion of public and private investment in infrastructure over the next decade.

To help the states and territories, the Government has introduced an Asset Recycling Initiative. It's an incentive for them to privatise existing assets and to reinvest the proceeds into new economic infrastructure. Asset recycling should reassure the taxpayers who paid for the assets in the first place that their investment is being preserved and their legacy built upon. I'm pleased to say that every state and territory has signed the National Partnership on Asset Recycling that will help them to build the infrastructure they need, including, it should be said, public transport infrastructure.

It is cooperative federalism at work – as is the National Partnership Agreement on Land Transport Infrastructure which will make roads safer for truck drivers and for all the vehicles that share the roads with them. This is a five year agreement and the funds will flow this year to the states that have signed up.

We promised that big new projects would be underway within 12 months of a change of government and we are delivering. In New South Wales, Australia's biggest road project, WestConnex, has begun, with geotechnical work already underway across Stage 1 and Stage 2. Stage 2 of WestConnex, which duplicates the M5 East, will begin ahead of schedule because the Commonwealth will provide a concessional loan of up to $2 billion on top of the $1.5 billion we committed for Stage 1.

WestConnex will create almost 10,000 jobs during construction and when complete it will by-pass 52 sets of traffic lights. It will reduce travel times for the 100,000 motorists who use the motorway every day by up to 40 minutes and it will take 3,000 trucks every day off Parramatta Road.

As well, the Commonwealth and the New South Wales Government are working together to complete the Pacific Highway upgrade by the end of the decade. In just the past year, 32 km of the highway has been duplicated, including the Sapphire to Woolgoolga upgrade, and now 397kms or 60 per cent of the final highway length is complete.

The duplication of the Pacific Highway, combined with the North-Connex in Sydney, means that, by the end of the decade, at most there will be just two stretches of traffic lights between Melbourne and Brisbane.

In Victoria, the Commonwealth is investing $3 billion toward Melbourne's East West Link. The East West Link will create more than 6,000 jobs during construction and it will reduce travel time by up to 20 minutes for commuters travelling from Geelong to the city and beyond. Stage 1 alone is expected to allow 100,000 vehicles each day to bypass 23 sets of traffic lights.

And on 29th September, the Victorian Government signed the contracts to build Stage One of East West Link – the link has been inked – so there can be no turning back from this major project that will help tens of thousands of Victorians every day.

In South Australia, the Commonwealth has committed $944 million to upgrade the North-South Road Corridor. This project will crate 1,000 construction jobs and early work is already underway on Ashwin Parade.

In Western Australia, the Commonwealth has committed $174 million to widen and strengthen the North West Coastal Highway, which is the main link between Geraldton, Carnarvon, Karratha and Port Hedland and construction will commence in the next month.

The Gateway WA is on track and the Commonwealth is providing $615 million for the 40km Northlink WA project. Planning is underway and construction will commence in 2016.

Planning is also underway for the $1.6 billion Perth Freight Link project funded with $925 million from the Commonwealth.

In Queensland, five major projects have been completed on the Bruce Highway – at Gin Gin, Mackay, Cairns, Calliope Crossroads near Gladstone and at Burdekin and the last section of the Townsville Ring Road will start within 12 months.

Early works have begun on the Gateway Motorway upgrade and the procurement process is underway for the Toowoomba Second Range Crossing, so that major construction works can start next year. The Commonwealth's commitment of up to $1.28 billion is the largest ever federal contribution to a single Queensland regional road project.

In Tasmania, the Commonwealth has committed $400 million to the Midland Highway and the Westbury Road Upgrade will be completed by the end of this year.

In the Northern Territory, the duplication of the first of the sections of Tiger Brennan Drive has been completed. The Commonwealth has committed a further $77 million towards upgrading Northern Territory highways with planning already underway.

In addition to these major road projects, the Government is spending $2.1 billion on the Roads to Recovery Programme and funding a $565 million Black Spot Programme to improve the most dangerous stretches of road throughout our country.

Then there's the Heavy Vehicle Safety and Productivity Programme providing $248 million to increase the number of rest areas and improve connections to freight networks.

There's also the $229 million National Highway Upgrade Programme for practical improvements such as shoulder and centreline widening, ripple strips and wire rope barriers.

And the Government is providing $300 million for the Bridges Renewal Programme to upgrade deteriorating bridges across the nation.

Airports are our gateways to the world. For more than 50 years, governments have talked about a second airport for Sydney. Finally, and not before time, the talk is over. We've taken the final decision that Badgerys Creek will be the site of Sydney's second airport – or, as I prefer, Western Sydney's first airport.

The Government has commenced consultations with the Sydney Airport Group. We are working up the commercial model and the airport concept designs and construction should begin in 2016. This airport is irrevocable – it is going ahead and construction should begin in 2016.

By mid-century, the new airport could generate a $24 billion increase in our gross domestic product and 60,000 new jobs in Western Sydney – it's the centrepiece of our long-term vision for Western Sydney – and heeding past lessons, it will be a case of roads first, airport second: the roads will be built before the first plane has landed.

A $3.6 billion, 10 year partnership with the New South Wales Government is underway, starting with the upgrade of Bringelly Road. So together, our road package and the airport will give Western Sydney the modern infrastructure it deserves.

In Hobart, environmental and design studies for the extension of the runway at Hobart Airport are underway. This $38 million upgrade will help Hobart to become the gateway to the Antarctic and give the potential for direct flights to Asia.

As well, planning work and consultations are currently underway on the Inland Railway between Melbourne and Brisbane which would significantly improve freight productivity compared to the coastal line via Sydney.

The Government is also getting on with the job of rolling out the NBN so that Australians will have access to very fast broadband as soon as possible, at affordable prices and the least cost to taxpayers and this Government has connected more premises in just one year than the previous government did in five. An independent Cost-Benefit Analysis of the NBN found that this Government's multi-technology approach will deliver net economic and social benefits of almost $18 billion.

Now the Government is determined to end the dam-phobia that has largely stopped the construction of new dams for the past three decades. Water is a priceless asset especially when the vagaries of our environment make it so scarce. Strengthening our water storage capability is essential if our country is to grow. We do need to build the right dams in the right places and most of these dams should be feasible without government support. But we are looking at some modest seed funding to help break the anti-dam mindset.

Just as we promised to end the analysis paralysis and get projects moving on the ground, we also promised a long-term vision for Australia's infrastructure needs and a comprehensive plan to deliver it.

We've passed legislation to make Infrastructure Australia more independent, robust and transparent, with a Board appointed CEO, so that states, territories, industry and the community can be confident it's working in the national interest, and not just the Commonwealth's interest.

To see our nationally significant infrastructure needs more clearly, we've tasked Infrastructure Australia to develop a 15 year infrastructure plan.The plan will cover all economic infrastructure – transport, energy, communications and water. It will evaluate projects receiving more than $100 million in Commonwealth funding to help clarify our country's infrastructure priorities for the future. It's reform to build the right projects at the right time for the right price. The work done to make costs and benefits more transparent should build deeper engagement by private investors in infrastructure.

Australia is not alone in facing a greater need for infrastructure investment. Almost every country needs more and better infrastructure to underpin jobs and growth, and almost every government lacks the resources to underwrite that investment. Governments do not have the money to deliver on their own and as this year's G20 President, Australia has made boosting private-sector investment in infrastructure a priority. We're driving a Global Infrastructure Initiative for quality investment across the G20 and beyond – and part of this initiative, is a new global infrastructure hub that we hope will be based in Sydney.

This Government is committed to building the infrastructure that we need to get products to market faster, to speed up the wait for freight, and to get employees to work and home again with less time wasted in traffic.

Nothing boosts confidence like cranes in the sky and bulldozers on the ground. It's an unmistakable sign of faith in our future. So, next year, I look forward to reporting further progress in delivering the projects we promised in our plan to build a strong and prosperous economy for a safe and secure Australia.

'We are now readier to take the longer view'
Sydney, 5 November 2014

Prime Minister Abbott delivers the inaugural Bradfield Oration, in honour of Australian engineer John Bradfield (1867-1943), to an audience of leaders from industry, business and politics at the Sydney Museum of Contemporary Art. He notes that Bradfield's greatest achievement, the Harbour Bridge, took decades to plan and build, a time span that still applies to current infrastructure challenges.

I love this city: our harbour, our beaches, and our bush. On a good day at Manly beach, just 15 minutes from where I live, you can surf among the dolphins. On the other side of my street, is Garigal National Park. Forestville is just 15 minutes from the CBD, at the right times, yet you can walk for two minutes, and not be able to see a single house; possums promenade along the power lines, lorikeets swarm on the balcony, and bush turkeys invade the back garden.

Much of Sydney is a city in a national park. It's the bush and the water that gives Sydney its unique character and should never be put at risk. It is truly one of the very best places on earth to live – until you have to move around – when you're often stuck in some of the world's longest car parks.

I grew up in Chatswood, within a good walk of the railway station. Dad could walk to work, children walked to the station and mum had a short drive to the shops. But beyond the inner city, for Sydneysiders living further than a decent walk from a railway station, you depend on a car – or an irregular bus service – and either way you need a decent road.

As a student, I struggled through clogged roads from the north shore to the inner west. As a commuter, I braved traffic jams to reach a station without a decent car park. And as a prime minister, like everyone else with somewhere to go at the wrong time of day, I inch through gridlock to get to the airport.

The first home I owned was in a one lane street that turned into a race way every two minutes when the lights changed at the intersection of the Princes Highway and Canal Rd. That's Sydney's problem: it's a city of over four million people – tipped to reach six million within two decades – with roads designed for two million; and the decent roads we do have still don't actually join up.

Bad roads add hours to your day and stress to your life; bad roads mean you're late for work and spend less time at home; bad roads mean more smog from vehicles in gridlock and more suburban streets turned into traffic canyons. That's why, as long as I've been able to travel, I've dreamt of a Sydney that all of us could move around much more freely.

It's the job of state governments to plan and deliver infrastructure; it's the job of local governments to provide municipal services and create attractive communities; and it's the job of the national government to end the talk and to get things built.

As a citizen, I want a friendly neighbourhood that's hard to change beyond recognition; I want a state government with a plan for my city and the determination to make it happen.

As prime minister, though, my job is to build prosperity for all of us; in part, through securing the first world infrastructure that green activism, policy procrastination, and misguided priorities have so far stopped.

As an infrastructure prime minister, my job is to work with the premiers to ensure that our national roads, freight, power, communications and water systems are no longer holding us back. And as the infrastructure prime minister, it's a particular honour to present this first Bradfield Oration – the first of many, I hope.

No other engineer has made such a mark on our city, on our state and on our country as John Bradfield. As a senior public works department engineer for almost 40 years, Bradfield transformed Sydney – and ultimately Australia. He helped to design the Burrinjuck and Cataract Dams in New South Wales, the Story Bridge in Brisbane, Sydney's City Circle railway line, and – his signature achievement – the Sydney Harbour Bridge.

A bridge over Sydney Harbour had first been proposed to Governor Macquarie by Francis Greenway in 1815. A century later, nothing had happened. For over a century, politicians had talked and residents had dreamed of a bridge between Dawes Point and Milson's Point – after all, it was only five hundred metres. It was John Bradfield who finally supervised the bridge's construction – from conception to completion.

The Sydney Harbour Bridge is one of the marvels of our city and one of the greatest feats of its time. Its principal designer was a profound talent with dogged persistence, compelling eloquence and an inspiring vision.

Bradfield was the first doctor of engineering from Sydney University and won the university gold medal. His doctoral thesis title reflects his life's work: "The city and suburban electric railways and the Sydney Harbour Bridge". In a quirk of history, his examiner was another engineer of genius: Sir John Monash.

As a former Premier Jack Lang observed of Bradfield, when Sydney's population was scarcely one million, he was "the first man to plan for…a city of two million people".

As we celebrate Bradfield's vision, we should also gratefully acknowledge the civic leaders who invested in it and helped to make it happen.

Long before he had completed the Bridge, Bradfield confided to his diary: "When I visualise the future, I feel that I was born 30 years too soon because the achievement of today will be but a stepping stone for greater feats necessary for the development of this great city". This is our challenge: not to play catch up but, like Bradfield, to plan for the future.

In 1932, when the bridge opened, there were under 200,000 registered vehicles in the whole of NSW. In its first year, the Bridge carried only 11,000 vehicles a day. Bradfield did not envisage infrastructure for his time alone but for our time too. His thinking was not for today or even for the next decade; it was for the next half century and beyond. Our challenge is to be as forward thinking in our time as Bradfield was in his.

In his day, there were two Sydneys divided by water. Today, there are two Sydneys divided by travelling times: one Sydney for people who can get to work within an hour; and a tougher, more stressful Sydney for people who spend over two hours a day travelling. People in the west, the south, the central coast and even the northern beaches can feel as cut off from their destinations as those who lived on the lower north shore in the pre-bridge years before 1932. Our challenge is to ensure that getting from one side of the metropolitan area to another is as easy as Bradfield made getting to the other side of the harbour.

The success of Sydney is fundamental to our nation's economy. Sydney contributes over a fifth of Australia's GDP. As our largest city – with leading financial services, tourism, education, health and manufacturing – it contributes more to our national wealth than any other place in Australia. It could contribute even more if road congestion didn't cost an estimated $6 billion a year.

Ask yourself how much has congestion cost you and your family in lost time, extra fuel, or wear-and-tear? I don't doubt our transport economists – but suspect that $6 billion is a very conservative figure indeed.

Congestion, of course, is not unique to Sydney. Traffic jams plague all our big cities. People leave earlier and earlier for work – and leave later and later for home – all in increasingly vain attempts to miss peak periods.

It's why I am determined to be the Infrastructure Prime Minister building the roads of the 21st century – because movement is what distinguishes us from previous generations and more ease of movement, like more disposable income, is one of the litmus tests of prosperity.

In the Budget, the government committed a record $50 billion to new transport infrastructure.

Thanks to the asset recycling fund – which will add 15 per cent to any proceeds of privatisation that are reinvested in economic infrastructure, including, should the states choose, urban rail – this budget is forecast to generate a record $125 billion of public and private infrastructure investment over the next decade.

My aim is cranes in our skies and bulldozers on the ground.

Commonwealth funding is driving the East West Link in Melbourne – where stage one alone will generate nearly 4000 jobs and save the occupants of 100,000 vehicles 15 minutes a day.

There's the full North-South Road Corridor in Adelaide within a decade.

There's the Perth gateway project, the Swan Valley Bypass, and the Perth freight link project.

There's the Gateway Motorway upgrade in Brisbane, the Toowoomba Second Range Crossing and major works to fix the Bruce Highway throughout coastal Queensland.

There's the upgrade of the Midland Highway in Tasmania and key roads in the Northern Territory.

But the biggest road projects are rightly in New South Wales – because in the decade after the Olympics the state government was out to lunch, to put it at its kindest.

The work in Sydney starts with Australia's biggest road project. WestConnex will eliminate up to 52 sets of traffic lights from 100,000 journeys a day – giving back to each vehicle's occupants 40 minutes that would have otherwise been wasted in traffic jams.

Then there's the upgrade of the Pacific Highway and the completion of NorthConnex – so that by decade's end there will be only two stretches of traffic lights between Melbourne and Brisbane.

And after 50 years of talk, a decision has now been made about Sydney's second airport site – or, as I prefer, western Sydney's first airport. This airport will happen – but so will the road and rail links to make it work and they'll be built before the first planes land.

You can tell that this government is serious because we haven't just announced the airport, we're already building the roads – such as Bringelly Rd where site works start soon. It's "roads first, airport second". The largely-Commonwealth funded western Sydney infrastructure plan will produce more than 50 kilometres of high quality roads with motorway standard interchanges.

The new airport is essential because the numbers flying into Sydney will almost double over the next twenty years – and they can't all land at Mascot which is struggling to cope and has been for years. Without another airport for Sydney, the national economy is tipped to be $34 billion smaller in 2060 and NSW will miss out on almost 60,000 jobs.

If Western Sydney is to be a city in its own right rather than a dormitory for somewhere else, it needs its own airport. The Western Sydney airport should become Australia's principal air freight hub and the centre of a massive business park.

The new airport is going to plan. Consultations with the Sydney Airport Group are underway. A commercial model and the airport concept designs are being worked up. And construction should begin in 2016.

Not much that governments do matters half a century on. The decision to build the western Sydney airport will permanently change our city and our country. It shows that we are no less capable than our parents and grandparents of seizing the moment and shaping the future.

Tonight, we remember John Bradfield for his bridges, railways and roads, but should not forget the dams he built as well.

A government determined to end the analysis-paralysis that's delayed western Sydney's airport should also end the dam-phobia of the past thirty years. Dams, after all, are the cheaper, more environmentally friendly alternative to the desalination plants which Bob Carr once called bottled electricity.

We shouldn't forget that aviation was also one of John Bradfield's interests. One way to sustain enthusiasm for the new airport could be to name it after a champion for Sydney and I can't think of a better candidate than John Bradfield. I suspect that many other Sydneysiders might think so, too, and I hope that finding out might be something that the *Telegraph* will take up.

So, it's too soon to say of airport decision-making that it's all over bar the shouting. The predictable objections might slow it down but they won't stop it because it is so obviously an idea whose time has come.

The announcement generated far less opposition than expected. Perhaps western Sydney's growth has made the need for its own airport almost self-evident; perhaps people are now resolved to be larger and better this time than the last time this issue was considered; perhaps we are now readier to take the longer view and negotiate difficulties rather than be defeated by them.

In any event, it's a new sign of purpose in our national life that this government is determined to build upon.

13

TRADE, AGRICULTURE & REGIONAL DEVELOPMENT

'Freedom is less a threat than an opportunity'
Davos, Switzerland, 23 January 2014

Addressing his first World Economic Forum as Prime Minister, Tony Abbott reiterates his faith in open markets and free trade as the key to greater global prosperity, cooperation and peace.

For more than 40 years, this World Economic Forum at Davos has been an important contributor to global progress. It has brought together some of the best thinkers and most important decision-makers: not to dwell on problems but to focus on opportunities.

As 2014 begins, it's easier to be optimistic. In the United States, economic growth is set to rise from under two per cent to almost 3 per cent, with a million jobs created in the last year. China's growth is moderating but likely to remain over 7 per cent. Even the Eurozone is finally growing again.

Of course, the recovery remains fragile. The US taper will need deft management. Around the world, over 300 million young people are neither working nor studying and the global economy needs 30 million more jobs just to restore employment levels from before the Global Financial Crisis.

The challenge, everywhere, is to promote sustainable, private sector-led growth and employment – and to avoid government-knows-best action for action's sake.

It's worth noting – if only to remind ourselves of the good that can be done – that in the past few decades, more has been achieved to reduce poverty than in any other period in history. In countries such as China, India and Indonesia many hundreds of millions have been lifted from subsistence to the middle class. Despite the (Global Financial) Crisis, worldwide, income per person is still up by over 60 per cent in the past decade. The global middle class is growing from 1.8 billion now to over 3 billion in 10 years' time.

This progress is partly due to better science and technology; and partly to the constant aspiration to do better. Mostly, though, it's been driven by the intellectual and philosophical conviction that freer trade and smaller government will strengthen prosperity; the instinct that empowered citizens can do more for themselves than government will ever do for them.

Essentially, officialdom has begun to grasp that human freedom is less a threat than an opportunity. As soon as people have economic freedom, they create markets. Markets are the proven answer to the problem of scarcity. They rest, as Roger Scruton has recently observed, "upon the kind of moral order that arises from below as people take responsibility for their lives, learn to honour their agreements, and live in justice and charity with their neighbours".

Even though the Crisis was the gravest economic challenge the world has faced since the 1930s, it was not a crisis of markets but one of governance. It was the G20 which helped to coordinate the actions which prevented another great depression. The challenge, as we continue to work through the weaknesses that brought on the Crisis, is to strengthen governance without suppressing the vitality of capitalism.

The Crisis, after all, has not changed any of the basic laws of economics. The lesson of recent history, whether it's the collapse of Soviet-style communism, the phenomenal growth of Asian economies, or the slow and painful recovery from the Crisis of 2008 and 2009 is that real progress is always built on clear fundamentals.

You can't spend what you haven't got. No country has ever taxed or subsidised its way to prosperity. You don't address debt and deficit with yet more debt and deficit. And profit is not a dirty word because success in business is something to be proud of. After all, you can't have strong communities without strong economies to sustain them and you can't have strong economies without profitable private businesses.

Above all else, policy-makers need to understand that every dollar government spends comes from the people, either through taxes and borrowings; or, over the past few years, through the process known as quantitative easing which is not indefinitely sustainable.

A certain level of government spending is necessary and good. In words attributed to Lincoln, government should do for people what they can't do for themselves – and no more.

Richer people, stronger countries and a better world all depend upon policy-makers' grasp of these fundamentals and there's no better place to reiterate them than the World Economic Forum – creator of the global competitiveness index as well as this conference.

As always, stronger economic growth is the key to addressing almost every global problem. Stronger growth requires lower, simpler and fairer taxes that don't stifle business creativity. And stronger growth requires getting government spending under control so that taxes can come down; and reducing regulation so that productivity can rise.

In the decade prior to the Crisis, consistent surpluses and a preference for business helped my country, Australia, to become one of the world's best-performing economies. Then, a subsequent government decided that the Crisis had changed the rules and that we should spend our way to prosperity. The reason for spending soon passed but the spending didn't stop because, when it comes to spending, governments can be like addicts in search of a fix. But after the recent election, Australia is under new management and open for business.

To boost private sector growth and employment, the new Government is cutting red tape and reducing the tax burden by scrapping the carbon tax and the mining tax. We've established a once-in-a-generation Commission of Audit to re-consider the size, scope and efficiency of government. We're streamlining environmental approvals and have already ticked off new projects worth over $400 billion. We've successfully concluded negotiations for a Free Trade Agreement with South Korea and are working on agreements with Japan, China, India and Indonesia as well as wider ones such as the Trans-Pacific Partnership. With an ageing population, we're implementing measures to get more people into work: like a 'fair dinkum' (as we say in Australia) paid parental leave scheme to give mothers in the workforce their full wage for six months. We're investigating childcare changes that will respond to modern families participating in a round-the-clock economy. We're determined that fit working age people will work, preferably for a wage but, if not, as a condition of receiving unemployment benefits. We'll do more to keep people with temporary health conditions in the workforce, rather than on a pension. And we're accelerating the construction of major infrastructure, especially roads, because time spent in traffic jams is time lost from work and family.

Every country's circumstances are different but this is what we are doing in Australia to boost growth, participation and productivity. Some countries might find our example instructive, just as we have learned from others' experiences. Growth, however, is the result of global conditions as well as domestic policies. And this year, Australia is in a unique position to promote global growth as chair of the G20.

If the largest economies can individually achieve higher growth and can cooperate to achieve higher global growth, obviously, every country benefits. At St Petersburg last year, each G20 country agreed to prepare its own comprehensive growth strategy to feed into a G20-wide action plan.

I'm looking forward to respectful but robust discussion of each country's national plan. Each of us can learn from canvassing the problems that we all face; and even more importantly, the problems that can only be solved by countries working cooperatively together. This year's Brisbane summit will focus on a few key subjects because progress usually comes one step at a time. Australia's aim is a communiqué just three pages long explaining precisely how good intentions are being put into practice.

Like last year, this year's G20 must be more than a talkfest.

As always, trade comes first. People trade with each other because it's in their interest to do so. Every time one person freely trades with another, wealth increases. Just as trade within countries increases wealth, trade between countries increases wealth – that's why we should all be missionaries for freer trade.

At the very least, the G20 should renew its commitment against protectionism and in favour of freer markets. Each country should renew its resolve to undo any protectionist measures put in place since the Crisis. Better still, each country should commit to open up trade through unilateral, bi-lateral, plurilateral and multi-lateral actions and through domestic reforms to help businesses engage more fully in global commerce.

As a trading nation, Australia will make the most of its G20 presidency to promote free trade. Over time, everyone benefits because, in a global economy, countries end up focussing on what they do best.

A more global economy with stronger cross-border investment eventually helps everyone because it generates more wealth and ultimately creates more jobs.

Of course, money's tendency to flow to where taxes are lowest is a powerful incentive for all countries to keep taxes down. One of the side effects of globalisation is more ability to take advantage of different country's tax regimes. Different national tax arrangements have not always kept up with the rise of services and the pervasiveness of digital technologies. So, the G20 will continue to tackle businesses artificially generating profits to chase tax opportunities rather than market ones. The essential principle is that you should normally pay tax in the country where you've earned the revenue.

My hope is to have a really frank leaders-only discussion in Brisbane about the biggest issues we face, including digitalisation and its implications for tax, trade and global integration. Because taxes need to be fair, as well as low, in order to preserve the legitimacy of free markets. For the leaders of the countries generating 85 per cent of the world's GDP merely to agree on the principles needed for taxation to be fair in a globalised economy would be a big step forward.

Then, there's the worldwide "infrastructure deficit", with the OECD estimating that over 50 trillion dollars in infrastructure investment is needed by 2030. Developing countries need new infrastructure, developed countries need rebuilt infrastructure and almost every country is struggling to finance the infrastructure it needs. It should be easier to get big new road, rail, port and dam infrastructure off the ground – and we can do that through attracting more private capital through sensible pricing policies and better regulatory practices.

As an "infrastructure prime minister", my hope as G20 host, is to bring policy-makers, financiers and builders together to identify practical ways of increasing long-term infrastructure financing. What investors really need is greater confidence that governments won't change the rules after the investment has been made.

The G20 assumed its current form in response to the Crisis triggered by bad banking practices. So at the heart of the G20's work is building the resilience of the financial sector: helping to prevent and manage the failure of globally important financial institutions; making derivatives markets safer; and improving the oversight of the shadow banking sector. Financial regulation is always a work-in-progress but these reforms now need to be finalised in ways that promote confidence without eliminating risk. The challenge for authorities is to keep abreast of developments, not to lag behind them as they did pre-Crisis, and to maintain the public's trust.

On trade, tax, infrastructure, employment and banking, we owe it to our citizens, on whose behalf we attend international conferences, to maximise the specific outcomes from this year's G20.

Finally, governments must always remember that an economy is far more like an organism than a machine. A strong economy is far less likely to be one responding to central control than one spontaneously generating its own growth.

After all, government doesn't create wealth; people do, when they run profitable businesses. Government's role is always to nurture its citizens rather than to promote itself.

At the start of Australia's G20 presidency, the government and the people of Australia look forward to welcoming national leaders and international opinion formers to our country. I promise you: we will make your trip worthwhile. Australia is determined, as a responsible and committed G20 chair, to promote better global governance.

We will strive to build on the good work of Russia's presidency and lay the foundations for further progress under Turkey in 2015. Better governance, though, is not the same as more government. Ultimately, the G20 is not about us in government; it's about the people, our masters.

'That is what the world expects from us'
Brisbane, 16 November 2014

In his address at the conclusion of the G20 Summit in Brisbane, Prime Minister Abbott applauds the summit's key objectives of boosting growth, enhancing global economic resilience and strengthening global institutions. He notes the summit has also to its credit committed itself to global approaches to infrastructure, reducing the gender gap in workforce participation, developing better approaches to energy efficiency and reforming the financial sector to avoid another global financial crisis.

First of all, could I say what an honour it has been to chair this G20 leaders meeting here in Brisbane. This meeting of the G20 leaders is the most influential and significant gathering that's ever been held in our country.

The thing about the G20 is that it is large enough to be representative of the wider world and it's small enough to be effective. That's why the G20 is now such an important element in the global governance architecture.

The first thing I should do is to thank the people of Brisbane for their hospitality. It is an honour to host an event such as this, but it is also an inconvenience and I do want to thank the people of Brisbane for making all of the leaders and delegates and media and everyone else associated with this event so welcome.

Most of all, I want to stress that this year the G20 has delivered real, practical outcomes. Because of the efforts that the G20 has made this year, culminating in the last 48 hours, people right around the world are going to be better off and that's what it's all about: it is all about the people of the world being better off through the achievement of inclusive growth and jobs. That's what it's all about.

This Brisbane summit, and indeed the whole year of Australia's G20 presidency, has not just been about bold ideas, it's been about strong execution as well. We set a goal, we developed a plan and we believe we have implemented it.

I've been very heartened and encouraged by the very candid conversations that I've had with individual leaders and which leaders have had with each other. That's been a mark of this Brisbane summit: the quality and the candour of the exchanges that we've had.

I asked all leaders to attempt, as far as they could, to throw away the scripts and speak from their hearts and to a remarkable extent that's happened over this weekend. There has been a spirit of collaboration from all of the leaders and all of their teams and I very much thank them for that.

When Australia's presidency began, we identified three key themes. First, boosting growth and employment; second, enhancing global economic resilience; and third, strengthening global institutions.

We believe, I think all of the G20 members believe that we can do more for our people and for the wider world when we work together than when we work separately. In partnership, I believe that we have very substantially delivered on those three themes that we identified.

We've signed off on a peer-reviewed growth package that, if implemented, will achieve a 2.1 per cent increase in global growth over the next five years on top of business as usual.

The Brisbane Action Plan contains over 800 separate reform measures and if we do all that we have committed to doing, the IMF and the OECD tell us that our Gross Domestic Product will be, as I say, 2.1 per cent higher than it would otherwise be. We've published these measures, we've published these growth strategies, so that the world can see what we are committed to and the world can hold us to account. The OECD and the IMF will be regularly reviewing our progress towards achieving these measures to keep us accountable.

We're focused on policies to increase competition, to unshackle the private sector from unnecessary regulation, and to increase female participation.

On infrastructure, very importantly, we're launching a global infrastructure initiative to address the $70 trillion gap in infrastructure needed within 15 years by 2030. A key mechanism to drive this initiative is the Global Infrastructure Hub that will be located in Sydney. That will be funded by contributions from governments and also from the private sector.

We've had a 25 by 25 pledge by all G20 countries to reduce the gap between female and male workforce participation by a quarter – to reduce the gap by 25 per cent – over the next 10 years, and this has the potential to bring 100 million women into the global workforce – an extraordinary achievement if we can deliver on this, but it is a clear aspiration and it is an achievable, accountable goal.

Now, we absolutely want companies to pay their fair share of tax and we want them to pay their tax in the jurisdictions where their profits are earned. This is particularly important for emerging and developing economies and we're taking concrete and practical steps to achieve this. It's about the countries of the world, the people of the world, receiving the tax benefits that are their due and it's needed so that governments can fund the infrastructure and the services that people expect and deserve.

Australia's also focused on four areas of financial sector reform to ensure that the circumstances that led to the 2008 global crisis can never be repeated. We're working to strengthen financial institutions, to protect taxpayers from having to fund bailouts if 'too big to fail' financial institutions run into difficulty, to address shadow banking risks and to make derivative markets safer. It's so important to make the global institutions developed in the 20th Century relevant to the 21st Century.

The working session on trade was one of the most productive of this G20 weekend. It saw leaders unanimous in their view that expanding global trade will directly benefit countries and people right around the world. Trade is a key driver of growth, perhaps the key driver of growth, and we're focused on domestic reforms to facilitate trade as well as the importance of a strong global trading system.

Leaders also began a discussion – a very important discussion – which I know will be taken forward over the next 12 months by Turkey, about how the World Trade Organisation could work better to deliver the growth we need. There will always be political differences about the global trading system, but we can do better and we made a very good start towards WTO reform this weekend.

For the first time, G20 leaders have had a session dedicated to global energy issues. Leaders agreed that the issue of energy requires a significant ongoing focus. We endorsed landmark energy principles which will ensure access to affordable and reliable energy for all. They will ensure that energy institutions are more inclusive of emerging and developing economies, they will strengthen energy markets, enhance energy security, phase out inefficient fossil fuel subsidies that encourage wasteful consumption and, importantly, they will support sustainable growth and development. Energy, I am pleased to say, is now at the heart of the G20's agenda and G20 Energy Ministers will meet for the first time early next year to take this work forward.

We agreed to work together to develop better approaches to energy efficiency. The G20 Energy Efficiency Action Plan identifies six areas where increased global action will have real benefits for all. They are heavy vehicles, appliances linked to networks, building, industrial processors, more efficient electricity generation and, importantly, access to finance to fund that more efficient electricity generation.

Obviously, it goes without saying that G20 leaders – all of us – support strong and effective action to address climate change. Our actions will support sustainable development, economic growth and certainty for business and investment and we will all work constructively towards the climate change conference in Paris next year.

There were a number of other important international issues that were dealt with. Leaders expressed deep concern about the humanitarian and economic impact of Ebola and discussed practical measures to tackle the outbreak in Guinea, Liberia and Sierra Leone. We support the international response and have committed to do all we can to sustain and respond to the crisis.

It has been a weekend of achievement. Our focus has been the economy and how we can achieve inclusive growth and jobs. I believe that the G20 this weekend has shifted a gear from responding to events to setting an agenda for growth.

Our message to the world is that governments can deliver; that governments can, under the right circumstances, agree; that the world can be better; that governments can do better and that there can be higher growth and more jobs.

That is what the world expects of us. That is what our people want. They want higher growth and the jobs that higher growth will deliver.

So, what we have seen over this weekend is cooperation, accountability and concrete plans. I absolutely believe that the economies of the world, that the countries of the world, that the people of the world, will be better because we have met this way in Brisbane this weekend.

We all know as we look around the world that there are many problems and we spend so much of our time enumerating them, but my message to the people of the world from Brisbane, Australia is that there is hope that things can be better. There is a plan that's been endorsed by the leaders of the 20 largest and most representative economies. That plan will be so much better than what went before at delivering the growth and the jobs that the people of the world want and need.

Our challenge, of course, is to fully implement our agenda.

Another giant step in our friendship with China
Canberra, 17 June 2015

After a decade of negotiations initiated under his predecessor John Howard, Prime Minister Abbott signs a
watershed Free Trade Agreement with Australia's largest
trading partner, China. At the lunch to announce the deal,
he says Australians will now pay less for cars, clothes,
electronics and other Chinese imports.

This is a momentous day. It's a happy day between friends. It is the day
that we seal the deal that was made during last year's historic visit by
China's President Xi Jinping. We seize this opportunity of more trade
and more investment with China and we complete a trifecta of trade
deals with our major trading partners, not only China but also Japan
and South Korea – markets which together account for more than 60
per cent of Australia's export goods. We again show that Australia is
open for business and that we deliver more opportunities for Australian
companies and the people they employ.

Today, we realise the vision of former prime minister John Howard
who launched these negotiations a decade ago. At that time, China was
Australia's third largest trading partner and the Asia region accounted
for but 29 per cent of global trade.

Today, China is by far our largest trading partner and the Asia region accounts for 36 per cent of global trade. When these negotiations
were first launched, Prime Minister Howard said that they would be
complicated, he said that they would be challenging, and he said that
they would be difficult. But he also said that they were worth persever-
ing with. He said that our shared optimism and enthusiasm meant that
success would eventually be achieved and today we have realised that
vision and achieved that success.

I congratulate Chinese Commerce Minister, Gao Hucheng, and our
own Trade and Investment Minister Andrew Robb for the extraordinary
and historic work they've done.

I was indeed truly delighted to today receive a letter from President
Xi conveying his personal congratulations on the signing of the agreement. And I have passed onto Minister Gao a letter to President Xi in

response, conveying my great pleasure at what is the beginning of the next chapter in the relationship between our two countries.

This agreement will give our nations unprecedented access to each other's markets. It removes barriers to Australian agricultural exports across a range of products, including beef, dairy, lamb, wine, horticulture and seafood. It means duty free entry for 99.9 per cent of our resources, energy and manufacturing exports within four years.

But it's about so much more than just exporting more and reducing tariffs. Australian services providers: financial, education, health and aged care, will have new access to China's services sector – a sector that is already the largest contributor to China's GDP and is set to drive economic growth in coming years.

For China, this agreement liberalises the screening threshold for Chinese private sector investment in Australia and it puts Chinese businesses in the same position as those of our other major trading partners. And, of course, it means that Australian consumers will pay less for cars, for clothes, for electronics and for other goods imported from China.

We are a leading trading nation. Our prosperity depends on trade and the jobs and economic growth it creates. In only a few decades, China has emerged as a global economic leader – the world's second largest economy, the second largest trading nation and now, of course, a major global investor. But the rise of China is not just about economics – it's about people.

The Chinese economic miracle is quite simply the greatest advance in prosperity ever seen in the history of mankind and the unprecedented agreement that we have signed today will not only enhance trade between our nations but also two-way investment.

Far more than trade, investment in another country is a sign of trust. You don't put your hard earned cash into another country unless you are absolutely certain that your investment will be respected, that you are likely to make a reliable profit and that you will be able to repatriate the money.

The fact that China has over the years directly invested almost as much in our economy as it has in the United States – an economy around 12 times our size – is a sign of trust in Australia. And our investment of almost $58 billion in China, with its very different legal and political system, is much more than just a bet on the world's coming economic superpower; it's proof of our trust in China, because in our own lives, we know that it's not money or goods that sustains a friendship, it's trust.

So, this agreement is another giant step in the friendship between our two nations. Our friendship will continue to grow. We look forward to a shared future of prosperity based on trust and respect.

Today is a truly historic step forward in our comprehensive strategic partnership.

I hope all of you will remember today. One day we will be able to say to our children and grandchildren, that yes, we were there the day this extraordinary agreement was signed between our two countries.

'Nothing to fear and everything to gain'
Sydney, 30 July 2015

At the Boao Forum for Asia, a meeting of high-level delegates discussing regional economic co-operation, in Sydney, the Prime Minister's keynote address focuses on the benefits of free trade agreements such as the one recently signed between Australia and China.

This conference will cover many subjects, but improvement in all things depends upon improvement in one thing: our economy. So, that's what I want to address today – our economy, and the heart of our economy, which is trade.

A short walk from here, in Macquarie Place, is a statue of Thomas Sutcliffe Mort, a leading merchant of colonial New South Wales. Mort helped to start the international wool trade that was the foundation of our early prosperity. He also founded the Australian Mutual Provident Society, which became today's financial giant, the AMP.

I mention this because what we do makes a difference and because then, as now, prosperity was generated by trade. Then, as now, jobs were generated by trade.

Australians today are wealthier and our country is more prosperous and more influential because we have grasped the opportunities of trade.

As you all know, Bob Hawke was one of the founders of the Boao Forum. Better than many others and sooner than many others, he understood that Australia's future prosperity rested on our trade with China. Australia is now poised to realise the Hawke vision and to complete the work begun by Prime Minister John Howard over a decade ago, when the China-Australia Free Trade Agreement passes through our Parliament in the next few months and enters into force.

This is a decisive moment for the economic future of Australia. It is as vital to our long-term prosperity as floating the dollar and deregulating banking was in the 1980s. The FTA with China will change Australia for the better, it will change China for the better and it will change our region and our world for the better. It will secure the employment of generations of Australians to come. It will provide massive new markets for our entrepreneurs. It will provide investment opportunities that will enrich the Australian people and the Chinese people alike. It is an agreement that is fundamentally fair, giving our nations unprecedented access to each other's markets. It removes barriers to Australian agricultural exports including beef, dairy, lamb, wine, horticulture and seafood, so much so that Meat and Livestock Australia forecast that their sector will benefit by $11 billion over the next decade.

The FTA means duty free entry for 99.9 per cent of our resources, energy and manufacturing exports within four years, so much so that the Minerals Council of Australia says that this will remove nearly $600 million in costs from the bilateral minerals and energy trade.

Remarkably, China has agreed to Australia gaining the most substantial market access of any of its FTA partners apart from Hong Kong and Macau.

Australian banks will be able to expand branch networks in China, Australian fund managers will be able to invest overseas on behalf of qualified Chinese institutions and Australian insurers will be able to provide third-party motor vehicle insurance in China. Over 400,000 Australian workers are employed in financial services. This agreement makes their positions more secure and it will help open new opportunities in this vital sector.

For China, the FTA liberalises the screening threshold for Chinese private sector investment in Australia and it puts Chinese businesses in the same position as those of our other major trading partners.

To protect Australian investors in China, there's an investor-state dispute settlement provision. We've secured this protection for Australian investments in China, so it's only fair that we give the same protection to Chinese investors in Australia.

But I must say this: the FTA's critics have forgotten their history.

After all, we have investor-state dispute settlement provisions in our FTAs with South Korea, Singapore, Chile, Thailand and ASEAN. We have investor-state dispute settlement mechanisms in no less than 21 investment protection and promotion agreements and we've had an investor-state dispute settlement provision with China since the Hawke Government first signed a bilateral investment treaty with China way back in 1988. The evidence of some 27 international agreements is that these provisions protect Australian investments.

And likewise, the FTA's labour mobility provisions protect the integrity of our labour market while allowing businesses to get skilled workers here where labour shortages exist.

Everyone working in Australia will be employed under Australian wages and conditions and will have to meet Australian standards for qualifications. That's fair, that's reasonable and that's what we've agreed to.

The FTAs signed in the past year with Korea and with Japan as well as with China account for nearly 40 per cent of Australia's two-way trade in goods and services. Our Free Trade Agreements with South Korea and with Japan are only months old and yet we are already seeing increased exports, like a 34 per cent increase in frozen beef prime cuts to Korea and a 56 per cent increase to Japan in just 12 months.

Macadamia exports to Korea have more than doubled and Japan is importing 66 per cent more of our rolled or flaked oats. There have been increases in wine, in lamb, in horticulture and other products as well.

Here in Sydney, one business alone, RBK Nutraceuticals, has increased its export sales to just one major customer in Korea by almost 170 per cent in a year and it's now fielding more inquiries from China in anticipation of the FTA coming into force.

Barossa Valley winery, Seppeltsfield, has clinched deals that more than quadruple its sales of premium wine to China to four million litres, in fact, which is about 10 per cent of Australia's total wine sales to China.

So these businesses, and thousands like them across this country, are demonstrating that FTAs mean stronger Australian businesses and more jobs for Australians. Now, in an uncertain world, I'm often asked about Australia's jobs of the future. The answer is absolutely crystal clear: the jobs of the future will be found in the markets of the future. Our efforts to secure these free trade agreements are all about better markets, more trade and more jobs.

As you know, our Trade Minister, Andrew Robb, is now hoping to finalise the Trans-Pacific Partnership agreement. The talks are at their final, critical stage. If the Trans-Pacific Partnership is concluded, it will be the world's largest regional free trade agreement, accounting for around 40 per cent of the global economy and involving almost a billion people, with almost unlimited potential for our businesses.

These free trade agreements are too important for our country; they're too important for our businesses and too important for our children to be sacrificed at the altar of short-term xenophobic politics.

So, I hope that our opponents will end their flirtation with the ideas and the fears of the past. As the former trade minister, Simon Crean, put it: "World trade is a multiplier of economic growth. If people are looking for job opportunities and advanced incomes, the path to that is in opening up trade." It was, after all, Gough Whitlam who signed the first trade agreement with China 42 years ago last Friday.

Likewise, it was a vision for deep engagement with the region that drove Bob Hawke and Paul Keating. So right now, the Labor Party should recall its recent history and listen to the sane economic voice of people like Simon Crean and Martin Ferguson.

After all, a deal is a deal. To amend one part is to re-open it all with big risks to Australian businesses, Australian exports and Australian jobs.

This is a test of character for Labor which first welcomed the China FTA but is now trying to stop it. Freer trade is an essential part of any credible plan to build a strong, prosperous economy for a safe, secure Australia.

Freer trade will strengthen and deepen the relationship between Australia and the nations of our region. Australia has nothing to fear and everything to gain from freer trade. We gain and the world gains as well. Indeed, so much of our region's prosperity has been built on Australian coal, iron ore and gas.

I am proud to lead a country which has done so much to drive the extraordinary economic miracles that we have seen in the countries to our north over the last half-century. Australia can give the countries of our region the resource security, the food security and the energy security that we all seek for the future.

We are in the right place at the right time with the right spirit and as far as I am concerned, we must and we will seize this moment.

'We all need your industry to prosper'
Canberra, 1 October 2014

At the Australian Food and Grocery Council Forum, Prime Minister Abbott pledges greater support to industries and enterprises involved in the production of food and groceries through the abolition of the carbon tax, cutting red tape, building infrastructure, and delivering more job-ready employees through a new apprenticeship system.

It is good to be back here at the Food and Grocery Council. I've been a regular speaker at this forum for many years since I was the Minister for Workplace Relations back in the middle years of the Howard government.

In 2011 and again in 2012, I spoke at this forum and detailed our commitments to the food industry. On both of those occasions I promised to make sure life easier by scrapping the carbon tax. Well, the carbon tax is gone – and thank you for your enthusiasm. Its removal is just the start of building the stronger and more prosperous economy that we all want, with a bigger and more profitable food and grocery sector.

I also promised that we would cut red tape – and that indeed is happening. Earlier this year, we held the Parliament's first ever Red Tape Repeal Day to cut more than 50,000 pages of unnecessary government regulation and legislation. More than 9,500 unnecessary or counterproductive regulations and fully 1,000 redundant acts of Parliament were removed. We are doing it again – there'll be a second Red Tape Repeal Day on 29 October.

I also promised in my previous appearances before this Council, that we would help you get your products to market by building the infrastructure that you need – and we are doing that. The biggest infrastructure programme in Australian history is now underway. There is a $50 billion programme underway to build or improve major roads in our cities and national highways like the Bruce and the Pacific. We have finally resolved the question of Sydney's second airport – or as I like to say, Western Sydney's first airport, after 50 years of procrastination.

I promised competition reform – and Bruce Billson has just spoken to you on the progress we're making there. I promised that we'd improve the participation rate to make it easier for you to find the workers that you need. We've introduced employment incentives for older workers and for long-term unemployed young people. We're expanding Work for the Dole. We are committed to a fair-dinkum paid parental leave scheme that should mean that more mums are participants in our economy as well as participants in our society.

When I've met with owners and managers of food businesses around Australia, you've told me how difficult it is to get job-ready employees. So we're moving to a new apprenticeship system that's employer-led and outcome focused, designed to ensure that we increase the present completely unsatisfactory completion rate for apprentices.

I promised that we'd get the Budget back under control – because we need to control debt rather than let debt control us. That's exactly what we're doing. We are tackling the legacy of debt and deficit that we inherited.

Your *State of the Industry* report highlighted the need to reduce energy, transportation and regulatory costs – and that's what we're doing. Through our deregulation measures, through repealing the carbon tax and through building the infrastructure of the 21st century.

As we reduce your costs and improve your competitiveness – it should mean less cost of living pressure on Australian families, it should mean more jobs and more exports for our country.

So we are, as best we can, honouring our commitments to the food and grocery industry. But keeping commitments is just the start. Our Economic Action Strategy requires constant work, constant improvements, never resting on our laurels. Our message to you today, is that we have a vested interest in the success of your industry.

It is an industry with unlimited potential. You turn over some $114 billion dollars a year; you employ more than 300,000 people. You're exporting more than $27 billion worth of product every year. Our job – my job – is to make it easier for you to do your jobs.

As your report points out, the best way to protect jobs in the food industry is through growth and exports. When I said on election night that Australia was under new management and, once more, open for business, I was acknowledging an iron law of public policy. You can't have strong communities without strong economies to sustain them, and you can't have a strong economy without profitable private businesses. Successful private businesses are central to the prosperity, to the life, to the decency, to the fairness, to the justice of the societies we live in.

It was my great predecessor Sir Robert Menzies who said at the opening of an Edgell factory back in 1959 that you can't truly understand the economic history of this country unless you go and seek to understand the life story and the life endeavours of the human beings who create their own businesses. Everyone in this room is familiar with what it takes to create businesses, either as a businessperson yourself, or as a facilitator of other businesspeople.

Businesspeople take risks, they put their economic future on the line for their business. They mortgage their homes, they risk their future to help others and we need to acknowledge what they do. Gordon Edgell for instance and his sons created an Australian vegetable manufacturing giant from just three acres of asparagus. Thousands of Australians today are following the same path – looking to the food industry to make their mark and their fortune. It's a tough industry – of course it's a tough industry, the vagaries of weather, of markets, of policy, but it's a dynamic industry too. Your industry is a modern success story.

Take Edgell – now Simplot, whose Managing Director, Terry O'Brien is your Chairman. This Government wants to give the Gordon Edgells of 2014 a fair go because all of you out there are having a go. You are reflecting what's best in our Australian character. We want to attract and retain big manufacturers like Simplot, because we need greater economic activity in the non-resources sector.

We need greater workforce participation, better infrastructure and stronger productivity growth. These are all about boosting our competitiveness, strengthening our economy, adding to our ability to have more jobs and more prosperity. The Industry, Innovation and Competitiveness Agenda is being finalised and we will as part of this agenda outline further measures to improve manufacturing competitiveness, encourage innovation and reduce regulatory costs.

I know another concern of yours, is the availability and price of gas for east coast manufacturers. I want to assure you that the Government, as part of the Energy White Paper, is looking at ways to help make the energy sector and energy prices more competitive – through a renewed focus on privatisation and deregulation. The Energy Green Paper, released last week, outlines our proposed policies to tackle this issue and I hope it allays some of your concerns.

As you can see, we are doing everything we can to be open to the businesses of our country. We want to work with business because we know that profit is not a dirty word. We know that without profit you can't survive. If you don't survive you can't employ, invest and create prosperity. I know that our food products are the best in the world. Our reputation for quality, purity and taste means that we can compete effectively in the world market, wherever we have the opportunity to do so. That's why we're doing everything we can to encourage more and freer trade. We have free trade agreements finalised with Japan and with Korea and we hope to do so soon with China. We were the first big agricultural exporter to secure a bilateral agreement with Japan. It's not about "catching up" to preferential treatment other countries have already secured, but about actually delivering to Australian exporters a first-mover advantage. It's a market – Japan – that our food producers know – it's our second largest, worth around $3 billion last year. Now it has more chance to grow, with tariff cuts for beef, for cheese, for sugar, for seafood and improved market access for many processed food exports.

There are also big opportunities for food exporters to Korea, with beef, dairy and wine, big winners from that Free Trade Agreement and tariffs reduced or eliminated on a whole range of horticultural products. Nearly all of my overseas trips have incorporated trade missions – with hundreds of businesses, including some in this sector, travelling with me. So, in Government, we are doing everything we can to open the doors for you – but in the end you still have to walk through them if we are to maximise the benefit of these arrangements.

Now before the election, we often spoke of Australia becoming the food bowl of Asia. In recent times, Agriculture Minister Barnaby Joyce has put the case that the markets and opportunities of Asia are so vast, that even if we doubled, tripled or quadrupled our production in fruit, in vegetables, in meat and groceries, we would still only be providing a fraction of the needs for food in our region. Barnaby is absolutely right. The markets there are so vast and the opportunities are so great – that there really is unlimited potential for this industry. Food and agriculture is not just an important part of our economic past, it is an absolutely vital part of our economic future. The only things that limit us are the physical constraints of our land and climate and our competitiveness as a country. That is why we need to lift our vision and continue to remove the impediments to Australia. This must be a growth industry that generates more exports, creates more jobs and feeds millions more people and I know you are up to this.

I want to thank you for your commitment to working with government to strengthen the foundations of our economy. My commitment to you is to keep working with you to remove any of the burdens that are holding you back – because I want Australia's food and grocery industry to prosper and succeed. We all need your industry to prosper and succeed and I pledge myself to do whatever I humanly can to make that possible.

*

14

DEREGULATION

'Our mission is not bigger government'

House of Representatives, Canberra, 19 March 2014

In this address to Parliament, Prime Minister Abbott points out that, thanks partly to the preceding Government, Australia now stands at 128th on the global index of government regulation. He pledges to repeal unnecessary laws and allow citizens to take control of their own lives.

This is the Government's first report on red tape and what we're doing to reduce it. Next week, the parliament will have its first ever repeal day: to abolish regulation and legislation that's outlived its usefulness or is doing more harm than good.

Cutting red tape is at the heart of this Government's mission: to build a strong and prosperous economy for a safe and secure Australia. Red tape is what officials wrap people in when they think that government knows best. Cutting red tape is a sign that this Government and this parliament want Australians, individually and in the community, to have more control over their own lives. It's an acknowledgement of the people, our masters.

Next week's repeal day will scrap more than 9,500 unnecessary or counter-productive regulations and 1,000 redundant acts of Parliament. More than 50,000 pages will disappear from the statute books. Removing just these will save individuals and organisations more than $700 million a year, every year.

The first repeal day will abolish the Australian Charities and Not-for-Profits Commission because people serving our community don't deserve a new level of scrutiny. It will abolish the Independent National Security Legislation Monitor because all relevant legislation has already been reviewed and the former government ignored all the Monitor's recommendations.

Redundant acts regulating – for instance – the 1970s conversion from imperial to metric measurement, governing state naval divisions (that became part of the Royal Australian Navy 101 years ago) and facilitating the construction of the Snowy Mountains Scheme (that was completed in 1974) will all go.

As a result of repeal day, films will only need to be classified once –

not again and again when they are reissued in DVD, blu-ray or 3D. As a result of repeal day, businesses won't have to re-apply to use agricultural chemicals and veterinary medicines because one approval should be enough. Universities will no longer have to submit capital asset management surveys in addition to other surveys which cover essentially the same thing. And jobs agencies will no longer be required to keep paper records of every applicant which, in one agency alone, occupied 336 filing cabinets. Businesses will no longer be required to administer the former government's paid parental leave scheme, saving them an estimated $48 million.

Associated with repeal day, national businesses will be allowed to operate under one workers' compensation scheme right around our nation rather than have to operate in up to eight.

Next week's repeal day will be the first of many. Under this government, there will be at least two a year – because we will make people's lives easier, not harder.

It's worth recalling that the first parliament of the Commonwealth of Australia passed just 513 pages of legislation – that's just half a page of legislation per day. That's worth contrasting with the last parliament, the 43rd, which passed half an Act of Parliament per day. Between 2007 and 2013, under the former government, some 21,000 new regulations found their way into national life. No doubt, some of these were good and necessary but some, clearly, were overkill at best.

Why should a long day-care centre with 15 staff and 75 places have to do paperwork said to cost, on average, $140,000 a year – which is $2000 a child or nearly $10,000 a staff member? The result of this is fewer child care services and higher prices for the ones that exist.

Why should a Sydney café that serves alcohol and has outdoor seating be subject to 21 local, 29 state and 25 Commonwealth regulations or sets of regulations? That's 75 different hoops to jump through that mean higher costs for businesses and fewer jobs for Australians.

Why should Australian medical researchers collectively put 500 years of work into preparing grant applications – of which only 20 per cent succeed? That's time not put into finding cures for disease.

Likewise, why should every Australian university be required to report more than 50 sets of data to the Commonwealth Department of Education and a further 50 to other government entities. Because, again, this is time and money that's not directed to teaching and research.

Of course, government should be confident that standards are maintained and that taxpayers' money is accounted for but it's too easy for officials to do their job at others' expense in the name of safety or accountability.

A reason why bricks and mortar retailing is losing out to on-line sales is the compliance costs that shops face – from planning regulations to product standards.

A reason why our farmers find it hard to compete is that one dollar in every six of their earnings, the NFF says, is spent on compliance.

About 60 per cent of Australian businesses are sole traders and 85 per cent have fewer than five employees. All too often, the local newsagent, dry cleaner, baker and butcher has to be the accountant, marketer, HR manager and cleaner for the business as well as the chief salesperson. They are virtually suffocating in red tape and it's well past time to say "enough".

On the World Economic Forum's global competitiveness ranking, Australia has slipped six places in four years, to 21st. Australia's ranking on the burden of government regulation, is 128th – yes, 128th in the world – nestled between Romania and Angola. On The Economist's productivity growth ranking, we come second last, just ahead of Botswana.

The first instinct of democratic politicians, confronted with a problem, is to promise to make it go away. Like a fence at the top of a cliff, sometimes regulation is necessary but there's a limit to what government should do to protect us from ourselves.

More regulation is not the solution to every corporate, community or personal failing. Sometimes, we just have to accept that mistakes are inevitable and that misfortunes are unavoidable. When someone in authority gets it wrong, the best outcome might be a timely resignation rather than more regulation. When it comes to making us act responsibly, good example may be better than more rules.

As Tony Blair has conceded, government can't guarantee a risk free life. "Ambiguity, uncertainty, the wisdom that comes with failing and changing your mind", he says, "are all essential to progress"; because "a risk averse public sector will stifle creativity and deny to many the opportunities to be creative".

Since day one, this Government has been cutting red tape. On day one, we began the process of scrapping the carbon tax. Repealing the carbon tax removes over 1,000 pages of primary and subordinate legislation and removes compliance costs from over 75,000 businesses. Repealing the carbon tax not only takes a $9 billion handbrake off our economy and gives a $550 bonus to households but will provide a direct red tape saving to business of $85 million a year.

And repealing the mining tax will save businesses more than $10 million in compliance costs.

Fifty-five announced-but-unlegislated tax measures will no longer proceed – including the previous government's $1.8 billion FBT hit on the car industry, and the cap on self-education expenses that would have hit tradies, nurses and teachers.

Every cabinet submission now has a regulation impact statement so that its potential impact on business, community groups and households can more readily be identified.

All Commonwealth government portfolios now have a dedicated deregulation unit, formed from existing staff, because it's sometimes more important to repeal old laws than to pass new ones.

Each cabinet minister is expected to consult widely before finalising new policy because the first law of government should be: do no harm.

At the December COAG meeting, all states and territories agreed to create one-stop shops for environmental approvals so that major projects will only need to be assessed once, not twice. There's already a one-stop-shop for offshore environmental approvals which the office of best practice regulation estimates will save businesses $120 million a year.

Soon, NH&MRC grants will run for five years – not three – so that successful medical researchers will spend less time filling out forms.

This government is making it easier for people to do business with government by reducing reporting requirements, by using credit cards more and by paying bills on time.

This government has also scrapped the aged care workforce supplement that forced providers to sign up to union-dictated enterprise bargaining agreements.

All these measures demonstrate our seriousness about reducing red tape and making it easier for people to go about their lives. But this is just the start, not the finish.

Every department and agency is conducting a comprehensive audit of the costs it puts on individuals and entities so that it can put a dollar figure on the cost of compliance and reporting and start reducing it every year.

Every department and agency will be required to contribute towards the $1 billion a year, every year, in red tape cost savings that the government is committed to deliver.

The Productivity Commission is finalising the indicators that will make red tape reduction easier to judge.

Not only will deregulation become a standing item on the COAG agenda but there'll be less red tape within COAG, with the number of ministerial councils dropping from 22 to eight.

The reviews that the government has in-train – into competition policy, workplace law, and the financial system – all have a deregulatory focus.

The White Papers that the government plans – into tax and into the federation – are both intended to reduce overlap and complexity.

We are carefully considering the former government's changes to coastal shipping and its changes to trucking rates to ensure that they make doing business easier, not harder.

For too long, governments have acted as if the Australian people work for them. People don't work for government; government should work for people. It's government's job to serve the people; not people's job to serve the government. In simple terms, we work for you. And we're working for you today by creating the biggest bonfire of regulations in our country's history.

Our mission is not bigger government; it's bigger citizens with more opportunities. To the Australian people, I say: this is about saving you money, saving you time, and trusting your common sense to make more choices about your life.

I am proud of the progress that the Government has made to date – but it's only the start of what is to come.

'We are suffering from regulatory overkill'
House of Representatives, Canberra, 22 October 2014

After the success of the first "Red Tape Repeal Day" on 19 March 2014, Prime Minister Abbott announces the second repeal day will include simplified tax returns and smoother interactions with the bureaucracy for people and businesses.

Today, bills are introduced for the second Red Tape Repeal Day. It is the second of many to come.

Every day, this Government is working to build a strong, prosperous economy for a safe, secure Australia.

Every day, we are seeking to identify ways to make life easier for individuals, community groups, charities – and businesses large and small. Our Economic Action Strategy aims to remove the burdens from business, make our country more competitive, and drive more jobs and higher living standards for all Australians.

Today, I am pleased to report that since the election, this Government has reduced annual red tape costs by over $2 billion. And this more than doubles our original commitment of a $1 billion a year cut in red tape costs.

While some regulation is necessary and nearly all regulations originally had some point, we are now suffering from regulatory over-kill. Between 2010 and last year an Act of Parliament was passed every two days. Under the former government, some 21,000 new regulations became part of our national life. And that does not include the regulations, laws and by-laws that were added at state, territory and local levels.

While it is easy to point to bizarre examples, like the ACT Government's attempt to require safety supervisors at sausage sizzles, the purpose of this Government is to look beyond the absurd. It is to identify the raft of red tape that adds costs without a commensurate public benefit.

Talk to any butcher, newsagent, dry cleaner or café owner and he or she will tell you that it is the accumulation of regulation that damages initiative, productivity and the willingness of people to 'have a go'. If red tape can grow incrementally, then it can be cut in the same way. That is what the Government is doing today.

When it comes to regulation, we are changing the culture of government. Deregulation units are now in place across government. Ministerial Advisory Councils have been established so that the people impacted by decisions can have a say on them. Portfolio regulation audits are underway. The performance pay of senior public servants now includes deregulation as a key performance indicator. The site – cuttingredtape. gov.au – has been established, allowing every Australian to make a contribution to the Government's deliberations on cutting red tape.

Regulatory Impact Statements are required for cabinet submissions because assessing the cost of any regulation is as important as knowing its benefits. Soon, a regulatory performance framework will drive cultural change within regulators and help to ensure that regulations are administered effectively and efficiently.

In March, we held the first ever Red Tape Repeal Day. On that day, nearly 10,000 unnecessary or counter-productive regulations and 1,000 redundant acts of Parliament were removed. That day we relegated some 50,000 pages of redundant regulation from the law books to the history books.

Since the first Red Tape Repeal Day, we've scrapped the carbon tax and the Mining Tax. Scrapping the carbon tax not only saves the typical household $550 a year, not only has it removed a $9 billion a year handbrake from our economy and provided a direct red tape saving to business of $85 million a year.

Each Repeal Day is an opportunity to reduce or eliminate regulation and legislation that has outlived its usefulness or does more harm than good. And today, we add to this, with almost 1,000 acts and regulations to be scrapped – more than 7,200 pages. These changes, large and small, are about making people's lives easier.

We are a government freeing up businesses so that they focus on the people they are meant to serve.

We will make it easier for bricks and mortar shops to compete with online stores by reducing their compliance costs – because, all too often, the retail sector has to interact with multiple agencies from local, state and national government.

We're making it easier for Australian Apprenticeship Support Network providers, who will no longer have to maintain some 3 million paper files and waste money every quarter doing so. By reducing administrative costs, these service providers can better focus on assisting apprentices and employers in meeting the skills Australia needs.

We are also making life simpler for users of managed investment schemes, who will no longer have to undertake two separate 'know your customer' checks before they can complete their applications because one check should be enough. Every year, there are over 500,000 new applicants for these schemes. Every duplicate check costs a managed fund around $40, as well as the time the customer spends providing the same information twice.

In healthcare, we are reducing the time taken to list medicines on the PBS, to improve access to vital, life-saving medicines.

And we're delivering a one-stop shop for environmental approvals. Reducing these approval delays is expected to result in regulatory savings to business of over $426 million a year.

Our Industry Innovation and Competitiveness Agenda is promoting lower costs, better skills, and the 'have a go' ethos that is so much a part of the Australian character. By reinvigorating Australian businesses, we've reinvigorated the economy.

Deregulation is an essential part of that agenda because 'bubble wrapping' our creative minds in red tape stifles innovation and flexibility. Importantly, the Competitiveness Agenda included proposals to reduce duplication of our regulatory arrangements where trusted international standards have already been met or trusted international assessments have been made.

Our guiding principle is that if a system, service or product has been approved under a trusted international standard or risk assessment, then Australian regulators should not impose any additional requirement, without a demonstrable reason to do so.

We are already seeing the benefits of this. For instance, the Therapeutic Goods Administration has just advised Cochlear – who make the bionic ear – that all its products are eligible to use European Union certification to streamline TGA certification, and that implementation will begin from next month. This change, according to Cochlear, will mean thousands of people in Australia and overseas will have access to the very latest devices, sometimes up to a year earlier than may otherwise have been the case.

We're making it easier for small to medium exporters to finance their export activity, now that the Export Finance and Insurance Corporation has the flexibility to lend directly for all types of exports – not just capital goods – reducing business costs and processing time. As well, EFIC's adoption of accelerated execution processes for some transactions could shorten processing time by 40 per cent and this could save an average of $5,000 per export contract.

These measures will make it easier for entrepreneurs to transform ideas into reality, and create an environment where small businesses can do more.

And with changes to the Corporations Act governing the administration of general meetings, the management of Australia's largest companies can spend more time focussed on managing their company than managing their shareholders by making it harder for activists to make vexatious requests for shareholder meetings.

We're making these changes because people don't work for government, government should work for people. It is government's job to serve the people; not people's job to serve the government.

We are a country of people who work hard, pay their taxes, volunteer in their local community and save for their retirement. And where we can make it easier for people to spend their time as they choose, rather than waste it filling out forms, we should.

A working mother, for example, who doesn't want to be contacted by telemarketers during her spare time, will be able to register both her home and her mobile phone numbers on the Do Not Call Register. We're now also making sure she doesn't have to remember to re-register every eight years by keeping her numbers on the list indefinitely.

This same mother could also benefit from the rollout of the *myTax* online portal, that pre-fills individuals' returns, so they don't have to spend hours flipping through the pages of a paper tax return. For over 250,000 people, this programme should reduce the time taken to submit a tax return.

And the broader *myGov* system means that Medicare, Centrelink, and Child Support customers can obtain information, make claims, and access services, without having to visit a service centre in person, or spend time on hold on the phone.

Cutting red tape is about making life easier. It means anything from less time in airports waiting in queues because of SmartGate, to more forms of identification that marriage celebrants may accept. Cutting red tape should mean less time in queues, less time filling out forms and less time searching for information.

These changes, and other changes since September 2013, have removed over $2 billion in annual red tape cost. But this is the start, not the end.

We are not only cutting red tape, but changing the culture that fosters and encouraging it. Regulation should not and must not be the default option for policy makers because more regulation is not the answer to every corporate, community or personal failing.

We are a country with highly skilled, highly capable people running our businesses, helping community groups and making our country better. We are putting more trust in them, more trust in them to make the right choices, and we know that our people are up to the task.

I am proud of the progress that we have made so far, and I pledge there is more to come.

15

WOMEN

'We stand for all the women who work hard'
Adelaide, 15 August 2015

In this address to the 70th anniversary lunch of the Liberal Party's Federal Women's Committee, the Prime Minister says more needs to be done to revive the party's proud history of female participation but draws the line at quotas.

It is good to be here to help celebrate the 70th anniversary of the Federal Women's Committee and to honour the work of women in our Party.

That tradition began more than 70 years ago when Sir Robert Menzies sought to unify the conservative side of politics. The Australian Women's National League was one of the strongest of the groups that Menzies summoned to discuss the formation of our Party. In return for joining the new Liberal Party, League President Dame Elizabeth Couchman insisted on the equal representation of men and women in senior party positions, at least in the Victorian division.

This was the first occasion that a quota was established for female political representation anywhere in Australia – and it happened in the Liberal Party and under our founder. It entrenched the place of women in the structures of our Party and provided a springboard for some to enter parliament.

The first woman ever to be elected to an Australian parliament represented the conservative side of politics; the first women to be elected to parliament in most states and in the House of Representatives were Liberals; and Liberal women were the first to achieve ministerial rank at state and national level.

Women like Enid Lyons, Annabelle Rankin, Ivy Wedgwood, Marie Breen and Margaret Guilfoyle were trailblazers for our country and for our Party. In more recent times, people like Margaret Reid, Kathy Sullivan and Julie Bishop, my deputy, have added to the litany of firsts for Liberal women.

Menzies' declaration, back in 1944, that "men and women will, side by side, be members of this organisation", reflected his aspiration to create a party that was beholden to no one and open to everyone.

Menzies was ahead of his time when it came to female participation and representation. He understood that if the Liberal Party was to become the party of aspiration then it had to be the party of aspiration for all.

Ever since, we have tried to be the party that embodied people's hopes for a better life and confidence in their own capacities to achieve it.

Ever since, Liberals have believed in an Australia that's better tomorrow than it is today.

I am proud to lead a party that's not a collection of union officials but of Australians from all walks of life who want to have a go.

We're the party of Dame Enid Lyons – the first woman to enter the ministry. We're the party of Neville Bonner and Ken Wyatt – the first indigenous people to take their places in the Senate and the House of Representatives. We're the party of teachers and nurses and police officers; of soldiers and farmers and business people.

In our party, you don't have to serve your time as an office bearer in order to enter parliament; our party prides itself on choosing the best and the most electable candidate for every seat, and not just taking the factions' pick.

It's precisely because merit should be all that matters, that I ask myself: why isn't our party selecting more women members of parliament? Why isn't our party, as relatively advanced on this today as we were 70 years ago? Why haven't we remained ahead of our time in promoting women; and is that one of the reasons why we no longer attract the majority of women voters? On this anniversary, we owe it to ourselves and to those who have gone before us to pose this question.

As many of you know, I grew up in a household of strong women. My mother went to university and entered a profession at a time when that was not common for women. At the family dinner table, I had to hold my own with three strong-willed and opinionated sisters. You often hear one of my opinionated sisters right now.

I live in a household of strong women who were raised and educated to believe that there should be no artificial barriers to their achievement. I work with strong women – who help to keep me aware of the ways that women can still be made to feel like outsiders.

Our party must always be a welcoming forum for women to argue their case, to win on their merits and to realise their ambitions because they're very good at their job.

Yet there is consistently low female representation across our party. There are relatively few women in leadership positions in the lay party; there are relatively few women in the parliament; and because there are relatively few women in the parliament it's harder to get more women into the cabinet.

Regrettably, the percentage of Liberal women in both chambers has plateaued since John Howard came into office. In the national parliament, women hold one in five of our seats in the House of Representatives and about one in six in the Senate; or to put it the other way, men hold four in every five of the House seats and five in every six of our Senate seats.

It's hard to believe that politically-committed and meritorious conservative men outnumber like-minded women by at least four to one. Naturally, I do acknowledge differences between men and women – but when it comes to political aspiration, we're just not that unlike.

Equally with men, women are interested in jobs, growth and community safety. Equally with men, women aspire to be all they can be. And equally with men, women have at least as much faith in their own judgment and capacity than in the benevolence and omniscience of officials.

I love this party, as you do, and I want it to be the very best it can be; and that has to include a determination to give a fair go to politically interested and able women. If even the Australian Army can become less blokey, then so must we. If the leaders of Telstra, the Commonwealth Bank, Woolworths, Rio Tinto, and Goldman Sachs can be "male champions of change", so must the men of the Liberal Party.

To be serious about winning elections, we must be more serious about engaging, pre-selecting, and sending to parliament the representatives of 50 per cent of the electorate.

Today, the Menzies Research Centre is releasing its report, Gender and Politics, pointing out that the lack of female representation is reducing our capacity to reach voters. It's a statement of the obvious – but it needed to be said – and it now needs to be addressed.

As it happens, governments often hold themselves to account by setting targets. For instance, this government has a target to create a million jobs within five years – and, two years on, I can report that we are on track to meet that target. We have a target to cut a billion dollars a year every year from red tape costs – and we're meeting that target and helping our country's small businesses along the way. We have a target to return the Budget to a strong surplus within a decade – and we're on track for that target too. We have a target of zero boats – and we've met that over the past year. We have emissions targets – that we've more-than-met to date – and this week, we announced further targets for 2030. And we have targets for public servants and for directors of government boards in order to make government more representative of the people it serves.

So it would be entirely reasonable for our party to have – not a quota – but a target to increase the number of women in the parliament and in our government at every opportunity.

Of course, the right representation at any time depends upon the choices available. Of course, it's up to every pre-selection panel to choose the best candidate regardless of gender. But if we don't get the percentage of women up, we will be letting ourselves down. At every election, at every reshuffle, we should aim for a higher percentage of women than before.

Right now, federal Vice President Rosemary Craddock is preparing a report to the Federal Executive on making our party more representative. I have asked Senators Cash, in her capacity as minister assisting me for women, and Reynolds, as a former Assistant National Director of the Party, to support this report by ensuring that the views of all our female members of the House of Representatives and the Senate are included.

As a member of the Federal Executive myself, I hope that the report will canvas specific steps to lift our female parliamentary representation and propose specific targets and goals for the years ahead.

If we lift our female representation, we should improve our overall representation and maximise our longer term chances of consistently winning elections and holding government.

We need to have a platitude-free conversation inside our party about how we can make more of ourselves by making more of those women who are natural Liberals. Every one of us needs to be alert to encouraging smart, liberal conservative women to consider a future in public life. This is not abandoning our history but being true to it. After all, it was Menzies himself, who said that we stand for the "forgotten people" and it was Howard who said that we stand for "all of us".

We stand for the women who start their own businesses – and we should want them to stand for us. We stand for the mums who seek a better future for their families – and we should want them to stand for us. We stand for all the women who work hard, pay taxes, volunteer in our communities and save for their retirement. We stand for them; we stand with them; and we should want more of them to stand as our representatives – for our party's sake and for our country's.

Seventy years ago, the federal Women's Council was founded largely thanks to the tenacity of Dame Elizabeth Couchman. Dame Elizabeth never made it to the Senate despite Menzies' observation that "she would have been the best cabinet minister I could have wished for". Her legacy, though, has been to ensure that the women who followed her had a stronger voice in our party and more opportunity to pursue the political career that she was denied.

So today, we recommit to that legacy and to making this great Party of ours the very best that it can be.

From 'unreconstructed bloke' to feminist
Parliament House, Canberra, 4 March 2014

Addressing his first International Women's Day as Prime Minister, Mr Abbott attributes his evolving views on women to the household he shares with four women – his wife and three daughters.

I have to say that, once upon a time, I may not have felt quite so comfortable addressing a breakfast like this as I do now. As my wife, Margie, quipped some time ago, "what is it that turns an un-reconstructed bloke into a feminist? Three daughters."

And it is true that my views on policy towards women have changed and evolved in response to watching friends of mine, watching colleagues of mine and in particular looking at my daughters grow up and thinking what would I want for them?

What would I want for these beautiful, intelligent, sensitive girls who have so much going for them and who deserve a world which recognises all of their talents and wants to give them every possible opportunity.

Now, they are growing up in Australia and, regardless of your circumstances, Australia is the best country in the world for everything.

Anyone who is in Australian has won the lottery of life and if you look at our country and the deal that it gives to women; it is obviously pretty good. It wasn't so long ago as a Sydney-sider that there was a female Lord Mayor, a female Premier, a female Prime Minister, a female Head of State in our Governor General, a female Monarch, obviously, and indeed the richest person in our country was female.

So, this is a nation which has smashed just about every glass ceiling, but we need to do more – we need to do more.

Now, I am not here to give a party-political broadcast this morning but I do want to say to you that I believe a fair dinkum paid parental leave scheme is an idea whose time has come.

I pay tribute to the former government for beginning the process of giving us a fair dinkum paid parental leave scheme.

As you know, the Howard Government, of which I was proudly a minister, introduced the baby bonus. The baby bonus was what you did when you didn't want to have a paid parental leave scheme and back in my un-reconstructed days I was a strong supporter of the baby bonus. I still am for people who are not in the workforce – for parents who are not in the workforce.

The former government, to its credit, converted the baby bonus into the beginnings of a decent paid parental leave scheme and I think now we need to go further.

Now, it's always a bit disconcerting when something happens that you don't expect. It is a little disconcerting when a conservative, when a traditionalist such as myself, comes up with something which is not regarded as a conservative and a traditional position.

It is a bit like when Nixon went to China, conservatives thought, "my God, has he suddenly abandoned the faith?" Progressives thought, "my God, is China no longer a progressive country?" The truth is this was a historic breakthrough. This was one of those moments when people from all sides of politics needed to realise that a watershed had been reached. So, it is, I like to think, with the Coalition support for a fair dinkum paid parental leave scheme.

Just imagine if a progressive had come up with this idea. The usual suspects would have been cheering and saying about time. But because a conservative has come up with this idea so many people are saying there must be something wrong with it.

Well, I say, don't oppose it – embrace it. Don't oppose it – embrace it. Let's drop this silly guilt by association and let's get on with something which is unambiguously good for the women of our country, for the families of our country and for the economy of our country.

The more we can ensure that women are economic as well as social and cultural contributors, the better for everyone.

I celebrate International Women's Day. I celebrate this month of March which is a month to focus on women and their achievements. And I say let's turn good intentions into real action. Let's get on with a fair dinkum paid parental leave scheme. Let's give every woman a chance to combine family and career. It is good for all of us.

16

LEADERSHIP, DIRECTION & GOVERNANCE

'It's not the system which is the problem'
Parliament House, Canberra, 26 August 2014

At the launch of Paul Kelly's *Triumph & Demise: The Broken Promise of a Labor Generation*, about the self-destruction of the Rudd and Gillard Governments, Prime Minister Abbott resists the temptation of triumphalism and instead applauds Kelly's evenhanded and considered treatment of events.

Paul Kelly and I go back quite a long way. Back in the late 1980s I was a relatively young editorial writer at *The Australian*. Paul, even then, was the guru in chief of the press gallery and I was often instructed by editor, Frank Devine, not to write our editorial of the day without first discussing it with Paul Kelly.

I was, relatively young and quite junior. Paul was the sage of Canberra. He was unfailingly courteous, unfailingly patient with the precocious colleague in Sydney and he kept talking to me even though from time to time I had the temerity not to agree with the Kelly line.

This is the thing about Paul Kelly: you never read a Kelly column, you never have a conversation with Kelly which is not utterly instructive. I have benefited enormously, not just from Paul's friendship but from his wisdom.

As a neophyte political staffer, having moved from *The Australian* to the office of the then Leader of the Opposition John Hewson, I recall receiving a special visit from *The Australian's* political correspondent in chief.

It was about 5.30 one Friday afternoon. It was quite unusual for a person of such gallery seniority to pay a special visit to the then Opposition Leader's press office but Paul came in. He sat me down and he said "I have a little test for you. Who is the most successful Opposition Leader of the post war period?" I said, Gough Whitlam. He said, "Here is a harder question for you – why was Gough Whitlam such a successful Opposition Leader?" And I scratched my head for a few moments. Paul said, "He was a successful Opposition Leader not just because he won elections but because he set agendas and he set agendas by making considered, powerful, thoughtful speeches which helped to shape the whole political culture in which he operated and indeed all of us operated".

I am not sure that I have been able to follow Paul's advice but I certainly accept it. If you don't set the agenda, you can't successfully run a government.

The tragedy, if I may say so, of the former Government, which is chronicled in Paul's book; the tragedy for itself, because I think in the end it was at the heart of its failure, the tragedy for our country, because it is in our national interest for all our governments to succeed, regardless of their political persuasion, the tragedy of the last Government was that it was much better at politics than government. It wasn't able, in the end, to set the agenda even though it was very good, at least early on, at generating headlines.

Over 40 years, Paul Kelly has been our foremost political commentator but certainly our finest historian of contemporary politics. *Triumph and Demise* reinforces his standing as our finest historian of contemporary politics.

Everyone who is interested in public life, everyone who is interested in Australian politics, should read this book – not just read the book, they should assimilate the book, they should learn from the book.

This is the first considered draft of the history of these times.

There's been an abundance of journalism about the last six years, but, inevitably, daily journalism lacks perspective.

We've seen some books written about the last six years. Inevitably, by partisans – by participants. It's been advocacy, it's been partisanship, sometimes it's been score settling; it hasn't been history. Paul has given us the first considered draft of the history of these times.

I wish to leave the judgements of those times – the judgements on the Rudd/Gillard era – to Paul, the author, and to his readers. Yes, Paul is critical – very critical – of the former government. What shines through though, even when he is critical, is his generosity to all of the participants in our parliamentary and public life.

Even when Paul is being critical, he sees the strengths as well as the weaknesses of the participants in our national drama. He sees their qualities as well as their flaws, and it's this generosity of spirit as well as perceptiveness of judgement which sets Paul apart from so many of his fellow contemporary journalists.

Not for Kelly, the sourness which so often contaminates so much commentary. Not for Kelly, the shallowness which is the subject matter

299

of so much commentary. He is interested in the big picture, in what really matters, not in just the gossip of the day or of the week.

There is one substantial issue with which I do take issue with Paul. Paul suggests, in a very important final chapter of the book, that our system is in trouble and because our system is in trouble, our country might be in trouble.

Paul suggests that the relentless negativity of our contemporary conversation, the culture of entitlement that he thinks has sprung up over the last decade or so, means that good government has become difficult, perhaps impossible.

There is no doubt that good government today is harder than ever before, in part, because of the 24/7 media cycle, which politicians inevitably need to feed. It's difficult to avoid trivialising what shouldn't be trivialised when it has to be spoken about and spoken about differently one hour from the next.

I was watching Sky just the other day, as you do, and at about 5.50 there was David Speers interviewing Stan Grant about the events of the day, and then shortly after 6 o'clock we had Stan Grant interviewing David Speers about the events of the day. As a political junky it is riveting television! For a political tragic, everything that they said to each other was worth listening to. But, it's easy to lose sight of the fundamentals that shape our nation when we are this immersed in commentary on commentary.

The system that produced the Rudd/Gillard government is the same system that produced the Hawke government, the same system that produced the Howard government. The Hawke government was undoubtedly the best Labor Government in our history, and along with the Menzies government, the Howard government can lay claim to being the best conservative government in our history.

If this system could produce, in the recent past, two outstanding governments, there is no reason why it can't, in the near future, produce other outstanding governments. It's not the system which is the problem; it is the people who, from time to time, inhabit it.

Our challenge, at every level, is to be our best selves. The challenge for all of us and everyone in this room today as part of the system, is to lift ourselves so that we see the system at its best, not the system at its worst.

The mission, if I may say so, of the current Government, is to demonstrate, through its action, ultimately through its record, that the last six years – the six years between 2007 and 2013 – is not the new normal; that it was in fact just a passing phase.

Our challenge – the challenge of the current Government – is to show that the age of reform has not ended, it was merely interrupted.

I believe it is absolutely critical for our country that we succeed in this task, and if we do succeed in this task, I am sure that no one would be happier than Paul Kelly himself.

'We've laid a strong foundation'
Canberra, 2 February 2015

Sixteen months after being elected to Government, the Prime Minister outlines his team's impressive achievements to a lunch at the National Press Club in Canberra - including the release of an Australian journalist from an Egyptian prison, the abolition of two debilitating taxes, a record number of new companies and stopping the boats – and says there is still much to do.

As a former journalist myself, it would be remiss of me at such a gathering of journalists not to express my personal delight and our nation's relief at the overnight release of Peter Greste and to reiterate our support, as a Government and as a people for a free media and a free press.

I particularly want to place on record my gratitude to Egypt's President, el-Sisi, for the understanding he has shown every time I have discussed with him Peter Greste's predicament. His role in Peter's release cannot be underestimated.

I also want to thank the Foreign Minister for her tireless advocacy on Peter Greste's behalf. And so, today, as we begin this important address, we should remember Peter Greste's ordeal. I say to Peter's family: you never gave up hope and your strength is an inspiration to all of us.

At the outset I want to let all of you know that, as you would expect, over the summer, I've been talking to hundreds of Australians from all walks of life – in the street, on the beach, in cafes, even at the pub; and I've been talking with my colleagues.

As every Australian agrees, to live here is to have won the lottery of life – because we are as free, fair and prosperous as any country on earth. But these are testing times for our country.

2014 was a tumultuous year that's reminded us to expect the unexpected.

Thirty eight Australians were shot out of the sky by Russian-backed rebels.

A death cult, claiming justification in Islam, is creating a new dark age over much of Syria and Iraq.

And the terrorism it inspires has hit Melbourne and Sydney.

It was an anxious year for our well-being, as well as for our security.

At last, the US is growing, but Europe is stagnating, and China – our economic locomotive – is now growing at its slowest rate in a quarter of a century.

And the price of iron ore – our biggest export – has halved in just over a year.

In troubled times, people expect more of government, not less – and we have to deliver.

That's why a government with the plan and the will to strengthen our economy and to protect our nation is so important.

This government is more determined than ever to make the changes our country needs.

This government will deliver Australia's economic future because only a Coalition government can.

As Liberals and Nationals, sound economic management is in our DNA. We've done it before and we are doing it again. More than ever, in troubled times, government has to protect our people and stand up for Australian values.

This government would hardly have taken the political risks it has without the conviction that some change is absolutely unavoidable if our country is to flourish.

To create more jobs and more opportunities for families, we simply have to build a stronger economy. A stronger economy is the foundation of a stronger Australia. And if the economy is stronger, everyone's life is better. A stronger economy helps everyone who's doing it tough:

- parents wrestling with school fees and health costs.
- small business people anxious to keep their staff
- seniors whose superannuation has to fund their retirement
- volunteers wondering if they can still afford to serve the community
- young people looking for their first job and their first home.

Building a stronger economy is the fairest thing we can do because it means more jobs, higher wages, and more government revenue to pay for the services we need. During 2015, our priority will be creating more jobs; easing the pressure on families; building roads; strengthening national security; and promoting more opportunity for all – with a new families policy and a new small business and jobs policy.

But we need to be candid about the challenges we face. The drift of the Rudd-Gillard-Rudd years cannot continue. Standing still on reform means going backwards on living standards.

Just a few years back, under the Howard government, we were quite literally the envy of the world.

In 2007, we had a strong and sustainable budget with a $20 billion surplus and $50 billion in the bank. After six years of Labor, the deficit had blown out to $50 billion and gross debt was skyrocketing towards $667 billion. Under Labor, government was spending too much; borrowing too much; and paying out too much dead money in interest alone. We can't wait for a crisis – like Europe – to address this problem because the solutions then will be much worse than the solutions today.

Our problem is not that taxes are too low; our problem is that government spending is too high. We are writing cheques that our children and grandchildren will have to meet through higher taxes, higher interest rates and poorer services.

Right now, we're borrowing $1 billion a month just to pay the interest on debt that the former Labor government ran up. That's right – one thousand million every month to pay Labor's interest bill – that's a brand new tertiary hospital that could be built every single month if Labor's interest bill did not have to be paid. And without structural change, within a decade, we'd be borrowing $3 billion a month just to pay the interest on Commonwealth debt.

So let's spend the money we have to on the things we really need; and let's borrow where we must, to invest judiciously in a stronger Australia for the future – but let's stop borrowing just to meet the ordinary expenses of government.

Reducing the deficit means that interest rates will stay lower. Reducing the deficit means that taxes can be cut. Reducing the deficit means more confidence in the economy. And reducing the deficit is the fair thing to do – because it ends the intergenerational theft against our children and grandchildren. We've never been a country that's ripped off future generations to pay for today. And under my government, we never will.

On election night, I declared that Australia was under new management and once more open for business. Since then, new projects worth over $1 trillion have received environmental approval. The carbon tax is gone – so every household, on average, is $550 a year better off.

The mining tax is gone – so Australia once more is seen as a good place to invest. Big new road projects are now getting underway to overcome commuter gridlock – and the new Western Sydney Airport is finally to be built after 50 years of indecision.

After 10 years of talk, free trade agreements covering more than 50 per cent of our exports – with China, Japan and South Korea – have been finalised with better markets for Australian farmers and lower prices for Australian consumers. The live cattle trade that Labor closed down in panic over a TV program is booming again. There are now 15,000 new trade support loans because apprentices finally have the support that's long been offered to university students. At last, the NBN is rolling out, reliably and affordably. And despite the argy-bargy, in every sitting fortnight since last July, the Senate has passed at least one major piece of legislation. And, of course, the illegal boats that just kept coming and coming under the former Labor government have all-but-stopped.

The Abbott government has stopped the boats – and only this government will keep them stopped. The Abbott government has scrapped the carbon tax – and only this government will keep it scrapped. My position on carbon taxes has been crystal clear since day one as party leader. There will be no carbon tax under a government I lead.

At the election, the economy was weakening, the budget was haemorrhaging and unemployment was rising. Today, despite headwinds overseas, the economy is stronger, the budget is improving and the jobs market has strengthened. Jobs growth in 2014 was triple the rate in 2013 – with 4,000 new jobs a week. New housing approvals are at record levels. The registration of new companies is the highest on record. Economic growth is now 2.7 per cent, up from 1.9 per cent a year ago. Petrol prices are nearing 15 year lows, home loan interest rates are low and stable, and the September quarter had the biggest fall in power prices on record.

But I'm not here to defend the past – I'm here to explain the future. People are sick of Australian citizens – including people born and bred here – making excuses for Islamist fanatics in the Middle East and their imitators here in Australia. It's not good enough just to boost the police and security agencies, which we've done – by restoring the millions ripped out by Labor – and to improve data retention, which we're doing. We have to tackle the people and the organisations that justify terrorism and act as its recruiting agents – such as Hizb-ut-Tahrir. We have already made it an offence to advocate terrorism and made it easier to ban terrorist organisations. If cracking down on Hizb-ut-Tahrir and others who nurture extremism in our suburbs means further legislation, we will bring it on and I will demand that the Labor Party call it for Australia. The police and the security agencies have told me that they need access to telecommunications data to deal with a range of crime, from child abuse to terrorism, and – as far as I am concerned – they should always have the laws, money and support they need to keep Australia safe.

And with the world still feeling the global financial crisis, people are anxious about our economic sovereignty. I am a friend of foreign investment but it has to come on our terms and for our benefit. The government will shortly put in place better scrutiny and reporting of foreign purchases of agricultural land and better enforcement of the rules against foreign purchases of existing homes so that young people are not priced out of the market.

These laws were not legally enforced by the former Labor government – not once.

This year, the government's budget focus will be on strengthening the economy. Because we have done much of the hard work already, we won't need to protect the Commonwealth budget at the expense of the household budget.

As the intergenerational report will show, more is needed to put the budget on a credible path to a sustainable surplus – but as New Zealand has demonstrated, a good way to achieve this is not to make any unnecessary new spending commitments.

We will always be looking for ways to make government more efficient and to crack down on waste. Governments should never spend more than they must because every dollar government spends is a dollar you don't spend, now or in the future. So any new spending will strictly be directed to making the economy stronger so that long-term revenue increases.

Before Christmas, I said that over the break I'd be better targeting the proposed paid parental leave scheme and scaling it back, in a families package focused on childcare. I admire stay-at-home mums, as Margie was when our children were young, but support better paid parental leave to maximise young people's – like my daughters' – choices to have a career and to have a family too.

I accept, though, that what's desirable is not always doable, especially when times are tough and budgets are tight. As the Productivity Commission has said, and as mums and dads around Australia have reminded me, the focus really does have to be on childcare if we want higher participation and a stronger economy. So a bigger parental leave scheme is off the table.

Values and beliefs are important but the most important consideration of all is what will best help families at this time. I know that many women in many families are working just to pay the childcare – because that was the Abbott family's experience when Margie first went back to work after becoming a mother. Childcare fees skyrocketed 50 per cent under Labor which abandoned its promise to build 260 new centres. More affordable and more available childcare means less pressure on the family budget. More parents in the workforce mean that more people will make a bigger economic contribution as well as a social contribution to our country.

Women, after all, are our country's most under-utilised source of skills and entrepreneurship – if female participation in Australia were six per cent higher, at Canada's level, GDP would be higher by $25 billion a year. So a better childcare policy is good economic policy as well as fairer family policy. We'll now consult widely on a way to improve the system of multiple payments, keep costs down, and put more money into parents' pockets.

As well as a families package, we're also working on a small-business and jobs package.

I admire people who take risks, have a go and employ others. If you're a small business owner, it's likely that you've mortgaged your home in order to invest, employ and serve the community. Quite literally, you have put your economic life on the line for others.

Every big business started off as a small business. The new industries of tomorrow are likely to be started by the small businesses of today. The best antidote to sunset industries is sunrise ones – and these are most likely to emerge from an enterprising small business.

At the heart of our small business jobs package will be a small business company tax cut on July 1 – at least as big as the 1.5 per cent already flagged. More jobs and better paid workers will only come from more profitable employers in a better position to employ people. Every new worker is generating revenue – so spending to get unemployed people into work; on childcare to keep parents in the workforce; on infrastructure to get people to their jobs; and on a small business tax cut to create jobs will help to get the budget back towards the surplus our country needs.

Economic growth is the best and fastest way to restore the surplus. I hope that 2015 will see a more honest national conversation between all of us with Australia's best interests at heart.

I want this year's white paper process – on reforming the federation and on tax – to demonstrate Australians' potential for change for the better rather than just politics as usual.

Finding ways to make every level of government more efficient, more effective and more accountable is in every Australian's best interest and shouldn't be an excuse for cheap shots.

Everyone who wants members of parliament to lift their game has an interest in governments taking more responsibility for the services they provide, instead of passing the buck.

We will also be inviting constructive debate across the political spectrum on all options for a better tax system to deliver taxes that are lower, simpler and fairer. Unlike previous debates, we won't pre-empt the outcome by ruling things in or out before the process has properly begun.

I do assure you, though, that this government wants to be remembered for cutting the overall tax burden, not for increasing it – for abolishing existing taxes, rather than imposing new ones.

As for the GST – it can't and it won't change unless all the states and territories agree.

It can't and won't change unless there is political consensus. That means – leaving aside any minor administrative changes – that the base and the rate of the GST won't change this term or next unless it's supported by the likes of Bill Shorten and the Labor premiers.

Both white paper processes will be open and constructive: stakeholders will be consulted, submissions will be published; any hearings will be open, and the states will have senior representatives on steering committees. Everyone who wants a say will have one – and the people will have the last word at the ballot box.

Sooner or later, all responsible members of Parliament have to put the long term national interest ahead of their short term political interest and there's no better time to start than now.

So far, this government – and only this government – has had the courage to tackle the deficit, to protect our borders, and to build a stronger and more prosperous economy. As I said so many times before the election, we will end the waste, stop the boats, scrap the unnecessary new taxes and build the roads of the 21st century.

And the results? Waste – down. Boats – stopped. Carbon tax – gone. Roads – under way. Sixteen months on, we've laid a strong foundation – but there's more to do and we're determined to get it done.

Our country is at an important economic crossroads. There's a mess to clean up after six years of Labor chaos. The Rudd-Gillard-Rudd years cannot become the new normal lest Australia join the weak government club and become a second rate country living off its luck.

You elected us to set Australia up for the long term.

You elected us to be an adult government focused on you, not on ourselves. You elected us to make the decisions needed so that everyone who works hard gets ahead, aspiration is rewarded, and our children can look forward to more opportunities than we had. You elected us to keep you safe and, with every fibre of my being, I am focussed on our national security challenges here and overseas.

Standing up for Australian values is something I have done all my life. Leadership is about making the right decisions for our country's future. It isn't a popularity contest. It's about results; it's about determination; and it's about you.

Australia deserves the stable government that you elected us to be just 16 months ago.

You deserve budget repair, no return of the carbon tax, no restart of people smuggling, and no in-fighting. We promised that we would do our best to keep you safe. We promised you hope, reward and opportunity. That's what the Abbott government is working to deliver for you.

'Our duty is to leave behind a greater nation'
Sir Henry Parkes Oration
Tenterfield, NSW, 25 October 2014

Delivering the Sir Henry Parkes Oration in honour of the man dubbed the "Father of the Federation", Prime Minister Abbott reflects on the challenge to balance power between the states and Canberra, and announces a steering group to guide reform.

It's great to be here at this place where history has been made, because on this day, in this place 125 years ago Sir Henry Parkes made a speech which started the process towards creating a Commonwealth of Australia.

He'd been to Queensland for a meeting, the meeting hadn't been a great success, so he wanted to salvage – as I understand it – something from that trip. So, after being on the train for some seven hours from Brisbane, he called in here to Tenterfield, he came into this building and he gave a galvanising speech – a speech which echoed, if not around the world, certainly around our country.

Then we had no national government. Then, as we've been reminded earlier this evening, we had six colonies, each of them with a prime minister. No army, no unified railway, an embryonic sense of Australian-ness, but no nation that we could call our own, no government that was our national government.

That was then – these days are different. We certainly have a national government and yet we have an unsatisfactory system of governance, because all too often wherever you look – whether it be the roads, the schools, the hospitals – it's hard to know who is in charge. That is what bedevils modern Australia in so many areas of our national life – who is really in charge?

So, just as here in this hall 125 years ago, Sir Henry Parkes started a process that gave us a nation, I hope tonight that we might start a process that will give us a more rational system of government. He launched from this hall the federation that was right for those times. Let us relaunch the federation tonight in a way that is right for these times.

Now I was very pleased to receive some months ago the invitation

310

to give this address in memory of Sir Henry Parkes because for many years now I have regarded our federation as having come to a sorry pass. For many years now, as a practitioner of government, as a minister in government, I have thought that we could do better. And the Coalition I have the honour to lead said before the last election that we would start a process with the aim of trying to ensure that once more for these times, as in those times, every level of government will be sovereign in its own sphere and that process is formally begun tonight.

Let me begin tonight, not with Sir Henry Parkes, but with a contemporary now lost in his shadow who helped to make possible Parkes' achievement as a founder of our federation. When Parkes lost his seat in the New South Wales parliament earlier in 1882, Edward Whereat – then just elected as the member for Tenterfield – resigned his own seat in Parkes' favour. Whereat himself explained this extraordinary act of magnanimity by declaring that Parkes "would be listened to with more attention in one moment" than he would be "if he spoke for 20 years". This remarkable piece of political selflessness exemplifies the spirit that's needed for many of our biggest issues to be resolved.

In an atmosphere of rancid partisanship, few great national questions can ever satisfactorily be decided. It was in negotiation and compromise, as much as the dogged pursuit of principle that led to our federation and produced our Commonwealth. The fathers of our federation were often political opponents but they worked together patiently for the greater good, on the understanding that getting something invariably meant giving something too.

The constitution they created over a decade of horse-trading entirely pleased no one but it's served well enough to shape a nation that is as free, fair and prosperous as any on this earth. Indeed, it's this very readiness to give and take with opponents of good faith; this ability to understand the other person's point of view, and to concede something to it, that has enabled us to resolve differences peacefully and to work more-or-less harmoniously together for more than a century in ways that have eluded less successful countries.

After all – at least in countries like ours – most contention is not between good and evil but between decent people arguing over the best way to achieve a better outcome. Any debate about the future of our federation needs the same give and take if it is to produce significant change. It needs to resemble the kind of measured debate that we can have over national security or about indigenous recognition rather than the debate we've had over the budget for instance or the carbon tax – because reforming the federation is not something that one person, one party or one parliament can determine alone.

Because it involves numerous governments of different political persuasion, reforming the federation will require people from across the usual political divides and from different levels of government to work together over an extended period of time.

Rethinking the conventions about which level of government is responsible for the delivery of particular services or the revenue measures to which particular levels of government should have access will require a readiness to compromise and a mutual acceptance of goodwill that's rarely achieved in our highly partisan system.

Without a measure of consensus, any change requiring legislation is unlikely to secure parliamentary passage and the whole exercise could turn out to be futile. Without an element of consensus, any change that's actually achieved could be reversed at the earliest opportunity and therefore hardly worth doing. But, reforming the federation does matter, it is worth trying to achieve and this Government is determined to make the case for change.

What's needed now is not a final answer but a readiness to consider possibilities, to engage in debate, and shoulder our collective responsibility for making our country all that it can be.

When Parkes gave his celebrated address in this very room 125 years ago – the address that is now taken to have galvanised the federation movement – his main focus was the self-evident benefit of one national army and one national rail gauge. As we know, our country has now had a national army for more than a century; and a standard gauge railway line has linked our mainland capitals for fifty years.

The problem, then, was to create a nation from six colonies. The problem now, is to create a more rational system of government for the nation that we undoubtedly have become. It's to realise, if possible, the self-evident benefits of less waste, less overlap, less duplication; it's to end the blame game by trying to ensure that voters know who's really responsible for the things they don't like; and it's to harvest the multi-billion dollar benefits in better services and lower costs that would come from successful reform.

Lack of "big bang" reform would not be a disaster but it would be a disappointment and it would be a failure of this generation of politicians.

Of course, the Australian people, deep down, could actually prefer the messiness and ambiguity of our current arrangements because they make it harder for governments to change what we've learned to live with.

The federation we have – for all its flaws – has spawned a vibrant democracy, a strong economy and a cohesive society that millions of migrants have chosen to join.

And the federation is being reformed – incrementally – all the time: through the agreements that the Commonwealth and the states make, or decline to make with each other; and the unilateral decisions that all governments make that impinge on the role of other governments.

Reform of our federation will happen. Either we will have organised reform or ad hoc reform, it will be cooperative change or it will be coercive change. But change will come and I say let's manage it together. After all, asking ourselves "what can be done better?" is at the heart of all progress.

We would be failing in our duty not to consider better management of the "dog's breakfast of divided responsibilities" that characterises this Australian federation today. It's not entirely dysfunctional – our country couldn't succeed if it were – but it's plainly not optimal either which is why reform is worth striving for.

A hundred years ago the states were clearly responsible for funding and operating public schools, public hospitals, public transport, roads, police, housing and planning. Under our constitution, the states are still legally responsible for them but a century of encroachment has left the Commonwealth financially responsible for vast services that it doesn't actually deliver and can't really control.

After two decades of "cooperative federalism" and any number of agreements at Council of Australian Government meetings, we still have tradesmen who cannot operate across state borders because their qualifications are not automatically recognised in other parts of Australia.

Yet there is hardly a problem that doesn't produce calls for "national leadership" and there are few challenges the states face which don't

generate calls for Commonwealth financial help. We do tend to see ourselves as one country rather than a collection of states and instinctively
we want our governance arrangements to reflect that.

I was health minister between 2003 and 2007 and the practical experience of trying to make a coherent system from out-of-hospital Commonwealth-funded treatment, on the one hand, and largely state-funded
public hospital treatment, on the other, turned me from a philosophical
federalist into a pragmatic nationalist.

In those days, debate over public hospitals that the states ran but the
Commonwealth funded was a constant game of pass-the-parcel with
each level of government blaming the other for the system's shortcomings. Many conditions would indeed be better treated outside public
hospitals; but that would mean the Commonwealth rather than the
states funding them – so funding arrangements rather than public health
considerations could end up driving policy.

Now, all of this hasn't stopped the provision of truly world class
health services: yes, people often wait longer than they should for elec-
tive procedures or pay more than they would like for them; still, the
common sense and decency of treating professionals and the pragma-
tism of health administrators in the field mean that for most people,
most of the time, it works tolerably well.

It would be better if one level of government was responsible for
funding all health services – but that would mean the Commonwealth
giving Medicare, the PBS and aged care to the states; or the states giving public hospitals to the Commonwealth. Either the states would lose
relevance or well-respected national service provision would be frag-
mented.

And so we go on, with the states providing public hospital services that the Commonwealth part-funds; the states complaining that the
Commonwealth is short-changing them; the Commonwealth complaining that the states are using that as an excuse. And the people complaining that no one really knows what's going on.

In 2005, sick of the financial straitjacket imposed by the Commonwealth-state health care agreement, the Beattie government in Queensland sought to charge a co-payment to public hospital patients. The
Howard government, in which I served, refused to amend the Medicare
agreement; it was a regrettable denial by the Commonwealth of one
state's attempt to be an adult government.

Now I remain a pragmatic nationalist – but the states exist, they have wide powers under the constitution and they can't be abolished; so – rather than pursue giving the Commonwealth more authority over the states, as I proposed in my 2009 book, Battlelines – better harmonising revenue and spending responsibilities is well worth a another try.

Back then, my thinking was that the states should become subordinate legislatures to the Commonwealth: in a parallel to the way local councils are subordinate to the state governments. But I now doubt that any such constitutional change could succeed; and, in any event, it's a good principle to propose the smallest change that will actually tackle the problem – that's why resolving the mismatch between what the states are supposed to deliver and what they can actually afford to pay for is worth another go.

That's what my colleagues and I meant when we said repeatedly, before the last election, that we would launch a federation reform white paper was meant to make each level of government more "sovereign in its own sphere".

Collectively, the Australian states currently spend about $230 billion a year but raise only about $130 billion from their own taxes; of the rest, about $54 billion comes from the GST, a tax that the Commonwealth collects but the states spend; and a further $46 billion comes directly from the Commonwealth under specific purpose payments or national partnership agreements.

The Commonwealth, for obvious reasons, is focused on expenditure restraint so that taxes can come down and the economy can grow; the states, for their part, know that their various services have to keep up with greater demand and better technology.

Can a more rational and better managed system be devised; or is change more trouble than it's worth? Is it inevitable that Commonwealth spending restraint will produce more user-pays arrangements in state institutions? Or, preferring a reorganisation between governments to a fight with the public, can the Commonwealth and the states better align their revenue with their spending?

To address "vertical fiscal imbalance" we could either adjust the states spending responsibilities down to match their revenues, or we could adjust their revenues up.

The first approach involves the current spending responsibilities being redistributed so that the Commonwealth would take on more and the states would deal with less. It wouldn't necessarily mean the Commonwealth taking over responsibility for delivery of functions currently carried out by state and territory Governments.

Nor does it imply a "one-size-fits-all approach" to service delivery. It could lead to a situation where funding for such services was delivered through an individual entitlement supplied through a market – along the lines of the NDIS.

Alternatively, the Commonwealth could stop funding programmes in areas of state responsibility and stop using its financial power to influence how the states deliver services. In that case, the Commonwealth would be ready to work with states on a range of tax reforms that could permanently improve the states' tax base – including changes to the indirect tax base with compensating reductions in income tax.

Then there's the issue of "horizontal fiscal equalisation" which is supposed to give each state and territory a similar capacity to provide public goods and services. It's basically about giving everyone 'a fair go' – but it has to be fair to the states making the financial contributions as well as to those receiving them, to those who give as well as those who receive. It should be possible to make these arrangements more equitable between the larger states with the smaller states no worse off.

So this federation reform process is proceeding in parallel with a tax reform process which makes this a once-in-a-generation opportunity for all first ministers, all levels of government to address the issues bedevilling our federation.

Together, the Commonwealth and the states should be prepared to look at all our existing taxes to make them lower, simpler and fairer. Might the states be prepared to accept responsibility for broadening the indirect tax base; might they be prepared to surrender some of their responsibilities to the Commonwealth; might there be new funding formulas that wouldn't solve the blame game but could at least give it a new and more realistic starting point?

At this stage, no one should be asked to play the "rule in or rule out" game, because that's guaranteed to generate fear rather than hope.

This government is determined to avoid anything that increases the overall burden of tax. We're not going to have a pointless fight sponsoring change that the states aren't even prepared to consider – because, if it's to happen properly, reform of the federation has to be owned by the states as well as by the Commonwealth.

The steering group for the White Paper reform process includes the heads of all first ministers' departments and the ALGA CEO. Initial discussions about the scope and timing of the Federation Reform white paper dominated this month's COAG meeting. The states and territories have begun preparing their initial submissions. Before the middle of next year, but after the upcoming state elections, it's my intention to meet with all the premiers and chief ministers solely to discuss reform of the federation.

I anticipate a green paper in the second half of next year and the white paper in the run up to the election so that its work can inform the proposals that this Government decides to take to the people.

Tonight, I announce a further group to guide and test the public servants' work comprising: former South Australian Labor premier John Bannon, former Victorian Liberal treasurer Alan Stockdale, Vice Chancellor of the Australian Catholic University, Greg Craven, Business Council CEO, Jennifer Westacott, former Western Australia Attorney-General Cheryl Edwards and Queensland Public Service Commission Chairman, Doug McTaggart.

The fundamental test that all parties and all levels of government will face over the next year is this: are we prepared to have a rational discussion about who does what; or do we think that the current arrangements, perhaps with some adjustments at the edges, are the best that can be managed under the circumstances?

Either way, it will be good for our system: we will end up with a more rational division of authority and responsibility; or we will be forced to stop complaining about a system that we're not prepared to change. Either way, we will have grown as a country.

Inevitably, this reform process will test the mettle of all Australia's first ministers (and indeed alternative first ministers): obviously it will test our willingness to compromise as well as our determination to pursue important objectives; it will test our capacity to reconcile a local perspective with the national one, both of them important; and it will test our readiness to overcome institutional self-interest because this can't be about us – it has to be for our country.

For all of us, this will be quite a challenge – but it's worth doing to see whether and to what extent we're up for it.

Our duty, our solemn duty is to leave behind a greater nation – now let us rise to it.

We heard earlier this evening the words of Sir Henry Parkes in this very hall calling us to rise to the greatness that was the United States of America. Well, that's a different country, this is a different time. Nonetheless, we should put no limits on what we can achieve and surely in this great Commonwealth of ours it is possible to achieve a better system of government than we currently have.

17

EULOGIES & TRIBUTES

'It was impossible to dislike such a man'
Parliament House, Canberra, 21 October 2014

On the death of his Labor predecessor Gough Whitlam, Prime Minister Abbott recalls some humorous encounters and says we all have much to learn from such political giants.

In every sense Gough Whitlam was a giant figure in this Parliament and in our public life.

He was only Prime Minister for three years – three tumultuous years – but those years changed our nation and one way or another, set the tone for so much that has followed.

Whether you were for him or against him, it was his vision that drove our politics then and which still echoes through our public life four decades on.

He was a gifted student. He saw war service in the Royal Australian Air Force. He was a brilliant young barrister before entering Parliament in 1952.

He became Leader of the Opposition and helped to establish his credentials by courageously reforming aspects of his party organisation.

After 23 years of Coalition government Australians wanted change. It was time, as the famous campaign song proclaimed – probably the only campaign song that anyone can now remember. Whitlam represented more than a new politics. He represented a new way of thinking, about government, about our region, about our place in the world and about change itself. 1972 was his time and all subsequent times have been shaped by his time.

His government ended conscription, recognised China, introduced Medibank, abolished university fees, decolonised PNG, transformed our approach to indigenous policy and expanded the role of the Commonwealth, particularly in the field of social services. These were highly contentious at the time. Some of these measures are still contentious, but one way or another, our country has never been quite the same.

Members of his government displayed the usual human foibles, but support it or oppose it, there was a largeness of purpose to all his government attempted, even if its reach far exceeded its grasp, as the 1975 election result showed.

He may not have been our greatest prime minister, but he was certainly one of the greatest personalities that our country has ever produced. And no prime minister has been more mythologised.

I dare say that most of us who met him have a Whitlam story. I introduced myself to him one day in 1978 at an event at Sydney University. "I've heard of you," he said. "You're some kind of a Liberal."

"I'm actually supposed to be DLP," was my response.

"DLP," he boomed. "That's even worse."

At another university event, I asked him about the book *Matters for Judgment*.

"I'm very pleased," he said, "that Sir John Kerr has gone into print because it has set up a great clamour for the truth, which only I can provide."

Gough Whitlam was a playful man. Even while making what he thought was the essential political or philosophical point.

Years later at an airport lounge, I found myself discussing an issue of ecclesiastical governance with him, involving the then Catholic Bishop of Wollongong. He sent me a note on the back of a boarding pass which I might share with the House. "Some pilgrims in Rome from the Gong found some churches to which to belong, in St Peter's no less, they at last could confess Bishop Murray had got it all wrong."

In person, it was hard to disagree with and impossible to dislike such a man – however much one might question his policies.

Of course, throughout his public life, he was supported by Margaret. Herself a formidable personality and a gracious adornment to our national life.

Gough Whitlam is gone – but not forgotten. He will never be forgotten.

His was a life full of purpose. Proof, if proof were needed, that individuals do matter and can make a lasting difference to the country they love.

It's worth recalling an exchange of letters between Gough Whitlam and his distinguished predecessor Sir Robert Menzies.

Sir Robert Menzies wrote to the incoming Prime Minister in 1972 and he said, "You have been emphatically called to an office of great power and great responsibility. Nobody knows better than I do what demands will be made upon your mental vigour and physical health. I hope you will be able to maintain both and send you my personal congratulations."

To which Gough Whitlam graciously replied: "I was profoundly moved by your magnanimous message on my election to this great office. No Australian is more conscious than I how much the lustre, honour and authority of that office owed to the manner in which you held it with such distinction for so long. No Australian understands better than you the private feelings of one now facing the change from the years of leading the opposition to the burdens and rewards of leading our nation. You would, I think, be surprised to know how much I feel indebted to your example, despite the great differences in our philosophies."

We all have much to learn from the giants of those times.

'The best response to evil is good'

Parliament House, Canberra, 9 February 2015

Addressing the House of Representatives, Prime Minister Abbott describes the recent Lindt Café siege, in Sydney, as a "testing day for our country" and reaffirms the nation's revulsion towards those who promote hatred and terrorism.

The 15th of December last year was a testing day for our country. It was a testing day for the police and for the security and emergency services. It was a testing day for the people of Sydney, witnessing an atrocity unfold in a café known to many Sydneysiders in the utterly familiar surrounds of Martin Place. Above all, it was a testing day for the men and the women held in the Lindt Café and for their families.

So today, we welcome to the Chamber the men and women held in the Lindt Café as well as the families of Tori Johnson and Katrina Dawson. The thoughts and the prayers of 24 million Australians – and many millions more around the world – were with you on that terrible day. And I want to assure you, we are still with you – we are still with you as you come to terms with that horrific experience.

Every day must be a struggle for the Johnson and the Dawson families. We grieve with you and we hope that you draw strength and comfort from the support of the people of our country.

We are so glad that you are here, in the home of our democracy, in the very cradle of that noble idea that men and women can make their own choices for their own lives provided that it doesn't hurt anyone else.

Australia is a peaceful country. We are a beacon of hope and liberty throughout the world. Sydney – our largest city – is so cosmopolitan and diverse that anyone can be at home there. In this country, our differences demonstrate our freedom and our willingness to lend a hand and to get along makes this the best place on earth to live.

This is what was threatened on the 15th and 16th of December last year. This is what we are determined to uphold and defend at home and abroad every single day. The best response to evil is good. The best response to terrorism is to live normal lives, because that shows that we might be threatened but we will not be changed.

The Martin Place siege, I regret to say, was inspired by that death cult, now rampant in much of Syria and Iraq, which is a travesty of religion and governance and which should never be dignified with the term Islamic State.

The Martin Place siege was the act of terror that we hoped would never occur in this country.

I want to assure the men and women in the Gallery, I want to assure all Australians, that this Government, as well as our state counterparts, are determined to learn from what happened at the Lindt Café on that dreadful day.

We are considering the Commonwealth-State review which will be released, with our response, before the end of the month. There is also a NSW Coronial inquiry that's underway. But the first duty of government is to keep our citizens safe. And while no one can promise that a brutal act of terror will never occur again, these inquiries will identify what we can do to further protect our people and our country.

I pledge that I will do whatever I humanly can to help keep our people safe. That's why this Government has boosted its spending on our security and intelligence services. That's why members of the Australian Defence Force, even now, are currently working with the forces of other nations to disrupt and degrade the ISIL, or Daesh, death cult. Air strikes, including our own, have hit it hard, stopping its momentum and degrading its forces.

This death cult has declared war on the world and the world is both hitting back and reaching out. In the days after the atrocity against Charlie Hebdo, the people of France responded to the brutality of Islamist extremists by walking arm-in-arm through the streets of Paris.

Likewise, in the days after the Sydney siege, Australians responded by carpeting Martin Place with flowers. Tens of thousands brought tributes, including a bride who had interrupted her wedding day to do so. Manal Kassem's floral tribute was a reminder that Muslim Australians were as affronted by the events of the 15th and 16th of December as every Australian. She reminded us, as did all who responded during those difficult days, that for every person who seeks to impose extremism and violence there are countless more who will stand against them.

Australia did not stand alone. I do want to place on record my thanks to the many national leaders who called in response to the terrorism in Martin Place. I do want to assure the House that we will defend ourselves against those who seek to do us harm, but we will always do so in keeping with our values – our Australian values. Those values are embodied in this institution and in our shared adherence to liberal thought and to democratic pluralism. We stand for the right of individuals to choose their own paths and to live their lives free of fear. We stand against organisations or individuals that promote hatred here or recruit vulnerable Australians for terrorism abroad.

We have already made it an offence to advocate terrorism and made it easier to ban terrorist organisations and if we have to seek further legislation, we will.

This is the first sitting day of the Parliament for 2015. This year, like every other year, there will be moments of contention, partisanship, bitterness, and drama, but there will also be moments of profound unity where our shared love of country prevails over everything else.

This is such a moment.

In April, some in this Chamber will travel to Gallipoli to pay tribute to the courage and resourcefulness and determination and sacrifice of our forebears a century ago. But today, we need not look so far, or travel so far, to see resilience, courage and decency. We look to the Gallery – and we see modern Australia. We see young and old, men and women of diverse backgrounds – and in them, we see the courage and the resourcefulness and the decency that we saw in other generations in another context.

Greater love hath no man or woman than to lay down their life for their friend. We salute Tori Johnson and Katrina Dawson. We salute everyone touched by the siege – touched by this atrocity.

I commend the motion to the House.

'This giant is surely one of us'
Parliament House, Canberra, 23 March 2015

On the death of former Liberal Prime Minister Malcolm Fraser, Prime Minister Abbott recognises his predecessor's liberal humanitarianism and staunch anti-communism, and reaffirms his place in the "broad church" of the Liberal Party.

It is fitting that we celebrate the life and legacy of our 22nd prime minister here in this chamber because this very building is one of his achievements.

He was prepared to endure jibes about politicians spending money on themselves because he understood that Australians would come to appreciate a parliament house that reflected our pride in ourselves and in our country.

He foresaw a building that would be the "crowning achievement of the parliamentary triangle" and, along with the National Gallery and the High Court, that were also started on his watch, would reflect the modern nation we had become.

He was right – and of course, as so often happens in our public life – his government wore the brickbats for starting it and another government gained the credit for opening it.

The Fraser government conferred self-government on the Northern Territory, established the Commonwealth Ombudsman and enacted our first Freedom of Information laws.

After the Hilton Hotel bombing, his government established the Australian Federal Police; and it set up the national crime commission following the Costigan enquiry.

His government commissioned the Campbell Report which laid the foundations for the eventual deregulation of the financial system.

Like all good farmers, Malcolm Fraser was a conservationist. His government banned sand mining on Fraser Island, banned drilling on the Great Barrier Reef, set up the Great Barrier Reef Marine Park and had this wonder of the natural world heritage-listed.

He was a liberal humanitarian who worked against white minority governments in southern Africa; and a staunch anti-communist who tried to keep our sports stars from the Moscow Olympics after the Soviet invasion of Afghanistan.

At the height of the Whitlam turmoil, he'd said that he'd like to see sport rather than politics on the front page – and when he imposed the Olympic ban he managed to realise that goal!

Fraser was not an avid social reformer, like Whitlam; nor a mould-breaking economic reformer, like Hawke; but he gave the country what we needed at that time: he restored economic responsibility while recognising social change.

His government passed the Northern Territory Land Rights Act and he was the first prime minister to visit the Torres Strait.

He established the Special Broadcasting Service and began large-scale Asian immigration to Australia by accepting 50,000 Vietnamese refugees fleeing communism.

In 1983, Malcolm Fraser left parliament proud of his government and its achievements; as he said at the time: Australia is handed over... in as good or better condition than any other Western country in the world.

For a long time after 1975, Malcolm Fraser was largely defined by the blocking of supply, the dismissal of the Whitlam government and his subsequent electoral vindication. Neither Whitlam nor Fraser ever resiled from the positions they took at that time, yet they ultimately came to see the good in each other.

Some years ago, Whitlam observed, with characteristic wit, that Fraser had supplanted him as the principal bogey man of the hard right – and that this second usurpation had been easier to take than the first!

As the Hawke government implemented market-driven reforms, a sense grew, especially among Liberals, that the Fraser government might have marked time.

In the late 80s and early 90s, Malcolm Fraser offered himself to be federal president of the Liberal Party and twice it didn't work out. As the Howard government implemented reforms such as the GST and privatisation; expanded mandatory detention to stop the boats; and joined US-led military coalitions in Afghanistan and Iraq, an estrangement grew between him and the party he'd led for eight years, for most of that time triumphantly.

John Howard has famously observed that the Australian Liberal

Party, unlike its namesakes elsewhere, is the custodian in this country of both the liberal political tradition and the conservative one. There is, in fact, a third tradition that our Party represents, as vital as our liberal and our conservative philosophies: a dedication to service and to repaying good fortune; the working out in this world of the Gospel notion: to whom much is given, much is expected.

Melbourne Grammar, Oxford, and a grandfather who was a senator no doubt helped to crystalize Malcolm Fraser's instinct to serve. Fraser's shyness, born of a lonely childhood, often made him seem remote but it also created a keen sympathy for the outsider.

Duty and service came naturally to him – he was a man to whom becoming a member of parliament, if that opportunity presented itself, would seem the most natural thing in the world.

His political allegiances might have been instinctive as much as philosophical but he was the true and authentic representative of an honourable tradition.

My first contact with Malcolm Fraser was to lobby him for voluntary membership of the Australian Union of Students. Because he had not been consulting papers at the time, Senator John Carrick advised me afterwards that the meeting had probably gone well – because the prime minister was focused on the discussion and not on something else.

In the early 90s, I persuaded both Malcolm Fraser and his one-time nemesis, Liberal-turned-Australian-Democrats-founder Don Chipp, to join the Victorian Council of Australians for Constitutional Monarchy.

When I asked them both to speak at the launch, Chipp said that "if that (expletive deleted) Fraser comes, I won't". A few months later, Malcolm settled the matter by joining the republican side.

I made it my business to renew contact with him on becoming party leader in 2009. We had some long talks; we often disagreed but I appreciated his wisdom born of experience.

He had a long and active life after leaving parliament. He brought Care International to Australia in partnership with his long-time Liberal Party federal director, Tony Eggleton.

Throughout his life, he enjoyed steadfast support at home. Tamie Fraser once said that "the best thing about being the prime minister's wife is knowing that it won't go on forever". Her legacy continues through the Australiana Fund that helps to furnish the four official residences. All subsequent Australian prime ministers and governors-general have benefited from her work.

To Tamie, to the Frasers' four children, Phoebe, Mark, Angela and Hugh – and to their grandchildren – I extend the condolences of the parliament and the people of Australia, and I also extend to them the gratitude of our party.

Yes, today I say "thank you" to them because my party has not said "thank you" often enough to their husband and father.

For most of his life, Fraser was a classic representative of our party.

He was conservative when he declared that "the values and principles by which we live, the human relationships which guide us, and the values to which we aspire as Liberals will not change".

He was liberal when he stated that "each man, from the street cleaner to the industrialist, (has) an equal right to a full and happy life...to go his own way unhampered so long as he does not harm our precious social fabric".

And he was, above all, an Australian patriot, when he declared at his first pre-selection that "I could not enter this fight if I did not love Australia".

He was never considered a popular politician although he won three elections, including the two biggest landslides in Australian history.

Years ago, when I was helping to draft the Fightback! document I sought to include a few observations that were critical of the Fraser government. My senior collaborator, David Kemp, rightly chided me on the grounds that it's hard to disown your past without diminishing your future.

In a sense, today's proceedings are a farewell – to this complex and driven man, to this forceful and effective leader, to this rare public personality who gained the support of all points on the political spectrum, but almost never at the same time.

But we Liberals owe him more than that; our challenge is not to say goodbye; it's to be more magnanimous in his death than we were in his life, and to acknowledge this giant who is surely one of us.

18

POSTSCRIPT:
I HAVE RENDERED ALL

'I want our Government and our country to succeed'

Courtyard at Parliament House, Canberra,
15 September 2015

After losing the leadership to Malcolm Turnbull in a Liberal party room vote, the deposed Prime Minister calls a press conference to thank the Australian people for the honour they had bestowed on him, and to outline his Government's proud record.

This is not an easy day for many people in this building. Leadership changes are never easy for our country. My pledge today is to make this change as easy as I can. There will be no wrecking, no undermining, and no sniping.

I have never leaked or backgrounded against anyone and I certainly won't start now. Our country deserves better than that. I want our Government and our country to succeed. I always have and I always will.

I have consistently said – in Opposition and in Government – that being the Prime Minister is not an end in itself: it is about the people you serve.

The great privilege that I have had is to see the wonder of this country like few others and I want to thank the Australian people for giving me the honour to serve.

Yes, this is a tough day, but when you join the game you accept the rules. I have held true to what I believed and I am proud of what we have achieved over the past two years. 300,000 more people are in jobs. Labor's bad taxes are gone. We have signed Free Trade Agreements with our largest trading partners – with Japan, with Korea, and with China. The biggest infrastructure program in our country's history is under way. A spotlight is being shone into the dark and corrupt corners of the union movement and Labor's party/union business model.

We have responded to the threats of terror and we have deployed to the other side of the world to bring our loved ones home. The boats have stopped – and with the boats stopped, we've been better able to display our compassion to refugees. And despite hysterical and unprincipled opposition, we've made $50 billion of repairs to the budget.

Of course, there's much that I had still wanted to do: constitutional recognition of Indigenous people – getting the kids to school, the adults to work and communities safe. I was the first Prime Minister to spend a week a year in remote Indigenous Australia, and I hope I'm not the last. Then there's the challenge of ice and domestic violence, yet to be addressed.

Australia has a role to play in the struggles of the wider world: the cauldron of the Middle East, and security in the South China Sea and elsewhere. I fear that none of this will be helped if the leadership instability that's plagued other countries continues to taint us.

But yes, I am proud of what the Abbott Government has achieved. We stayed focused despite the white-anting.

Of course, the Government wasn't perfect. We have been a Government of men and women, not a government of gods walking upon the earth. Few of us, after all, entirely measure up to expectations.

The nature of politics has changed in the past decade. We have more polls and more commentary than ever before – mostly sour, bitter, character assassination. Poll-driven panic has produced a revolving door prime ministership which can't be good for our country and a febrile media culture has developed that rewards treachery.

And if there's one piece of advice I can give to the media, it's this: refuse to print self-serving claims that the person making them won't put his or her name to; refuse to connive at dishonour by acting as the assassin's knife.

There are many to thank for the privilege of being Prime Minister. First and foremost, I thank my family for allowing me to be the absentee spouse and parent that politics entails. I thank Margie for her grace and dignity throughout my public life. I thank my party for the privilege of leading it. I thank the armed forces who are serving our country and defending our values, even as we speak. I thank my staff who have been absolutely unceasing in their devotion to our party and our country, especially my Chief of Staff who has been unfairly maligned by people who should have known better.

Finally, I thank my country for the privilege of service.

It is humbling to lose, but that does not compare to the honour of being asked to lead.

In my Maiden Speech here in this Parliament, I quoted from the first

Christian service ever preached here in Australia. The Reverend Richard Johnson took as his text, "What shall I render unto the Lord for all
his blessings to me?" At this, my final statement as Prime Minister, I
say: I have rendered all and I am proud of my service.

My love for this country is as strong as ever and may God bless this
great Commonwealth.

Acknowledgements

We wish to acknowledge the following people for their invaluable assistance in the composition of this volume, *Abbott: As Delivered*.

First, we wish to recognise the Executive Director of the Menzies Research Centre (MRC), Nick Cater, for providing us with the inspiration to embark on the timely project of researching and publishing a series of noteworthy speeches by Australia's 28th Prime Minister. With this publication brought to fruition, these selected speeches of Tony Abbott can be read firsthand, and appreciated as a catalogue of his substantial policy achievements in office. Nick's encouragement and guidance throughout this project has been invaluable and much appreciated.

We would like to thank our colleagues at the MRC, Fred Pawle and James Mathias for their encouragement and abiding interest in this publication.

We especially appreciate the genuine interest and enthusiasm of the former Prime Minister himself, the Hon Tony Abbott. At all times, We have valued his generous encouragement and support behind the project.

We are very grateful to the Rt Hon Stephen Harper of Canada for his Foreword. Written by a contemporaneous statesman of Tony Abbott, and a leader of one of the most effective, recent centre-right governments in the English-speaking world, this foreword provides a fitting adornment to the volume.

With the style and presentation of the volume, we are indebted to the assistance of Fred Pawle. His creativity, flair and journalistic eye have provided valuable input into the formatting and layout of the manuscript.

In bringing this volume to print, we are grateful to Dr Anthony Cappello and the team at Connor Court for overseeing the process of publication with their professionalism and precision.

We conclude by offering our profound appreciation to our families and friends who have supported us through this endeavour with their love, good humour, interest and encouragement.

David Furse-Roberts and Paul Ritchie
Sydney
February 2019

Index